A PATTERN OF LIFE

A PATTERN OF LIFE

The Memoirs of an Indian Woman

SHUDHA MAZUMDAR

Translated and edited
GERALDINE H. FORBES

MANOHAR
2024

First published 1977
POD reprint 2021

Reprinted 2024

ISBN 978-93-88540-69-8

Published by
Ajay Kumar Jain *for*
Manohar Publishers & Distributors
4753/23 Ansari Road, Daryaganj
New Delhi 110 002

Printed at
Replika Press Pvt. Ltd.

Dedicated in devotion to the lotus feet of Bhagawan Sri Satya Sai Baba who is *Satyam, Sivam* and *Sundaram.* His is truly the embodiment of all that is True, Good and Beautiful. By his Grace I have found the Path.

Foreword

When my husband, R.C. Casey, became Governor of undivided Bengal in 1944 we lived for two years in Calcutta. There, one of my first Indian friends was Mrs. Shudha Mazumdar, the distinguished translator into English of the *Ramayana.* She was a woman of much perception and warmth and had many interests and affiliations. I had then known few Indian women in any intimate way and she had met few Australians.

When we came to Bengal we, as Australians, knew little of India and of the sensitive, gifted Bengalis who lived mostly in the vast delta where the mysterious, intricate shifting waterways shaped so much of their thought and vision. Shudha Mazumdar, through her warmth and generosity, did much to interpret for me the Indian mind. She even taught me a little Bengali.

The period covered by this book begins in Shudha Mazumdar's childhood and finishes towards the end of 1930. Her parents were dissimilar in outlook. Her father, a landowner, was attracted to Western ideas and manner of living and he was, to a degree, unorthodox. Her mother was an orthodox Hindu and clung to Eastern ideas and beliefs. The book follows the development of an observant child, maiden and wife through her early family life (fascinating in its detail and discipline) into a time of change and adjustment.

The time was one of unique interest which saw the growth of nationalism and the emergence of such great figures as Motilal Nehru, the father of Jawarharlal Nehru and Mohandas K. Gandhi. A book of this kind is unlikely to be written again because of the generation it deals with and the period it covers. With intelligence, curiosity and compassion, it takes us through aspects of Hindu family life onwards into a changing world.

Shudha Mazumdar writes beautiful, clear and imaginative English. She is indeed an outstanding writer as well as a rare and beloved human being.

MAIE CASEY

THE LADY CASEY
BERWICK, VICTORIA, AUSTRALIA
7 November 1973

Contents

Note on Transliteration

There is no set transliteration scheme used for this work. In all cases an attempt has been made to use the most common spellings for the Indian words used. Since this book is intended for a general audience, it was felt that using the common forms would be of more value than forms that are acceptable according to one of the transliteration system.

Introduction

I first met Smt. Shudha Mazumdar in 1970 while searching for information about her great-uncle, Jogendro Chandra Ghose. After one or two meetings, the conversation shifted to Shudha Mazumdar and she began to talk about her life in the family home in Kidderpore and with her husband in the districts of Bengal. As the story unfolded it became more and more fascinating. Smt. Mazumdar was born at the turn of the century, married at age thirteen as was then customary but had matured to lead a life quite different from that of her mother. As a matron she had become a respected and prominent social worker with much of her life centered on people outside the home. As I grew more interested, Smt. Mazumdar suggested sharing with me 'some things' she had put on paper. This turned out to be over five hundred manuscript pages about her life. When I returned to the University of Illinois I brought these memoirs with me, reread them and showed them to a number of my colleagues. They agreed they were a find and in the summer of 1972 I returned to Calcutta to edit them with Smt. Mazumdar's approval.

Seven years later, with more experience and greater understanding of the changes that have affected the status of Indian women, I continue to see these memoirs as highly significant. They are a woman's story of the period, 1900-1930. For India, this was a dramatic and exciting period which saw the rise of a nationalist movement, the advent of Mahatma Gandhi and the mobilization of thousands of men and women in the struggle against the British. This account is significant for a number of reasons. First, as a personalized account, it lends a vividness to the times, second, it can contribute to our understanding of the changes women experienced. In addition, these memoirs are a valuable 'case study' for assessing women's role in social change.

History, from one point of view, is the sum total of innumerable biographies. Political history generally concerns itself with the lives of great men and women. The stories of lesser individuals are overlooked, yet they include details that can be of value in rounding out the period and giving it a completeness. Many people have kept letters, diaries and written their memoirs, but these are much rarer in India than in the western world. Memoirs, like letters and diaries humanize the past. Through these materials it is possible to visualize the past and to feel the writer's emotions as he/she watched events happen. They do not tell the complete story, but memoirs give us the past in concrete and vivid terms.

These memoirs focus on a particularly interesting period in terms of the history of women in India. In these three decades, women first began to take an interest in politics, formed national organizations to present their social demands and mobilized on both social and political issues. The outline of these events has been presented by a number of historians but what we lack are detailed accounts written by the women who lived through this period. There are many questions that continue to be asked about the 'coming out' of Indian women. What were the 'traditional' institutions that shaped women's roles? What inspired those women who decided to move from home-centered lives to take a part in public activities? How did they justify these new roles? How did they mediate between traditional values and institutions and their new life styles? And, what impact did they have on society?

Shudha Mazumdar's *A Pattern of Life in India*, is the personal story of a woman who had fully experienced 'traditional' values and institutions and had 'come out' to join organizations designed to uplift Indian women. Through this one woman's life, one can obtain answers to these questions. It is possible to see this as a case study which could be tested for more general validity against the case-histories of other women of her generation.

These memoirs can also help us assess women's role in social change. Women, we are frequently told by historians, social scientists and Indian males writing their memoirs, were the stumbling blocks to modernization. In these memoirs we have an intimate look at Shudha Mazumdar, her mother, mother-in-law and a number of other women as they led their daily lives. The situations they faced and the choices they made can lead us towards a more complete look at women's role in social change.

Born in 1899, Shudha was the daughter of a wealthy and respected landowner, Tara Pada Ghose. His grandfather, Mohan Chand Ghose, had acquired his fortune while employed as a civil servant. He had then moved the family from Khulna district of East Bengal to the Kidderpore area of Calcutta, built a mansion and joined the landed gentry living in Calcutta. The Ghose family became the patrons of aspiring poets, writers and philosophers who reflected the society's interest in new ideas. One of the descendants, Jogendro Chandra Ghose, became the Leading Member of a society of Positivists who sought to import a modified version of Auguste Comte's philosophy into India as a modernizing ideology. When Shudha was born, the family controlled lands in Khulna and Twenty-four Parganas, were well-known for their charities and respected as pillars of the community. Shudha was brought up in an upper caste, well-to-do household where female seclusion was practised and female activities relating to religious ceremonies and food were germane to the family's status.

As was characteristic of many early twentieth century households in Calcutta, the style of life for males differed considerably from the style followed by the females. Shudha's father was highly Westernized, in outward appearance as well as philosophy and habits. He lived in an area of the house which included shelves of English books and a dining room, where he ate, in lonely splendour, attended by his Muslim servant. The women's compartments presented a direct contrast to this picture. For the women, meat was a taboo and Western styles and habits were looked upon as something one had to tolerate in the menfolk. While her mother 'tolerated' Tara Pada's habits, there is little to suggest that she approved of them or accepted this as the proper way to live. Like a good Hindu wife, she obeyed her husband—up to a point. When the question of her daughter's education became crucial, Shudha's mother had her way and the daughter's formal education did not go beyond the level sanctioned by society at that time.

Growing up was a pleasant experience for Shudha. Throughout her childhood she enjoyed the advantages of being the daughter of a *Zamindar* for she had an abundance of playmates and interesting places to play. Three brothers, two uncles, assorted relatives and servants peopled her world, playing with her and socializing her into a woman's role. The games she loved best were those she played with her brothers but these led some of the older females of the house to worry about her 'tomboy' inclinations. Most of her companions concentrated on preparing her for woman's most important event—marriage. In these memoirs one finds a fascinating account of the ceremonies young girls learn to perform, requesting a good and faithful husband like Shiva, and the vows they are taught to observe. While still a child, Shudha overheard the remarks of elderly relatives cautioning her mother that she was rapidly approaching marriageable age, and, more frequently, that some of her naughty acts would not endear her to the household of her father-in-law.

While preparation for marriage began shortly after birth, there was an opposing set of influences in Shudha's childhood. Her father, doting on his youngest daughter, seemed to behave quite foolishly—at least from the perspective of the women in the household and others who were concerned with arranging a good marriage for this child. He invited his darling daughter to his table, tempted her with bits of chicken cutlet and other dishes prepared by his Muslim servant, enrolled her in St. Teresa's convent (with British and Anglo-Indian girls) and taught her to recite English poetry. This was not unusual for the time, many fathers behaved like this with their daughters.* But, it was highly irresponsible. Tara Pada Ghose was a *Zamindar* and his family were concerned that Shudha's marriage

*For a more thorough analysis of the contradictory roles Bengali girls are taught *see* Manisha Roy's *Bengali Women* (Chicago, 1975).

be arranged with a family of equal or higher status. Girls belonging to the Brahmo Samaj, a reformist Hindu sect, were being educated at this time, but the practice was not as common among Hindus and particularly not those from West Bengal. Fortunately, at least in terms of the society's values and the opportunities available to the young Shudha, the mother's influence took precedence and the daughter was only allowed to attend St. Teresa's as a day-scholar, not as a boarder, as the father had wished. Within the home, relatives and servants trained Shudha in the art of cooking and the correct performance of religious and household ceremonies.

At age thirteen Shudha was married. Somewhat old by her grandmother's standards, she remained young enough to conform to the standards of the time. In a society which practised prepuberty marriage (in terms of formal ceremony), marriage of girls under age ten had been under attack. The Marriage Act of 1872 (which applied to non-Hindus only) set the minimum age for females at fourteen while the 'Age of Consent Controversy' focused on the minimum age for intercourse with a female, married or unmarried. The penal code was finally changed, and twelve, rather than ten, became the new age of consent. During the discussion of this topic and age of marriage, the fate of child-widows, injuries to child-brides and the impact of these practices on the nation's health became the primary issues. This had its effect and among the more progressive elements of society, a slightly older age for marriage became fashionable.

Marriage was the only sacrament for Hindu women and the only institution through which women could gain status. In addition, it was the most important institution for forging connections between families and for indicating relative status. Shudha tells here of her own marriage, a great and exciting experience, which she only partially understood in terms of its total significance. For her, marriage meant moving to a new place and acquiring a new family, and the beginning of a set of tests which would cause her to summon all her childish wisdom about woman's behaviour. Her husband's family were considerate, devoid of the evil mother-in-law stereotype, and complete with a playmate in the form of her husband's younger brother.

During the first year of her marriage, she moved from her father's home to that of her father-in-law, adjusted to her new role and began her acquaintance with her husband.

At her husband's home in Murshidabad, Shudha found herself among strangers who did many things differently. The food was cooked with different spices and the practices of the family were more consistently orthodox than those in her own home. The first encounter was frightening—she was on display and very fearful that she would make mistakes. But the mother-in-law and grand-mother-in-law were kind, they did their best to make the transition an easy one. Nevertheless, the shift in role was dramatic—from carefree child to responsible daughter-in-law—but her training and intelligence were obvious assets in making the adjustment and she soon pleased her new family.

When Shudha writes of her first impressions of her husband one can begin to understand what Indians mean when they say, "We marry first and fall in love later." This system, people patiently explain, differs from the marriage system in the West and is far more stable in the long run. It is not a particular man that the young Indian girl is taught to love, but rather an ideal, a concept that she thinks about from the time she is a small girl. Finally, she is presented with a husband and the transfer of devotion from the ideal to the real takes place. With Shudha, the love developed for her husband seemed to go beyond the expectations for an arranged marriage. The young husband and wife liked each other from the beginning and as they grew up together, mutual respect and the fun of being together developed into deep love and admiration.

Married life opened doors to a completely new kind of life. Her husband accepted a position in the Bengal Civil Service and was assigned postings in Bengal's district towns. Regarding Shudha, he had two options : long periods of separation while she remained with his family, or taking her to new and distant places where she would be without the comfort and security of the joint family. In this situation, Shudha proved her father's daughter. She had loved adventure stories and was anxious to explore the new life. His transfers took them all over rural Bengal where they lived as a nuclear family and made new friends and where Shudha became a woman quite different from her mother and grand-mother. Transfers from one town in the *Mofussil* continued until 1934 when Shudha's husband was posted to Calcutta.

Living in remote villages, Shudha and her husband developed a new pattern of interaction. Without the presence of elders there was no need to retain strict male-female separation. Shudha and her husband began eating together, spending their evenings talking over the day's events and experimenting with cooking recipes. All these activities shocked the servants (who belonged to the households of the parents) but they were not powerful enough to put a stop to the outrageous behaviour they observed. It was during these early years of marriage that Shudha and her husband were able to develop their relationship and that she was able to develop as a person. Her husband took over where her father had left off—he encouraged his young bride to read, write essays, and learn to play the harmonium. More than that, he encouraged civic-mindedness, an interest in getting to know other women and coming out of *purdah*. Her father would have been delighted with the actions of his son-in-law, but the women of both households would have been shocked had they known the whole story.

The old ways were not suddenly and completely abandoned; Shudha was the ideal daughter-in-law when necessary. She performed the necessary religious ceremonies and was careful to prepare foods correctly. Her careful training at her mother's hands made her aware of the importance of setting up a separate kitchen for her mother-in-law and taking pains to ensure that forbidden foods and their refuse did not contaminate the elderly lady's food. Shudha's sensitivity gained her the approval of her mother-in-law who seemed to overlook some other variations in the household pattern. When choosing a girl for marriage too much education was of no more value than complete illiteracy. The rudiments of formal education were desirable, but it was far more important that a girl know how to do housework and how to adjust to her position in her husband's family.

As a married woman, Shudha began to take an interest in a number of new activities. A next-door neighbour taught her Tagore's songs, a music master attempted to teach her to play the sitar, and Saroj Nalini Dutt's fledgling 'social work' *Mahila Samitis* claimed her time and attention. A woman, particularly a new daughter-in-law in an old and respected family, would not normally have had time for such activities. Family ceremonies and obligations, and the tasks associated with running a large joint household would have claimed most of her attention. Shudha had expressed great affection for her husband's family and had enjoyed living at Murshidabad but she enjoyed this new freedom. The most serious problem she faced was that of loneliness.

Child-bearing followed marriage. Within two years Shudha became pregnant and bore a son. In India, where marriage is almost universal, child-bearing is seen as the next logical step. A woman must marry, there is no other sacrament for her; from childhood she is socialized to 'serve' and placed under the guardianship of males—first the father, then the husband, and finally the son. The desire to bear children, particularly sons, can be seen in terms of the demands of a patrilineal society. But also, it is child-bearing that establishes a woman's identity, gives her status in the community and proves to her husband, her family and her community that she has come of age and is ready to take her place among the women. Shudha had two sons—widely spaced by accident rather than planning—and has given vivid details of the customs associated with child-birth and the after-care of the mother and child.

Social work began for Shudha Mazumdar when she responded to Saroj Nalini Dutt's invitation to join a group of ladies trying to form an organization; it became a lifelong habit. The women's organizations provided a social outlet, new contacts that eased the loneliness, and gradually the realization that women could band together to present their demands. In the early years, Shudha was a member of Mrs. Dutt's *Samiti* but when her husband was transferred, she became the moving spirit behind new *Samitis*. These organizations taught women the rudiments of parliamentary procedure and how to present their demands, for a female doctor or a girls' school, to men in power. These early efforts at 'social work' were also important for the diffusion of patriotism among women's circles and for the inculcation of a civic consciousness. While these rural women's societies have not yet been adequately studied, what we do know suggests they were very important in bringing women into contact with new ideas and helping them make the transition from family-centered roles to ones which involved intimate relationships with many people.

Shudha Mazumdar, like most Indian women of her generation, did not avoid what was considered woman's *dharma*. She married, had children and operated fully as a housewife. But other interests claimed her attention. On the one hand, there was social work activities, on the other, political events. Barred from any overt declaration of patriotism by her husband's position in the BCS, she attended the 1920 Congress session in Calcutta and avidly followed events reported in the newspapers. And, she was not above obtaining and reading proscribed literature.

Her interest in national events was clearly over-shadowed by her duties as wife and mother. Mention of Gandhi's speech at the Calcutta Congress is related by someone who did not recognize all the speakers, had to view the scene from behind a screen, and would frequently allow her mind to wander from the issues being discussed to catch a glimpse of costumes or simply marvel at the experience of being 'out.' Other political issues, e.g., *swadeshi* and terrorism, are considered, but a child's fever, the marriage of a relative or a village baby-show are seen as equally important. From one perspective, Shudha Mazumdar was out of touch with the important events which were happening around her. From another perspective, this was the reality of the woman's world. National events could not be seen clearly nor participated in fully from behind the screen. Family issues did come first, for on them hinged woman's status and position. Shudha was deeply concerned with her family, but like many other women of her generation, an interest had been awakened in the world outside and participation in that world had begun. Her interest in national events seems far more typical than that of a woman like Sarojini Naidu who had travelled and studied in England in the early years of the century and by 1925 was President of the Indian National Congress. Women played a part in the

Nationalist Movement from the early years—one finds evidence of their support through the observance of a non-cooking day in 1905. It was only in 1930 and the years following that women 'came out' in large numbers to march, picket, and attend public meetings. But their support prior to 1930, although less, was vital to the movement for they supported the husbands and nurtured the children.

As a matron, Shudha was involved with social work and politics but still burdened with responsibilities deriving from the joint family. She was given the responsibility of choosing a bride for her younger brother-in-law and in this case she operated much as had women of her mother's generation. Suddenly lineage, looks and horoscopes became overwhelmingly important and the achievements of the candidates dropped in value. The efforts to improve women's welfare, the political events of the day and her increased ability to express herself had altered her notion of an ideal sister-in-law but Shudha's choice had to please both her husband's family and her father's family. Finally, it was the traditional notions of an ideal bride which triumphed.

Throughout this period of married life, Shudha changed a great deal. The change was not only in terms of maturity, she had acquired a new public role through which she tried to help rural women modernize. This change necessitated an abandonment of the secluded life followed by many women of her class and status. When she came out of *purdah,* it was with her husband's blessing and the urging of Mrs. Dutt. Symbolically it was an important step, but in reality she had already begun her life outside the walls of the family home. Involvement with the world grew rapidly but family responsibilities were not neglected. This, I believe, is an example of the way many Indian women handled changing roles. They took care of family responsibilities and in fact, argued that one could not adequately fulfil the role of wife and mother unless one were educated and knowledgeable about the world. Mrs. Mazumdar did not argue that women should abandon traditional roles to work for social reform and political freedom, but rather that they should learn to combine the two roles, for the better development of society.

Shudha Mazumdar's memoirs are continued only until 1930. This does not represent the end of her life, but rather the end of a formative period. After 1934 the family lived, except for brief periods, in Calcutta and Shudha entered a new phase of her life. In Calcutta, she joined the national and provincial social organizations for women and began to work on this level for an improvement in women's status. During the years which followed, she held various posts in the women's organizations, met and learned much from other people and was finally sent to the International Labour Organization to attend a special conference on women and labour. Following this conference, Shudha travelled throughout Europe to study prison conditions at first hand. The conditions of women in prison had been one of her major concerns and to this day she continues to take an interest in their plight.

During these early years Shudha developed a deep concern for the hardships of rural women and began to work to ameliorate these conditions. Her first social work was in the *Mahila Samitis*, later she joined national organizations and has since been responsible for organizing new social welfare associations. Her concerns have been many: medical care, nutrition, economic hardships, and, in the case of women in prison, spiritual needs. Her work has always had a strong religious component and efforts have been more frequently chanelled into concrete work than towards petitioning for social change legislation.

There have been other preoccupations in Shudha's life since these memoirs were concluded. As a young woman she experssed a seriousness about religious affairs that some of her acquaintances felt was far beyond her years. Her mystical dreams, occasional moods of depression and questioning of the meaning of life, resulted in a search for religious experience. Shudha was at one time associated with the Ramakrishna Mission and in recent years, with Satya Sai Baba. He has become her trusted advisor and in his writings and teachings, Shudha has found comfort and fulfilment.

This is a woman who has never really retired. She sees her social work as the doing of good works, as an expression of her *dharma*. For her, there has never been any psychological conflict associated with going outside the home to encompass a larger number of people in her life. This was partly because Shudha lived separate from the joint family but also because she saw service, the doing of good works, as her duty. Her father, she tells us, was an extremely charitable person. Among the recipients of his charity were poor people from many areas and communities, he even sent money to the poor in England. Her mother, by contrast, limited charity to 'the family.' It was this tendency to concentrate on the needs of the family, rather than the larger world, that inhibited women joining organizations concerned with assisting non-related individuals. This was not true of Shudha and one might suggest that her father's early example had made an impression. What comes through clearly though is that her acts derived from a religious motive and seem more closely related to the concept of a woman's duty to serve than to a secular notion of humanitarianism.

At age 78 Shudha Mazumdar remains a vital and interesting person. Of late she has retired, due to poor health and her advancing age, but people who know her well will not allow her to retire. She is no longer active in social organizations but her phone rings constantly and she is besieged by a string of callers who want her advice. She has become a woman of great strength, one who is able to comfort, give advice and listen to the problems of others. Despite her pleas for a quieter existence, it is doubtful that those who have come to know her will want to comply. And, the twinkle in her eye assures one that she is not so ready for a life of complete serenity as she would have us believe.

What can these memoirs tell us? First, they include much about the national scene and developments from the perspective of a middle-class woman. She was keenly interested, followed events closely but was unable to participate directly. What we begin to see, then, is how certain major events looked to someone who was patriotic but not at the centre of activity.

There is much in these memoirs about the institutional framework that governed women's lives. It has been suggested by some social scientists that arranged marriage is the most important institution for maintaining the structure of Hindu society. When we look at women's roles, the joint family seems to be the most important institution for socializing women and for the maintenance of a particular role. The elders both transmit the norms and enforce them; when these elderly people are removed from the scene, some dramatic changes occur.

In these memoirs we have an excellent example of the way one woman's life changed. The details included make it possible to question what motivated this change and what type of obstacles existed. In Shudha's case, the absence of the joint family seemed very important. There was no longer anyone to keep the wife and husband apart and to prevent the development of contacts and friendships with non-family members. But the change Shudha experienced cannot be attributed totally to the absence of restraints. She was well-educated for the time and her father and husband had taken an interest in her development. Nor should her mother's influence be omitted. She had stressed the importance of learning traditional skills, but she also told her daughter stories of poets and kings and subscribed to one of the earliest magazines written for women. As a mature woman, Shudha did not break with custom or reject traditional values and institutions. This is a story of change, not revolt. Shudha continued to behave in traditional ways when it was required while adopting ideas and modes of behaviour from the 'modern world' with which she would be comfortable.

These memoirs can throw light on the general question of women's role in social change. Not only are women generally seen as traditional, they are regarded as extremely reluctant to accept social change. Evidence, if one looks closely, seems to point to the opposite conclusion. When the Brahmo reformer, Keshub Chunder Sen, joined the Brahmo Samaj, he was forced to leave his father's home. When the father died, Keshub's mother came to live with him and accepted the Brahmo Samaj. Examples similar to this are not difficult to find. Women actually seem to make some amazing shifts in behaviour and attitudes. Shudha Mazumdar went to Europe, following the death of her husband, to attend the meetings of the ILO. At that time she had abandoned jewellery and coloured saris for the austere dress of the Bengali widow. Faced with a winter trip to Europe she was persuaded to don coloured *saris*. This may seem like an insignificant adjustment, but in a situation where style and colour of dress indicate one's status, this adjustment represented an important change in attitude.

Women, these memoirs suggest, change fairly easily if the structural elements are conducive to such change. It is only in those situations where women are given double messages—to change, yet a change would deprive them of their place in society—that they seem to cling to tradition.

Shudha Mazumdar's memoirs can add much to a sociological study or an historical account of this period. This is an excellent story of a woman's development from the time she was trained to adjust to the family she would marry into until, as a matron, she devoted a large amount of her time to social activities outside the family circle. Her loyalties had transcended the family connection over the years as had her patterns of interaction. While one can watch her horizons widen, one also senses her firm commitment to the preservation of certain traditional values and institutions. Trained as a child to perform a few simple religious ceremonies, a deep and serious spirituality developed as she matured. Shudha Mazumdar does not idealize the old system or make polemical statements to defend a tradition which sanctioned hierarchies and defined one's status in terms of birth, but she does help the reader understand the role tradition played for women in a period of social and political change.

SYRACUSE
MARCH 1977

GERALDINE H. FORBES

1

'Wife brought to bed of a daughter. . . .' The entry was dated 22 March, the year 1899. I was only ten years of age when I found this item, written in English, in an old diary. My advent had been important enough to be noted down by my father!

Mohan Chand House in the Kidderpore area of Calcutta was our home. The family had landed property, some of which was in Sripur—a little village in Khulna district. In 1842, our ancestor, Mohan Chand Ghose, had moved from there to Calcutta and acquired the home. Later my father, Tara Pada Ghose, extended it and named it after my great grandfather.

The house was enormous. The front wing was Father's. It had an English dining room, a vast Victorian drawing room, a book-lined library, shady verandas and corridors, and a marble staircase that led up to the immense roof-terrace overlooking the Kidderpore Docks. On this side also was the office where the clerical staff worked at huge ledgers under the eagle eye of the manager, who had a superintendent to help him in the administration on the estates. They lived in a separate block which was called the *amla* quarters. Here they and many men and maid-servants of the house were provided with food and lodging.

Mother's rooms were situated in another wing. Father also had a suite here and so did each of my brothers after marriage. And here too was a cheerful little room, the accouchement chamber, where all the family had been born and were to be born.

Of a family of five, I was the youngest and seemed to be always in the background. My elder sister, thirteen years my senior, had been married a few months before my birth.

People always appeared to be occupied with her and her husband in some way or other, for though they lived in Howrah, they often visited us. There was one brother before and two others after her.

The youngest, then six years old, was much disgusted at my arrival. One of my earliest recollections is a quarrel with him. 'Why were you born?' he burst out, 'ever since you came, both mother and father have stopped loving me. I do not wish to see your face!' I took the words to heart and for a long time after used to pull my pinafore over my face whenever we chanced to meet. He was a terrible tease and took a particular delight in my discomfiture. But he was my only playmate in my father's vast house and I bore it all for fear of forfeiting his friendship.

As time went on, I grew more attached to him than to my other brothers and many were the games we had together. I had several dolls and played with them all by myself, but since it was imperative to have someone else when I wanted them to get married, I begged him to become the father of the groom. Long before the ceremony, we secretly prepared tiny earthen lamps and dried them in the sun. Then, with the kind help of the cook, who let us have some oil and rag wicks, we lit them on the wedding night. Placed in a long line, the little flickering flames made a brave show when the bridegroom was driven forth in state. He was an English sailor and his coach was a doll's wicker perambulator for which his legs were far too long.

Besides being the father of the groom, my brother was helpful in other ways. He became the horse that drew the coach and the musician who hummed tunes from Lobo's wedding band as he pranced along with the perambulator in tow. I never breathed freely till the bridegroom had reached his destination on the other side of the veranda. There I waited with the blushing bride, whose veil was lowered in accordance with the time-honoured tradition of Bengal.

My brother obligingly officiated as the priest as well, and later begged people to come and 'see the face of the bride'. The blessings, which were invariably in the form of small coins, were promptly pocketed by him. He argued that as the bridegroom's father, he was entitled to take all that was given to the bride, and I, never quite certain of my status in the matter, was compelled to relinguish my rights. Once, I remember, we felt strongly that we could not honourably accept these gifts without dispensing some sort of hospitality to those who attended the ceremony, and so decided to invite them to a *carai-bhati* [picnic] which would be the wedding feast.

Once again, the cook co-operated and made available to us one of his stoves on which to prepare the *khichuri* [rice cooked with lentils] but hovered over us to see that we did not set ourselves on fire. I do not know whether my brother parted with the cash to buy the foodstuffs or whether they were supplied by this obliging cook, but I do remember that there was a delicious *khichuri*. As I was stirring the mixture, weighed down with the importance of being a bride's mother, my brother came in. 'No onions', he warned, knowing my weakness for this edible root, for onions are considered 'unclean' and our guests were extremely orthodox.

Ours was a very quiet household and we saw little of the world outside the great walls surrounding the garden. Except for my mother's numerous relations and a few of my father's, we seldom had visitors. Sometimes, drawn in a closed brougham by a dappled grey horse of uncertain temper, I accompanied my mother on visits to her people. Something or the other was always happening to them: engagement ceremonies or weddings, babies arriving or functions connected with their coming. Then, of course, there were times when I heard that they were ill, but I was never allowed to go with her on these occasions; instead of me, she took with her a small basket of fruit or some such invalid food for the patient. The clan instinct was strong in her and she was always lending a helping hand to anyone who came from her father's or my father's village.

My father, Tara Pada Ghose, was a landowner—a *zamindar*, as they were then called in Bengal. Most of the ancestral property which my father inherited was in the area of the Sunderbans—the Sundari forests in the delta of the Ganges. His position as *zamindar* required him to visit these remote areas. In later years he used a motor launch, but in those days it was the *budgerow* [houseboat] rowed by many men, that took him on his tours over the rough rivers. Among his retinue also sailed his beloved horse Jack to enable him to visit his tenants in their scattered holdings.

My father took a great interest in his tenants and did not leave them entirely to the mercies of the overseers. Every cold weather—as we refer to winter time—I remember seeing many of the tenants arrive with their families. For weeks they lived in a separate portion of our great house. The women and children came to Mother and told her of all their wants in the village. Every afternoon, in a large tent with a top gaily coloured in orange and red, the men had an audience with Father.

When Father held court, he sat in a special chair on a raised platform, surrounded by the officers of his estate. One by one the peasants came forward with their grievances and he lent a patient ear to each one. They were now the guests of their landlord, and Mother kept careful watch to see that they were all fed amply and well. The women and children toured the zoo and Kali temple, bathed in the Ganges and visited the *jadu ghar* [home of magic], the museum. These activities delighted the children and their mothers, while the menfolk were busy with more important matters.

Apart from his estates, Father had two great hobbies, his health and his horses. He had four horses in his stables, and I remember so well the manner in which he fussed over their food and had them groomed in his presence. He was a familiar figure on the *maidan* [open field] riding there every morning, accompanied by his attendant with flying turban-tail. Once, near the Red Road, he was thrown. It was on his 72nd birthday, but he picked himself up and rode home.

'What made you do that, Mr. Ghose?' asked Colonel Denham White, our family physician, as he felt his patient's pulse. He had been called when Father discovered that his aches and pains were bad enough to keep him in bed. 'You could have returned home in your car. Was it not waiting for you as usual?' 'Yes,' Father replied 'but Jack would never again have acknowledged me as his master if I had.'

In a specially built gymnasium, he exercised regularly and kept magnificent health even in old age. I never saw him eat our food. He dieted according to every book on dieting, experimenting to discover what was best for him. His diet was composed, according to an English menu book, of meat and fish—boiled, baked or steamed—and vegetables. But there came a time when, much to Mother's distress, it was nothing but fruit and nuts. When he felt he was putting on weight he made drastic cuts in the courses. It was fascinating to watch the cooked meat and fish being weighed on scales at the dinner table, and to see bits being snipped off here and there to conform to the exact requirement suitable for his size and age according to the book he happened to be following.

Even though he did not partake of our food, a tray of little bowls containing many kinds of curries was unfailingly set before him by Mother. Sometimes he sampled them and commented on their richness, firmly convinced that this, together with the rice eaten with them, was the cause of all the illness in the country. The one Bengali food he ate with relish was *dahi* [yoghurt], and regularly each night Mother put a little bowl of milk to set for his lunch the following day.

He was also extremely fond of her *sandesh* [a milk sweet] which was served in tiny terra-cotta bowls sprinkled with rose petals as a special delicacy at his dinner parties. She was never present at these parties for we were all in *purdah* [seclusion] in those days in spite of Father's advanced Western ideas.

My father had lost his father in infancy and had been brought up by his uncle, Jogendro Chandra Ghose. This uncle was a remarkable personality. In his dress and in his living he was extremely orthodox, but in religion he was staunchly Positivist. He was a follower of the French philosopher, Auguste Comte, and considered Richard Congreve, the head of the London Positivist Society, his *guru.*

To Jogendro, Positivism seemed to be the ideal philosophy to tie together valuable Hindu social institutions and certain secular, rational concepts from the West. He began to write books and articles which explained his brainchild, 'Hindu-Positivism'. Having accepted the Positivist 'sacrament of maturity' in 1884, Jogendro was qualified to become the leader of the 'Society for the Study of Comte's Positivist Philosophy in India'. As leading member, Jogendro organized the festivals of the Positivists and carried on a lengthy and exhaustive correspondence with Richard Congreve.

I never saw my great-uncle, but many were the tales current in our family of his simplicity, courage, and absolute freedom from convention. This background was a strong influence in my father's life so that he in turn became unorthodox and immovable in his ideas.

My mother was the sweetest soul, but poles apart from my father. While he remained unorthodox to a degree, whole-heartedly adopting western ideas, she clung to the eastern ones. He had his ways of living and thinking, but she held firmly to her own.

My mother's people came from a nobler lineage than my father's because they had the blood of Maharaja Protapaditya in their veins. Protapaditya of Jessore was the pride of Bengal—the rebel lord famed for his valour and stubborn resistance to Moghul sovereignty! Stirring tales were told of how well he fought and was victorious in the sixteenth century, but, alas, was later conquered and captured. Guru Prasad Roy Chowdhury, my mother's grandfather, owned extensive land and property in Khulna, in the surrounding areas and in Calcutta. There can still be found a lane named after him in the southern part of Calcutta.

The family mansion was at Taki Saidpore by the broad Ichamati river. Here his son, Rajendra Nath, a much loved landlord, maintained the old traditions of charity and almsgiving, fulfilled all obligations to his tenants and dependants, lived honourably and died full of years leaving ten children to mourn his loss.

My mother was the eldest daughter. Her name was Giri Bala, 'daughter of the mountains', and it was an appropriate one. She had amazing strength and endurance; her mind was stronger than her frail and ailing body which never dominated her spirit. She had no tact, spoke the truth bluntly without mincing matters, and was immovable as a rock where her principles were concerned. She was a curious mixture of sentiment, practicality and courage.

The *Ramayana* and the *Mahabharata* epics were her favourite reading, yet she was passionately fond of the very popular historical romances of Bankim Chandra Chatterjee. In those days, she also loved the writing of Hem Chandra Banerjee and had learned most of his poems by heart. Many were the stories she told us about him, and in her jewelbox was a treasured pair of earrings that the poet had blessed her with when she arrived as a bride. His palatial home, which now has a rather desolate look, was very near ours and his family seemed to be the only one in Kidderpore with whom our women-folk were on visiting terms.

We learned from her of the famous visitors to the house for Jogendro regarded his special apartments as similar to a French salon. Mother had watched all this from a distance for she never appeared before the men. During the years, she had had glimpses of many who became famous—Henry J.S. Cotton of the Indian Civil Service; W.C. Bonnerjee, the first President of the Indian National Congress; Dwarkanath Mitra, the first Indian High Court Judge; and of course, Bankim Chandra Chatterjee and Hem Chandra Banerjee.

Mother told us in detail about the leading literati who gathered in our home—how they would read out their contributions to *Banga Darshan*, a popular Bengali monthly published by Bankim Chandra, and shout with laughter as some important personage was ridiculed without mercy. She loved those evenings and loved dispensing hospitality to the jovial men who gathered there. She was a young wife then, and being weary after the long day would sit nodding on the steps as she watched dinner grow cold. At times it was past midnight when she had finished serving the men and was able to have her own meal, but those were happy days for her.

We never tired of hearing how the poet, Hem Chandra Banerjee, once played a practical joke on her. To all who belonged to the coterie, he posted a doggerel in Bengali which, translated, would be something like this:

Tapsya fish just off the fire with piping hot *loochi*
Chipped potatoes, cauliflowers and young goat's meat
On a cold winter eve should you care to eat,
Then hasten to Number 14 Puddapukur Street.

Mother faithfully maintained the various rituals, functions and social customs that had been handed down to her by grandmother. In spite of my father's liberal ideas and Western way of life, in faith he was essentially a Hindu and it was here that he and my mother were one; both were religious and pious without cant.

Many of Mother's beliefs, to Father's rational mind, were mere superstitions, but he never seriously interfered or forbade anything she chose to do within our home. He had at one time tried his best to persuade her to eschew our age-old customs and to adopt Western ones, but she had been adamant in her refusal.

'At a very early age I was brought to this house by your mother to keep up its traditions. So as long as I am here I must be true to the things into which I have been initiated. Should you leave this ancestral home of yours and live elsewhere, then only in new surroundings and in altered circumstances, can I think and act according to your desires. Here, I am not only your wife, but the daughter-in-law of the house. . . ,' she had told him. And it was ever thus. She kept her faith and lived up to her beliefs, and rigidly adhered to family traditions she felt it her duty to uphold. We, the children, knew in some measure how difficult life was for her and how easy it could have been had she agreed to follow Father's wishes. But no, she had her own ideas of duty and those were of paramount importance to her. The legacy left by her mother-in-law lay heavily on her but she bore all with equanimity. 'A man may do whatever he chooses but that home is doomed where a woman follows her own desires,' was one of her favourite sayings. Generous to a fault, endowed with a priceless sense of humour, always self-restrained and fearless, she bravely stood up for what she considered to be true.

She had her own personal establishment including her kitchen, presided over by a Brahmin cook, and a retinue of servants for the daily work. She also had a private kitchen where she made her own tea and every day some dishes for us, no matter how many had been prepared by her Brahmin cook and Father's Muslim one. Pir Mohammed had a detached cottage in our compound. Here he cooked his *belati khana*

[English food] for Father's table and cared for the hens that fluttered about and squawked and laid their eggs in a specially built coop.

Although Mother never sat at Father's table, she never failed to be present when he sat for his meals in lonely splendour. It was nearly always long past midday before she had her own lunch and then only after her duties and her daily ritual of prayers and worship were complete. At night, the cook departed after having served us, leaving Mother's food in *dekacis* [pans] over the dying fires. Whether this kept it warm or not we never knew, for we were fast asleep before she had her frugal dinner, after her evening bath and prayers and after every one else had dined.

We had our food from the hands of her Brahmin cook but were occasionally allowed to taste the Western dishes from Father's table. But the pleasure was brief. Immediately after having eaten this food, I had to undergo a thorough wash and change every item of my clothing before I was permitted to touch anything in Mother's apartment. Unorthodox food was considered to be unclean, and therefore I was unclean until I had been thoroughly washed.

I remember that the youngest of my brothers was very much against my partaking of this unclean food. When I expressed my surprise as to why I should abstain when he and all my brothers ate it, I was loftily told that they were men, and it ill-befitted me, one of the inferior species, to even dream of acting like them. 'Does Mother or Didi [elder sister]* ever eat here, you stupid? You are a girl, so its a positive sin for you to eat fowl or their eggs.' I grew anxious and implored his advice as to how I could evade committing this terrible sin. 'I'll tell you what', he suggested sagely after much deliberation, 'when Father calls you at dinner time, make a wry face—like this,' and he painfully twisted his face, 'and say you have a tummy-ache.' Now I was particularly fond of the tasty dishes

*Siblings are referred to by kinship terms rather than their given names. Thus, Didi is elder sister; Dada, the eldest of elder brothers; Mejda, the second eldest of elder brothers; and Chorda, the youngest of the elder brothers.

prepared by Pir Mohammed, but what could I do? Even for their sake I dared not displease this despotic brother who could make life unbearable for me with his gibes and threats if I did not blindly obey him.

So the following day I repressed my unholy appetite and feigned an acute pain. Since Father was concerned, he did not press me much and thus I purchased the goodwill of my playmate by abstaining from custard pudding. But, the plan failed to work for long. 'Come now,' coaxed Father, offering me a piece of chicken cutlet on his fork one day, 'Have this wee bit, I am sure this will not hurt you.' The fragrance of the forbidden meat made me forget my vows. Docilely I accepted the offer while my brother looked daggers at me.

The handling of small coins was distasteful to Father, so Jamuna, his old servant, spent whole afternoons conditioning them. The copper coins were polished till they shone like gold, then each of them was neatly folded in a small square piece of white note paper. A few of these were always in Father's purse to be given away to the many lame and blind who begged in the streets.

He was very sympathetic to suffering and his charities were many and varied. He distributed largesse to needy Brahmins during the death anniversary ceremonies of his father and grandfather; doled out rice to the poor who lined both sides of the street in front of our gates every Sunday afternoon; sent sacks of rice to the somberly dressed Little Sisters of the Poor for their Home for the Aged and Infirm; sent cheques to the Bishop's wife, Mrs. Coppleston, to buy coal in the winter for the slum-dwellers of London; gave land to our village priest on which to grow the rice needed to support his family; and subscribed to countless causes. His purse was ever open for all charitable purposes. He made no distinction amongst his beneficiaries, whereas Mother's beneficience was solely for the people of the rural areas she knew.

So far as she was concerned, she had no doubt that charity should begin at home and, considering the unending needs of her own and Father's village people, it should definitely remain there. She was always amused at Father's charities and thought them just another of his foibles.

Father was always well-dressed, having an extensive wardrobe of European clothes tailored by the best English firms of Calcutta. He wore them with ease. A man of extraordinarily fair skin, a small 'French-Cut' beard as it was called in those days, and a tall distinguished frame, he was often mistaken for a European. A friend of my brother related that as boys, they would run to the gate to watch my father pass by in his landau, drawn by a pair of spirited horses and driven by a coachman flourishing his whip. The picture was completed by the two footmen who stood at the back of the coach, crying out to pedestrians to keep to the left as the coach turned corners. The jingling bells and snorting horses, the colourful liveries of the servants and the long gleaming landau with Father immaculately dressed in foreign clothes (complete with pincenez on his nose) was of perpetual interest to them. He said Father drove by at a certain hour in the afternoon with such exactitude that they sometimes set their clock to the time. 'Look, look, there goes the Frenchman. . . .' they would call to each other, and for a long time took him to be one.

Sometimes I was asked to accompany him on one of those afternoon outings that were considered to be so good for one's health. To sit primly dressed in my best frock and straw hat trimmed with pink roses, in silence, was something of an ordeal but of course I could not dream of refusing to comply with his wishes. It was boring just to sit and watch the passing streets and people. Father was always absorbed in his own thoughts and those were the days when little girls were to be seen and not heard. Once I was caught putting a peanut in my mouth and was gently reprimanded. Eating in public was simply not done. His code of good behaviour was never preached; we were left to exercise our own intelligence in the matter.

Mother, on the contrary, pressed her points by adding that it was necessary for a daughter of Bengal to do this, or not to do that, concluding most times with, 'Remember, you will have to go to your father-in-law's home and if you do not know these things you will be held in disgrace.' 'The father-in-law's home' assumed awesome proportions for young girls in Bengal; forever it was dinned into their heads what would be approved of there and what would not. To gain the approval of the revered elders of one's husband's family was an important item in the code of good conduct.

Father dearly loved and venerated my grandmother. She had been widowed at the age of nineteen, with a small daughter and this son who was then only a few months old. Her word was law in the household. Bitter sorrow and stern circumstances had been hers since early womanhood and they had helped to mould her character accordingly.

She did not quite approve of her only son's lapse from Indian ways of living, but being wise she made a compromise. He might do whatever he chose, but once a day he must have his food in orthodox style in her apartment. And it was so. As long as she was alive, Father was allowed to eat from Pir Mohammed's hands only at night. In the morning, his mother was not to be denied the pleasure of supervising her son's food, fussing over him in joy and coaxing him to partake of special delicacies prepared by her cook. She died in 1904, and I have but a dim recollection of her.

Father was deeply grieved. For a whole month following her death he obeyed the simple but severe customs laid down by orthodox Hindu society for those who sorrow for the dead. Living on a single dish of boiled rice and vegetables prepared by Mother in the morning, and only fruit and milk at night; wearing only those clothes that were absolutely necessary; and abstaining from any form of luxury or entertainment, he lived a rigidly austere life for the whole of the mourning month. Afterwards, he meticulously performed the elaborate rites of the *shraddha* ceremony for the peace of the soul of the departed, fed the poor in great numbers and distributed largesse to needy Brahmins and learned Pandits. After all was over, he returned to his normal way of living but was unable to reconcile himself to the loss of his mother. Leaving Calcutta, he travelled alone in North India for many weeks visiting Mathura, Hardwar and other holy places.

2

One day after Father had returned from his travels, I learned that I would be going to school. Mother packed a small tiffin box with pastries and sweets, and it was duly placed in Father's landau. Bursting with importance, I brushed my close-cropped hair, put on a clean frock and pinafore, and took my place opposite my father. Soon we arrived at St. Teresa's Convent School, and here I was admitted as a day scholar.

At that time, I was the only Indian girl amongst the English and Anglo-Indian girls at the school. Being quite ignorant of English, I had to speak in broken Hindi to make myself understood. The good nuns, who mostly came from Germany and France, knew some Hindi but not a word of Bengali. I made friends quickly and became very fond of school.

'It won't do to teach her English only', said Mother, so I was placed under the tutelage of one of her relatives and from him I received my first lessons in Bengali. I used to rise early in the morning and trot downstairs to the *amla* quarters for this instruction.

In a section of this detached building, separate from the clerks, lived distant relatives whose slender salaries forbade the luxury of bringing their families to Calcutta. Year in and year out they lived there, provided with food and lodging by Father, visiting their dear ones in distant villages only during holidays. Amongst these kinsmen were an uncle of Father's and another on Mother's side, the former lean and lanky, a teacher at the David Hare School, and the latter, not unlike Falstaff, a clerk at the Meteorological Office which Mother always insisted on referring to as the 'stormy office'.

These two were a jolly couple and had a room to themselves.

I was the pupil of the Falstaffian uncle and well remember one of his favourite modes of punishment. When I failed to answer his question in a satisfactory manner, I was lifted up to the top of a wall that partitioned their room from the next and left there with legs dangling miserably until my sin was sufficiently expiated.

Father did not approve of our visits to this portion of the house. In fact, except for Bengali lessons we were forbidden to enter the *amla* quarters, but my youngest brother and I found it difficult to keep away from the apartment of this corpulent uncle. Full of Bengali folk tales, an inexhaustible stock of grisly histories of ghosts and goblins and romantic and heroic stories from the ancient epics, he was a most engaging companion. The battles from the *Mahabharata* were a popular subject, and I was often asked which of the five Pandava brothers I would like for my future bridegroom. 'Go away', I cried, turning away my burning face, but so well did he extol the virtues of each of the five heroes that I found it hard to choose. We were never tired of hearing the exploits of the brave Bhima: of his giant size, his great appetite that was so hard to appease, his strong language vented on his enemies, and the manner in which he vanquished them. To my child's mind, it was he who shone with brighter light than the virtuous Yadhisthir or the valiant Arjuna.

On Saturdays and Sundays, when there was no school, we would steal through the cowshed in the silent afternoons to listen to uncle's wonderful stories. He was a born teller of tales and his graphic accounts, delivered with gestures and an abundance of eye movements, kept us spellbound. We did not dare to use the front door for Father might see us, but that slinking through the cowshed was a terrible business! I still remember how my heart hammered as I dodged the curving horn of Chandi. She was a beautiful cow with a large white spot on her brow and a most uncertain temper! But we were well aware of Father's disapproval, and this was the only other route leading to that magic world of delectable tales.

The vocation of every girl was to be a wife and a mother, and the ideal held up to her for her future life was *seva*, service to others. The blessings of the elders of the husband's home were considered to be necessary ingredients for her happiness and prosperity, and these were to be earned by services, however small, given in loving respect. It was the pride and privilege of a bride to serve but if she failed, her parents were blamed for her shortcomings and the mother bore the slur of having failed in her duty towards her daughter.

Since much would be required of the girl when she attained womanhood, a system of education began to prepare her for her future life from her earliest days. As nearly all things in India hinge on religion, this training was also centered in religious thoughts and practices.

It aimed at imparting an elementary knowledge of the basic ideas that were considered by a Bengali family to be good and true; it was accomplished through the medium of little rituals and prayers and fasts. These rituals had some connection with objects that were familiar to the child such as plant and animal life. By this system of training, the child was taught to be disciplined and dutiful and responsible. She who undertakes a lesson of this kind, is said to have undertaken a *brata*. The literal meaning of *brata* is vow. So the child takes a vow to do a certain thing which must be performed.

Many are the *bratas* performed by Hindu women regularly during certain times of the year, but there are also *bratas* which are only for the young unmarried girl. The child is left to do everything in her own way. Unlike the usual Sanskrit prayers that need a priest to prompt them, the *mantras* [sacred formula] used in performing these *bratas* are generally in simple Bengali verse which the child learns by heart and recites unaided.

The *tulsi brata* teaches the child how to care for the bush of Sweet basil that is so dearly cherished in every Hindu home. The cow *brata* makes her familiar with the four-footed friend whose milk not only sustained her in infancy but is still an important item of her daily food. There is another delightful *brata* called *punyi-pukur*, or the lake of merit, in which the child digs a diminutive lake and seating herself before it, prays to Mother Earth for the gift of tolerance and for the fortitude to endure all things in life lightly, as does Mother Earth herself.

The prayers are quaint and the requests are remarkable for their naiveté. Worldly bliss is sought in many forms. For instance, in one *brata*—the little devotee desires:

Cows in the cowshed, and
Corn in the Store-house
Vermilion between the parting of my hair
Every year a son, and
May not a single one die, and
Never may a teardrop fall from my eye.

Each *brata* has a tale of itself. At the conclusion of her *brata*, the girl must sit with her group of friends and listen to the legend that has been woven round it.

Even though my Positivist grandfather was no more, his wife was to live to a good old age and took a lively interest in family affairs. She looked with disapproval on my bare knees and frocks, foretelling sorrow for my mother, through me, if she persisted in allowing Father's Western ideas to permeate our household. So whenever 'young Grandmother' (for that is what we called her), came for a visit I was careful to stay away from her.

But one day she caught sight of me and said to my mother, 'Well, Bou [daughter-in-law], your daughter is growing up. Are you making her take an interest in any *brata niyamas*? She is old enough to make a beginning, or does her father desire to make her into a *pucca memsahib* [genuine foreign woman]?' Mother looked at me thoughtfully and nodded. 'Yes, she has just stepped into her eighth year. . . .'

The existence of the *atman*, the Godhead or divinity, within men is accepted as a fact by all those who are of the Hindu faith and it is believed that the highest good is the realization and the expression of that divinity. To achieve this, various spiritual disciplines and techniques were recommended by the sages and seers of ancient times.

As realization is attained through the mind, attempts are

made to train the restless mind from one's earliest years. The training is done according to certain rules, which demand regular practice and form the basis of the concept of *yoga.* The daily routine of the vast majority of Hindus (women in particular) is governed by rules which are in fact connected with those rules of discipline preliminary to *yoga.*

First, there is the visit to the toilet followed by a bath. Then, dressed in clean clothes, comes prayers or meditation and only after this is it possible to eat. This then became my morning routine at the age of eight and I have never deviated from it.

One of the most popular *bratas* in Bengal for the unmarried girl is Shiva *Puja* [worship]. The great God Shiva is the ideal male and many a maiden is blessed with the words: 'May you be granted a husband like Shiva.' He is well known for his deep devotion to his beloved wife, Durga, and for the havoc he wrought throughout heaven and earth in his wild paroxysm of grief when he lost her. As old as the hills, the beautiful legend has still the power to thrill many a girl of the Hindu faith and make her long for a husband, not as resplendent as Indra, King of the Gods, but as great as Shiva. For the Great Yogi cared nothing for earthly riches and dearly loved his wife. Mothers initiated their daughters in this *brata* for it was believed the benediction of Shiva could bring his devotee a husband as great-hearted and loving as himself.

Bysakh, the first month of the Bengali year, is considered to be an auspicious time to commence any *brata niyama.* So on the 14th of April (New Year's day in Bengal) Mother made me undertake my first *brata*, the Shiva *puja.* I was then eight years old and learned to perform the little ritual every morning before I went to school. For this, the first *niyama* was observed; that is, I had to have a good bath and wear a crimson silk *cheli sari*, the correct dress for the occasion, and not allow a sigle morsel of food or drink of any kind to touch my lips before the conclusion of the ceremony.

Rising early in the morning, I first bathed and changed and then I ran to the garden to pick some flowers and fresh young blades of *durva* grass with which to perform my *puja.*

The ritual had to be finished before I could have breakfast, and then, breathlessly, in frock and pigtail I was ready at the gate waiting for the school bus that arrived unfailingly at 8-30 a.m.

On the ground floor of mother's establishment was our *puja* room. No one was allowed to enter this sacred room with unclean clothes, and leather footwear had to be left ouside the doors. On its faded saffron walls were pictures by Ravi Varma, colour prints of various gods and goddesses with gilt frames tarnished by time.

On a large lotus, inlaid in black and white marble on the marble floor, reposed the beautifully wrought white marble throne of Lakshmi, the goddess of Fortune. On this was the *pali* of Lakshmi—the token of prosperity. The *pali* was a wickerwork basket, not unlike a Grecian urn in shape, filled with recently harvested golden paddy and some *cowries*, sea-shells used as currency in very ancient times and considered now to be symbols of wealth and good fortune.

Crowning this *pali* was another basket containing toilet articles of the goddess. In shape it was a miniature *pali*, usually made of wicker embroidered with sea-shells and trimmed around the edges with some red material. This is the emblem of happy wifehood which the young bride carries when she leaves her father's home for her father-in-law's. Besides the comb and mirror are lengths of gaily coloured ribbon for her hair, a pair of conch shell bangles, a *kajallata* (collyrium pot) with which to darken her eyes and the little vermilion box with its crimson powder that is cherished so dearly by every married girl in Bengal. From the moment she becomes a bride, vermilion begins to play an important part in her life.

After the marriage ceremony, her bridegroom dips the edge of a silver comb in the bright powder and marks the centre parting of her hair. After that day, every morning and evening for the rest of her life she renews the ruby red mark with the edge of her comb. Only when death takes her husband away from her does she rub off the mark and put away her beloved vermilion box forever.

Water from the Ganges was stored in a huge brass jar.

The great river Ganga (Ganges) that rushes from the snowy Himalayan regions, cascading down to the plains below, flows through Bengal on her way to the sea, making the land green and fertile. Loved and revered throughout India, the Ganga is spoken of as a goddess in Indian epics and her waters are considered very holy.

Facing the *puja* room was a small open courtyard, the floor of which was paved with cement, except for a square in the centre in which the earth was left bare. This was the place of sacrifice. Into this soft earth was fixed a very old, worn, forked piece of wood which was called the *hari-katha*. Here, once a year in October, (on the night of the full moon) during the Kojagori Lakshmi *puja*, a pure white goat was beheaded by the man who by vocation was entitled to perform this sacrifice. He was called the *karma* and as his forefathers before him, did this work for a small fee. This was the only sacrifice that was performed at our home.

Mother also had a *dhenki*. This was a huge wooden threshing machine which was fixed on the floor of the *dhenki* room and here Mother with her maids threshed the paddy and prepared the *chira*, parched and flattened rice, for the *pujas*. It was done in token quantities but anyone in the locality who needed some for ceremonial purposes came to have it made in our *dhenki*. The thud, thud of the *dhenki* as the crusher went up and down in the hole, threshing the grain, disturbed Father so it could never be used when he was in. I remember enjoying the fun to be had stepping on and off the end of the *dhenki* making it go up and down again.

In the *puja* room, Mother taught me how to make the necessary arrangements for the ritual with a set of small copper utensils I had been given. In the little water vessel I poured out some Ganges water and first washed the flowers, the *durva* grass, the leaves from the *bael* tree so loved by Shiva and *aconda* which was difficult to obtain in town, but sometimes supplied by our *mali* [gardener]. Daily he brought a fresh sprig from our *bael* tree, and from this I would select the unblemished, tender young three-leaved shoots. The *durva* grass had to have three blades too. The grass and the fresh flowers I picked from our garden were separately placed on the little copper flower plate. Crimson and cream sandalwood would then be separately rubbed with water on a stone slab and the paste thus formed scraped up into tiny little bowls. Finally, a handful of uncooked rice was carefully washed and heaped on another plate, and on this I placed a peeled banana. This was the *naibedya*, food offering.

In an earthen pot in a corner of the *puja* room was kept some soft mud from the Ganges and with a fistful of this substance I would mould my symbol of Shiva. I never could make this in a proper manner and was often in despair, for my Shiva would insist on being a crooked one, which boded no good for me. In a flat dish I put my Shiva on a sprig of *bael*, then I lit a little lamp and placed the food offering and the flower plate on either side, sitting on a small carpet to perform my ritual.

First I gave my Shiva a bath gently sprinkling him three times with a little Ganges water from the tiny copper shell-shaped vessel. Every time I did so I murmured, 'I salute thee O Shiva.' Then, dipping a few flowers and leaves in the sandalwood paste and holding them in my joined palms, I said a little prayer before making my offering. Briefly, some of the attributes of Shiva were mentioned, and it ended something like this:

Lord I am so small a maid
That hymns of praise I know not,
Aconda flower, leaves of *bael* and water from the Ganga
Be content with these my offerings,
O Bhola Maheswara.

Bhola is a name of Shiva, meaning, 'the oblivious one', for unlike other gods he is said to be oblivious of formal ritual and content with a wild flower or a leaf if it is offered with love and devotion. Maheswara is another name of Shiva, and it means 'great god'.

This offering too was made three times. Generally I closed my eyes trying to visualize Shiva with the patch of deep blue on his fair throat, the third eye of wisdom on his forehead and matted locks piled high on his head. There was such a picture of Shiva on the wall, with a slim crescent moon shining from above and a sweet little face peeping out from behind the moon. 'Who is that peeping out behind Shiva?' I had once asked. 'O that is Mother Ganga,' was Mother's casual reply. 'But why is she there?' I persisted. 'Because Bhagiratha begged her to come down to earth. She was pleased with his penance and prayers and consented to do so if he could make Shiva agree to receive her for otherwise the earth could not bear her weight. So Shiva, who is ever ready to help his devotees, bore the first impact of her mighty waters on his head. This made it possible for Bhagiratha to obtain salvation for the soul of his ancestors.'

'Tell me more . . . .' I begged breathlessly. 'I have no time, its all in the *Ramayana*, you must read it for yourself.' 'But that is all about Rama, Lakshmana, and Sita,' I protested, remembering that she had read aloud the 'Banishment of Sita.' 'Bhagiratha was an ancestor of Rama', was her short reply as she hurried away.

Every year for four years, I regularly performed my Shiva *puja* throughout the month of Bysakh. I had been told that I must not think of anything else while I performed my *puja* but this was a difficult order to follow. Once, I had devoutly closed my eyes as usual when offering my flowers and, on opening them, found to my surprise and awe that a full-blown flower had covered my Shiva like a cap. I ran to inform Mother and dragged her in to see the miracle; she smiled and said perhaps I had said my prayer with 'one mind' and that was the sign that the great god was pleased with me.

The fast of *nil*, another *brata*, was performed by my mother, *Didi* (my elder sister), and myself all together. This *brata* is comparatively simple. We had to fast until the worship of Shiva was over in the evening, and then we feasted on fruits and sweets prepared from milk. *Nil-Kantha*, which literally means, 'blue-throated' is but one of the many names of Shiva. Forever unselfish, it was he who had offered to take the bitter poison that was churned out of the ocean by the demons in their search for *amrita*, the nectar of immortality. Unable to swallow the poison, he stored it in his throat where the dark blue poison glowed through his fair skin.

To conclude the *nil brata*, we went at sunset with offerings of flowers and fruit, sweets and sandalwood paste on a tray to the temple adjoining our house. Each of us lit a little lamp and poured Ganges water, milk, and honey over the great black marble symbol of Shiva. After placing our offerings before it, we said our prayers.

There was another *brata* that Mother made me undertake. When roused, I was the unfortunate possessor of a fiery temper and stinging tongue, which in Mother's opinion was most unbecoming in a maiden and would mean endless sorrow for me at my future father-in-law's house. At the same time I was always blurting out things that were better left unsaid. When reprimanded, I justified myself with, 'But, it is true, Mother, so why should I not say it?' According to her, there was a proper time and place for truths, but I never could gain her perspective. After losing an argument, my elder sister once retreated with the comment that my tongue was not to be wondered at since I was born under the sign of Cancer; and she warned Mother of the dire consequences in store for me if nothing were done about it.

So, Mother at last decided upon the *Madhu-Sankranti brata*. For two successive years on the last day of each month, I had to give a small new bell-metal bowl of *madhu* [honey], and a silver coin to a holy man, and then take the 'dust of his feet' in salutation. It was hoped that by his blessings I would gain a honeyed tongue.

One of the important annual events in our house was Saraswati *Puja* to worship the Goddess of Learning. As Saraswati is the beneficent Mother who bestows knowledge of the arts and of letters, her devotees are mostly students and it is they who welcome her advent. My brothers were very keen on this *puja*, and long before the actual day, they were occupied with preparations for the function. A clay figure of the goddess has to be dressed and set up in an appropriate setting. The main task was making the *caal*, the background screen of split bamboo. The goddess would stand in front of this on a little platform protected on both sides by screens of bamboo. The whole edifice was first covered with coloured paper, then decorated with lotus blossoms cut from white and rose coloured tissue paper. Our *caal* was always the best in the neighbourhood and considered to be a suitable work of art.

We built the *caal* in a little room downstairs which was always kept locked. It was to be a surprise for the household and would only be brought forth the day before the *puja*. In this task my duties consisted of running endless errands, boiling the paste, hunting out the scissors when they got lost amidst the pile of paper shavings, and other humble tasks. But I was properly thankful for the right to remain within the room where all these fascinating proceedings went on. I was also permitted to join in making the multi-coloured paper festoons for decorations. On the eve of the *puja* day, the *protima* [image of the goddess] was brought home where it was greeted by the sonorous sound of the conch shell blown by Mother.

My brothers rose at dawn the next morning to gather leaves which they entwined with fresh flowers over the door of the *puja* room. The goddess on her pedestal looked serenely beautiful.

Around her, a miniature grove had been created with maidenhair fern, crotons and other potted plants. On either side were little lacquered tables (twenty in all) holding the food offering. There were large shining brass plates filled with fresh fruits, dates, nuts, and other dried fruits. Coconut sweets of many kinds, made by Mother, were a special feature. Varieties of them ranging from tasty red globules prepared with shredded coconut and molasses, to snowy white, feathery chips, so light and airy, and crescent-shaped affairs strewn with almonds, pistachios, and raisins, and flavoured with cardamom seeds were all present. Then there were fragile cream wafers stamped in delicate designs, sugar cakes, plates of *atap* rice, a kind used for *pujas*, and brown sugar piled up high and crowned with a banana. There were also bowls of milk and honey and yoghurt for the goddess. In wicker trays and tiny baskets were displayed delicious balls of parched rice, fried and rolled in golden syrup, crisp popcorn coated with molasses, and fresh scrunchy puffed rice, together with roasted gram treated with treacle, and every single item was Mother's handiwork.

The place on which the *protima* rested was decorated with *alpana*, a kind of free-hand painting of decorative patterns done for ceremonial purposes. It was traced on the patent-stone floor with deft fingers dipped in a thick paste of *atap* rice and water, the motif being the lotus blossom and bud. Mother's *alpana* was always lovely, and after completing it, she painted pairs of *Sri Charana*, beautiful footprints, from the door of the *puja* room right up to the *alpana* carpet she had spread to welcome Mother Saraswati. The goddess was supposed to step on these as she entered the room. On a small stool in front of the image, each of us had to place some of our books and a glass ink-pot with a reed pen. Blessed by the goddess, it was thought we would then prosper in our studies. I was fearfully weak in arithmetic and I never forgot to include my dog-eared book in the hopes of bringing about some improvement.

The *protima* was first of all consecrated by the priest. This little ceremony is known as the *pran pratistha*, instilling life. The priest invokes the spirit of the goddess into the *protima*, and from that moment till the *puja* is over, Saraswati is said to reside within the clay image and to receive the worship of her devotees. Until this was done, the image was referred to as *protima*, but after the *pran pratistha*, she was Devi [goddess]. As soon as the *puja* was over, the image was again called *protima*.

We had to fast until the *anjali* which was usually about 10 a.m. and followed the *puja* performed by the priest. For the *anjali*, family and friends gathered together and stood before the goddess. *Anjali*, the 'flower offering' to the goddess, was accompanied by Sanskrit *mantras*, repeated in unison. First came the *mantra* to meditate on, the *dhyan mantra*:

O Pure White One, seated on a white lotus
Bending so gracefully,
Thou art as beautiful as the young moon

In thy lotus hands thou holdest the book and the pen
Grant us the wealth of all learning and fine arts
O goddess of speech, I bow before thee.

Then the *pronám mantra* :

Hail to thee, goddess of the moving and unmoving worlds,
Pearls adorn thy breast, with beautiful hands
Thou holdest the *Vina* and the Book,
O goddess Bhagavati Bharathi, I bow before thee.

Then came the culminating prayer that we all loved to chant together; Father had taught it to me himself so I did not need the help of the priest. By this time a sense of intimacy has been established between the goddess and the devotee, who therefore feels no compunction in making his many demands. Assured of the Mother's all-embracing love, and knowing that she understands his frailities, the devotee says his final prayer.

A three-leaved *bael* sprig and a few flowers sprinkled with sandalwood paste were given to each of us. Placing them within our folded palms, we stood in a semi-circle around the goddess and chanted in Sanskrit:

Even as Brahma, the creator of man cannot be without thee,
Grant one also the boon of cleaving to thee.
The Vedas, sacred lore, song and dance and other arts are inseparable from thee;
O goddess, favour me so that I may attain perfection in all these fine arts.
Good fortune, good memory, the ability to grasp the truth,
Health and radiance, patience and contentment.
With these eight attributes of thine, sustain me O Saraswati.

This prayer, with its music and rhythm, never failed to cast its influence over us, and we all felt better and more hopeful at least as far as learning was concerned.

At the end of this prayer, the flowers and leaves were cast

at the feet of the goddess. Having prostrated ourselves before the goddess in salutation, we each received a flower from Saraswati's feet as a symbol of her benediction. The *puja* being over, *prasad* was distributed. *Prasad*, left-over holy food, consisted of the food offering which the goddess had partaken of.

Distributing the food offering was an immense task. All the members of the *amla* quarter and the friends and relations who had gathered for the ceremony received a sample of each item that had been offered to the goddess. Each one received his share on a piece of banana leaf. Some plates of *prasad* were also sent to our neighbours and a plateful was sent up for Father who would eat only one little piece. 'Prasad kanika matra', he would say with a smile, meaning that a tiny morsel of this holy food was sufficient for the purpose of breaking one's fast. After this, we all trooped to the store-room for the pastries and milk sweetmeats that had been arriving from the confectioners since morning.

Here we had a liberal allowance as the mid-day meal was generally late on this day. Cartloads of vegetables had arrived from father's Sunderban estates for the vegetarian feast to be served to friends and relatives invited to the *puja*. The kitchen hummed with the activities of Brahmin cooks hired specially for the occasion while the veranda near the *puja* room was crowded with remotely related aunts and cousins who sat peeling and chopping the vegetables.

Huge fires roared in the kitchen and over them hung giant cauldrons filled with various curries. On large wooden platters, flour and *ghee* [clarified butter] were kneaded by perspiring stalwarts to prepare the dough for *loochis*. First the dough was converted into little balls, then each ball was rolled out into a thin rounded patty. They were then dropped into boiling *ghee*. Fascinated, I watched the cook fry the *loochis*. He flung three, four, five cakes at a time into the wide vessels of boiling *ghee* and immediately each one became an enormous bubble. Swiftly he did them to a turn and drained them in big wicker baskets by his side. They were served at once to the important guests, for the *loochi* has to be eaten straight off the fire to be really enjoyed. The rest of us were served when they had ceased to look like so many little balloons, but we were hungry enough to enjoy them despite their deflation.

The *loochis* were served with *dal*, a thick mixture of gram boiled in fragrant spices, two or three kinds of vegetable curries, sliced egg-plant fried in mustard oil, and a chutney made of tamarind and dried fruit. The meal concluded with yoghurt and milk sweets.

On that day, all our food was served on large green pieces of banana leaves. Water was drunk from little terra-cotta tumblers and the curries and curds were served in tiny terra-cotta bowls. Afterwards all these bowls were thrown away as were the leaves. Because unglazed earthenware cannot be scrubbed and washed in a proper manner, one single sip from a cup of this kind is sufficient to render it 'unclean'. Potters make these little cups and bowls for a few *pice* each and they are always used when many guests assemble.

After the meal *pan* was served. *Pan* is an edible heart-shaped leaf, large and luscious, having a sharp sweet taste. It is a climbing plant grown with special care in cool darkened bamboo-fenced enclosures covered with palm fronds to shelter them from the sun's rays. The cultivators observe strict rules of personal cleanliness. It is believed that anything of any kind that it is likely to exude an offensive odour may be absorbed by the plant and affect the flavour of the leaf. The enclosures are guarded with great care and every precaution taken to ensure the correct texture, growth and delicacy of the leaf.

Pan leaves came in little bundles and had to be cleaned and sorted out. Each one was then prepared with a smear of lime, finely cut betel nut, and fragrant spices and then folded to form a tiny packet. A clove pierced through the heart of each *khili* as this packet was called, holding it firmly closed. Hundreds of these had to be prepared and were kept fresh by sprinkling them with rose water. After the meal these were served to the guests who chewed them with relish, for they make the mouth fragrant and are said to help digestion.

The task of preparing *pan* was usually performed by women only, and with other little girls I was often called to lend a hand in the work. I always tried to evade this task for the one thing that I detested in those days was sitting quietly. I underwent a good deal of upbraiding over this. 'What a tomboy!' Mother scolded, 'Sorrow is in store for you, my girl, at your father-in-law's house.' But usually I turned a deaf ear to all rebukes and bounded off to join my brothers in their boisterous games. I was a good hand at tops, cracked marbles with ease, and had acquired quite a name for myself in the kite contests of our quarter. I played half-back in our football team, and in the cricket season, batted and bowled without turning a hair. Once a cricket ball, catching me unaware, made my little finger black and blue. Clenching my teeth, I kept back the cry that rose to my lips for fear of being turned away from the game and jeered at for being a girl—a favourite taunt of my younger brother, but one that possessed the power to cut me to the heart.

What I enjoyed most on the occasion of the *puja* was serving. The cooks found it difficult to wait on all, so Mother and I, helped by an aunt or a cousin, would sometimes serve the women and children. With the end of my *sari* wound round my waist, I felt very grown up ladling out the curries. The wives of tenants of nearby estates arrived with strings of children and the little ones clamoured so much to be fed that we served them before the rest of the guests. At the end of the meal, my Falstaffian uncle—the keeper of the store-room—allotted two pieces of sweetmeat for each child, but these failed to satisfy them and they looked expectantly for more. So, to please my protégés, I did not hesitate to filch some more whenever uncle's back was turned. The mothers blessed me copiously as they departed with little bundles of sweets surreptitiously tied to the ends of their *saris*.

The feasting continued till late in the afternoon. At sundown we all assembled once again for *arati*, the evening ritual. The *puja* room was darkened with incense from the brazier, and its fragrance filled the room. Our eyes smarted, but it was a joy to be able to still see the beautiful face of the goddess.

My youngest brother was very fond of banging the gong at this time, for the sound of the gong is part of the ritual.

Ding dong dong dong ! he clanged in rhythmic strokes while the priest, standing on his strip of carpet, waved aloft the flickering five-flamed lamp in one hand, and tinkled a little bell with the other.

I, swelling my cheeks prodigiously, blew on the ancient conch shell with all my might. The others, with palms joined, murmured the prayers that came to their lips prompted by their heart's desires. This was the last ceremony. The *puja* was now considered to be over and the priest departed, suitably remunerated and accompanied by a servant who carried for him a big bundle of *prasad.*

At day-break the next morning, Mother bade farewell to the *protima*. The common clay had been sanctified by the presence of the goddess and, as such, was still held in reverence, just as a human body is after the departure of the spirit. The farewell was a formal ceremony. After her bath, Mother came in her cream silk red-bordered *sari* and bowed low before the *protima*. Very deferentially, she approached to touch the beautiful brow with vermilion; then breaking a sweetmeat, she touched this on the lips of the *protima* and also a tiny morsel of crushed *pan*. Finally, taking a winnowing fan in which stood a lighted lamp and other auspicious articles she moved it thrice before the *protima* in a circular motion and touched the image on the brow. Then she went down on her knees and bowed till her forehead touched the floor as she murmured, 'Come again Mother', and thus the last salutations were made.

At sundown, the *protima* was carried on many shoulders and, accompanied by torchlight and music, was taken in procession to be immersed in the waters of the Ganges. I have never seen just how this is done, for I was not allowed to go with my brothers. It was they who had the privilege of accompanying the *protima* in a country boat to the middle of the river. There, ropes were untied and the image, with its glittering *caal*, went into the bosom of the Ganges. We felt sad and the house appeared strangely quiet. It was as if Mother Saraswati had in truth visited us for a day, and her departure cast a gloom over all the family.

3

Time passed and I was growing. I was now almost nine years old. 'She is not learning any housework. . . whatever will she do in her father-in-law's home? lamented many a well-wisher to my mother. Those dark words were often repeated, but they failed to register with my mother and I went about as usual, giving little thought to the problems of domestic life. My time was divided between school and the carefree hours at home, and except for asking me to fetch and carry during the *puja* days and occasionally hand out plates of sweets to her guests, Mother made no effort to educate me. It was Dada, my eldest brother, who at last made her realize that it was high time to take me in hand.

'She is growing up to be a wild good-for-nothing', he complained, 'Let her learn something useful.' He turned to me. 'From tomorrow', he told me firmly, 'you are to wash your own clothes.' I quailed under his stern eye, and though I disliked this chore intensely I did not dare disobey him. Wasting soap and using more water than necessary, I washed and rinsed clothes in a most unsatisfactory manner and my arms ached as I hung them up to dry. Tuni-jhi, Mother's pert young maid, took pity and several times tried to secretly help but I waved her aside as I well knew what would be my fate if the news leaked to my short-tempered brother.

One Sunday, he caught me romping about in the garden and promptly led me into the house. 'Come and help mother, her cook is ill,' he said. In Mother's kitchen Bamun Pishi greeted me warmly with her toothless smile. 'You have done well', she told Dada. 'A girl has to learn all things; no one knows what destiny has in store for her. Yes, she must be able to do everything,' she wheezed, nodding her hairless head at me.

Many years ago, when she had been widowed at an early age, she had come from a remote village in the Rahr country to cook for my grandmother and had stayed on with us ever since. Although she was no relation, we addressed her as *pishi* [aunt], really meaning father's sister. And as she was a Brahmin, we called her 'Bamun' a corruption of the actual term. So she was called Bamun Pishi. Now she was in charge of the milk and vegetable section of Mother's kitchen. She had a flair for confectionery and was famous for her coconut sweets. I learnt to cut coconut shreds, cutting my fingers many a time in the process. But rolling the little balls of shredded coconut mixed with treacle made my mouth water!

Bamun Pishi knew how to make the most delicious crunchy *muri* [puffed rice]. Deftly sweeping the puffed grains, with a specially made little broom, as they sizzled on the hot sand in the shallow earthenware vessel, she filled several wicker baskets kept for that purpose. Afterwards the *muri* was poured into the huge earthen jar that stood in the corner of the store room. Some of it was tossed into a brass vessel filled with liquid *gur* [syrup] made from the sap of the date palm and shaken up and down till they were well coated with the sticky golden syrup. After rubbing some mustard oil on her hands she picked up a handful and one by one rolled them into small round balls. These crisp and tempting balls tasted heavenly. Sweets were mostly homemade in those days and Bamun Pishi was always busy preparing them. The open wood fire cast a rosy glow over her withered cheeks and I sat watching with my chin on my hands as the light of the flickering flames played over her kind old face. She cut all the vegetables for the innumerable dishes and it was from her that I learnt to cut them in various sizes and shapes according to the purposes for which they would be used.

Potatoes cut lengthwise went into the fish curry with the thin gravy, rounded ones to richer curries, small pieces to the bitter *suktani* that is served at the beginning of the meal, and those coarsely chopped unpeeled potatoes went into the *caccari* made with mustard paste and chillies. We sat together on the floor with the basket of vegetables between us. But before I was allowed to cut potatoes, I was first taught how to handle the many varieties of spinach. I learned to pick out the tender leaves for frying and select the spices for flavouring. Bamun Pishi was always ready with rhymes about this, and some of these rhymes were full of sarcasm. The housewife who was ignorant of the correct use of spices was jeered at with a rhyme which went something like this:

What a jewel of a housewife is she,
Who flavours with *jira* [cumin]
The sweet sour dish!

'Why, what should it be flavoured with?' I asked. 'Mustard seed of course!' she replied with asperity, 'And never forget that.'

Many were the rhymes she repeated and I listened with absorbed interest. Once she caught me peeling too much of the potato away with the skin. 'Don't waste so much!' she shrieked. 'That is not the way to pare vegetables. Whatever will your father-in-law's people say?' Then she went on to tell me about the good and bad housewife. 'Listen:

Where the housewife is an able cook
And can finely pare her vegetables,
It has been heard spoken,
That home is never broken.
She who lacks the sense of income and expenditure,
Is angry at good words,
Makes sharp retort and causes needless pain,
The husband of such a one can never home remain.'

I also heard from Bamun Pishi the legend of Khana and some of her words of wisdom. In the dim past, Khana was a learned lady who was cherished dearly in the home of her father-in-law. She was skilled in the science of astronomy and could foretell the future. Her father-in-law, a minister of the King, consulted her in secret about problems of State and her advice was so wise that the King held him in high honour.

But envious ones plotted his downfall and told the King about Khana. One day she was summoned to Court to be asked questions personally by the King, and Khana, to save her husband's father from disgrace, cut off her tongue. 'A piece of that tongue was eaten by the wall lizard, the *tik tiki*,' continued Bamun Pishi, 'and that is why, whenever the *tik tiki* cries 'Tik! Tik!' [right! right!] after anyone's words, they never fail to come true.

Khana's words are in rhymes and commonly quoted in the rural areas where people know them by heart, for most of them deal with the crops and the weather. I was hovering in the kitchen one evening when it began to drizzle and Bamun Pishi, watching the rain drops, dreamily said, 'We are sure to have a good harvest this year.' 'How do you know?' I retorted, for I was still sore at her refusal to let me have another pop-corn ball. 'Why, Khana told us about it,' and in a quavering voice she recited, 'Hail to the King of that land of merit, where it rains at the end of Magh. A plentiful crop of mangoes is followed by a good crop of rice and many tamarinds foretell floods. Should spade-chopped clouds appear in the sky and a light wind blow at times, then hasten O peasant to build your *aal* for rain is sure to fall! And they always come true, the words of Khana,' she concluded, nodding her head. She explained in answer to my question that an *aal* was a narrow embankment enclosing the peasant's paddyfield. This had to be kept in repair in order to retain the water needed for the crops.

Deploring my lack of knowledge of these fundamental matters and blaming my school for it, she wheezed, 'Whatever do they teach you there my child? The next thing you will be asking is whether paddy "trees" produce good planks of wood!' Here she cackled with laughter and I was duly chastised.

While teaching me a few rudiments of cooking she also introduced me to the 108 names of Sri Krishna, for these were what she crooned in her cracked old voice as the peeled potatoes and shelled peas. I never got all of them by heart, but I loved to hear her repeat them.

'But why so many names, Bamun Pishi?' I asked her once.

'And why should they be repeated?' 'How are we to be liberated otherwise?' she replied. 'In this Kali Yuga, this dark age of sin and sorrow, how are men to be saved if they do not call on Him? In olden days people indulged in elaborate rituals and almsgiving but all that is changed. Now men have to spend their time in searching for the wherewithal to sustain their very life—their thoughts are all occupied with the problems of how to fill their bellies with rice,' she sighed. 'Under these conditions the only way left is to hold fast to the name of God.' Here she chanted in a feeble voice words that never failed to fascinate me:

Worship the Name, fill the core of thy life with the Name.
Endless are the names of Krishna and limitless their power.
Worship the Name with devotion, for the Name is Sri Hari Himself.
Listen Listen, O brother, to the chanting of the Name
For hearing the Name will free you from sin.

In spite of Bamun Pishi's low opinion of the education that was imparted to me at the convent, school-going was a pleasure except for one or two things, and one was the problem of my hair. The trouble began when it had grown to my shoulders. Mother's notion of hair-dressing and that of the good nuns differed so widely that I was left wondering which course to follow. A bath was of course a daily function in the family, and according to Mother, a bath was only a bath if it included some water on the hair. Also, the top of one's head was thought to be peculiarly susceptible to heat and as such needed half an ounce of oil rubbed into the crown. Either Mother or the maid rubbed this well into my head. Now this meant that the hair was wet and had to be left loose to dry. But according to convent rules this was 'untidy', so often I was reprimanded and made to tie up my loose hair at school.

'Why do you bathe every morning' my schoolmates asked me. 'We don't. We only have a bath on Saturday or Sunday'. I told my mother this and begged her to allow me to do the same. She shuddered and said I was to do nothing of the sort and on no account was I to dream of adopting any of their ideas of personal cleanliness. The sanitary habits of all *firingis* [Europeans] were utterly deplorable. She considered them to be so unhygienic that she made me change into fresh clothes after a good wash when I returned home from school each day. 'But, why Mother?' I had protested, 'they all look quite clean.' 'Yes, that's just it,' she replied grimly, 'they look clean but they are not. They neither rinse out their mouths after a meal nor wash themselves at particular times each morning.' Then she went on to explain what she meant, and I too shuddered!

Apart from what I learned from my books, my education was definitely enlarged by the attitudes of the good Sisters of the Cross at St. Teresa's Convent. It was from them that I developed a particular aversion to costume jewellery. Not that I was addicted to it, except for a pair of slim gold bangles I never wore any ornaments at school. But one sad day I fell for a brooch of imitation stones which cost but a few annas from a roving Boxman. Seeing it pinned on my frock, a sweet-faced nun spoke to me about the inadvisability of disporting these trinkets. Her words and her manner left an impression on me which abides to this day.

I also came to know the correct procedure when referring to babies who are on their way to this world, but this was not so easily learnt. Like all other children of this country, I could not but be aware of the fact that mothers carried a baby somewhere in the middle of their bodies for a period of nine months before it was born. This was general knowledge because as soon as it became known that a newcomer was on the way, there was a spate of ceremonies and feasts in connection with the expected arrival. Constantly exposed to these rejoicings and the words of advice always given by more experienced women, I had come to regard child-birth as a natural occurrence in a married woman's life.

A new wing for mothers and their infants had been added to St. Vincent's Home, right next to our school. We were being shown round the building after the opening ceremony, and seeing rooms all furnished complete with baby cots, one of the girls facetiously asked, 'But where are babies?'

'Oh,' I said airily, 'They are all now in their mothers' tummies!' But to my surprise this witty remark of mine was received in marked silence and with queer looks from my schoolmates. Someone must have repeated my remarks to the Sister in charge, for she looked on me with cold eyes and was unnecessarily severe. My companions avoided me and I carried an aching heart for many days till, in the course of time, things once more became normal.

It was not until sometime later that my best friend, Ruby Goddard, helped me understand why I had been temporarily ostracised. She told me the stork story but added sagely, 'We all know how babies come. We are not so silly as really to believe that they are carried by storks but we are not supposed to know'. 'But why?' I asked in bewilderment, 'Shh . . . .' she whispered, lifting her finger to her lips, and I was left wondering.

At Father's request, I was given piano lessons after school hours. Since I began late, I only learned a few melodies like 'The Blue Bells of Scotland.' I loved to tinkle this tune whenever my fingers touched the keys, but my music teacher had other ideas; she felt that I should practise my scales. So, with a long pencil nearly as thick as a ruler, she used to point out the notes, counting aloud: 'One, two, three, four, . . .' Then, whenever I struck a wrong key, she would bring it down on my knuckles with a sharp rap. This happened quite often, for I would be tired and hungry, and my eyes smarted with tears. I also tried my teacher's patience sorely by hitting the keys too soundly. 'Don't thump!' was the fierce injunction I always heard during my lessons.

At the dress rehearsal of the prize distribution, presided over by the Lieutenant-Governor's wife, the names of the pupils were called out, and each girl had to come in the prescribed manner to receive her prize, which was then announced. The Sister in charge of this mock function must have studied the foibles of every pupil, for with a disconcerting sense of humour she made her helpless victims squirm by announcements like these: 'Miss Shudha Ghose, awarded the first prize for thumping on the keys!' or 'Miss Ruby Goddard, a special prize for tying a bow over her eyes!' All this was greeted with shrieks of laughter from those who had already passed the ordeal, and poor Ruby pushed away the offending bow while I felt like imitating Sita in the *Ramayana* and entering into the bosom of Mother Earth for shame.

But all this faded from memory on the great day of the real prize distribution when I became a bridesmaid at the 'Doll's Wedding.' The audience tittered as I pursed up my mouth and primly uttered my lines, 'Yes, very true, empty vessels make the most sound,' was my reply to one of the undesirable suitors who was recounting his many qualities in the hope of being favoured. I well remember the long white muslin and lace Empire gown, tailored by the Anglo Indian girls of St. Vincent's Home, that I wore for the occasion.

It was at this time I had my first experience of an English theatre, and it left an indelible impression on me. Charles Vane, a Shakespearean actor, had come all the way from London with his company, and Calcutta was agog with excitement—at least my brothers were. My father, who was an ardent admirer of Shakespeare, had purchased tickets many days in advance for a matinee performance of *The Merchant of Venice.* I was thrilled to the core and utterly loathed Shylock and loved the gallant Bassanio. I had been told the story in a very sketchy fashion by my younger brother and found it hard to follow the entire play, but the court scenes with Portia stirred me to the depths.

'Did you like the play?' Father asked me later, 'and did you understand it all?' To further our knowledge of English he spoke to us in that language and insisted on our doing the same. When I replied rapturously in the affirmative he opened his volume of Shakespeare at Portia's immortal lines of—'The quality of mercy is not strained. . . .' and read it out with much feeling. Then raising his eyes with a quizzical look he said, 'Do you think you could learn this by heart? If you can, this will be yours,' and he held up a silver coin.

I took the book and went up to the terrace and pacing up and down repeated the passage till I became word perfect. In the evening I went to him to claim my prize. But Father said, 'Not now,' and not until next morning was I given a hearing. Then Father was so delighted with my performance that not only did he give me the coin but, to my great distress, he made me recite the lines before all my brothers, while he commented, in glowing terms, on my delivery and diction, praising the good nuns for my feat. All this was torture to me for I well knew what was in store for me afterwards. And sure enough, as soon as we were away from Father's presence, my younger brother mimicked my speech and made such derisive remarks that even the rupee could not compensate for my torment.

His satisfaction at my discomfiture was short-lived however. He developed a temperature that evening, much to his disgust, and slight though it was, Father declared that it was inadvisable for him to go and see *Hamlet* the next day. The tickets bought were for the night performance and as the play was to be at that late hour and the subject not suitable for me seats had been booked for my brothers only. But when it was found that my younger brother could not go, it was decided that I should take his place. So I was made to miss school and put to bed after lunch to keep me from falling asleep at the theatre. But by afternoon my brother's temperature had dropped and he piteously requested me to plead on his behalf that he might now go to see *Hamlet*. 'Go and tell Father that I am quite well', he begged, 'there's a good girl. He loves you so much he is sure to listen to you.' I had slept the whole afternoon and looked forward to seeing those glamorous people at the theatre once again, so I hesitated.

'You won't like it either, this play,' he added earnestly, 'it's full of ghosts.' I recoiled, and hastened to Father and obtained the necessary permission. For the first time my brother hugged me in joy! He lifted me right off the ground in his arms and plumped me down suddenly on my feet, then tore off to spread the glad news to my other brothers.

On his return from the theatre he became a very realistic ghost. Stripping his bed of its sheet he draped himself in it and stalked about the house, pointing a stiff finger at nothing as he said in a ghostly voice, 'I can such a tale unfold. . . .' He caught me unawares one evening, and as I saw the tall white figure looming in front of me in the darkness, I yelled and fled. That night I cried out in my sleep, and he came to grief at last He was well scolded by my mother and from that time the ghost of Hamlet's father haunted our house no more.

My father's pioneering spirit had led him to plan his children's education by methods that were not usual in those days. When my two brothers were but six and eight years old he sent them as boarders to an English School in Darjeeling, then considered a very remote hill station.

Travelling was not easy and as the journey through the Himalayas was long and tedious, the school attracted but few people. My grandmother strongly disapproved of the boys being 'banished' at that tender age, but found Father, in spite of his devotion to her, quite adamant in his idea. And since the subject of the education of the sons of the family was considered to be outside a woman's domain, my mother's opinion could not have carried much weight. So, accompanied by an old servant called Kali, my brothers left and a few months later there occurred that which was referred to as the 'Darjeeling disaster'.

It was on a dark night when a terrible cyclone was raging. After thirty-six hours of continuous rain, great boulders and trees torn from their roots descended from Observatory Hill towards the town of Darjeeling. As the debris crashed down the mountainside it carried everything in its wake including the school. On that fateful night of September, the pupils of the school had been led out to take shelter in another house. Here it was so crowded that my brothers crawled under a heavy table. But this new shelter offered little safety and the landslide killed and maimed most of those who had taken shelter there. After the landslide had passed these two small boys were found unharmed under the table.

When the news reached us we learned that the school with all the pupils and residents had been swept away by the landslide. Later, my father heard that his sons had survived and were being sent to Calcutta. He went to meet the train. The station was filled with weeping parents, relatives, and friends searching for their loved ones amidst the maimed and injured children brought in by this special train. Father looked into all the compartments, but nowhere could he see his little sons. In despair he went to make enquiries and found both the boys in the Guard's Van, they, being the only ones uninjured, had been placed in the Guard's charge and travelled with him. For many days after this my brothers hardly spoke a word as it took time to erase that grim experience from their minds. They soon became day scholars in Calcutta and were never again sent to boarding school.

Then came my turn to be responsible for causing my parents pain. I had made many friends at school and one of them, then a boarder at St. Vincent's Home, had encouraged me to live at the school. She painted in glowing colours the charms of a boarder's life, enlarging on the 'fun' that was to be had there. Being a lonely child, I was possessed with a great longing to join her. I was then about nine years old and one day I crept to Father and from behind his chair expressed my wish to become a boarder. Time passed and I had nearly forgotten all about my desire, when one day at tiffin time I was told to come to the Home for my food.

I went with alacrity, but my heart sank when I saw the coarse rice and heavily-spiced egg curry served to me. Hilda, my boarder friend, gobbled up hers with relish but when I tried to eat I found the food so hot that it literally burnt my mouth. Realizing I had become a boarder at last, I felt a lump in my throat. The afternoon lengthened, I lost interest in my lessons and began to feel homesick and forlorn. Suddenly one of the Sisters called me from the class and led me to the parlour. Here, to my surprise, was Mother, who had never before come to the school. It was always Father who periodically met with the Sisters to know how I was progressing. With Mother was my younger brother and one of my grown-up cousins known as Peludada. Peluda, as we called him, looked sheepish, while Mother appeared quite at ease.

'Is this your mother?' Sister Superior asked me with a worried look. I nodded vehemently. 'She wants to take you home, do you wish to go with her?' 'Yes,' was my joyful reply. All I remember after that is that Mother took me by the hand and saying some words in Hindi to the Sisters, led me to the waiting carriage. Closing the carriage doors, Mother proceeded to dress me in a *sari*, and without any explanation for her conduct went on to say that it was necessary to wear this as we were going to the wedding of Susama Didi, the daughter of my widowed Pishima. Pishima was my father's only sister and if anyone had the last word with Father, it was she.

Stern and forbidding, she wielded great influence over him in the absence of my grandmother and he was devoted to her. I remember Mother was scared of her and so was Father. For me it was never a pleasure to visit her as there were no children in the house and the atmosphere was heavy, but a wedding was a different matter altogether. I cheered up when the sound of wedding music greeted us as we entered the gates. Mother took me straight to Pishima.

Pishima looked at me with approving eyes, taking in the *sari* over my school frock and said it was well that I had been brought away from that boarding school of the Memsahibs. She also added that Boku—that was her pet name for my father—must have lost his head completely to think of putting his daughter into such a place.

Feeling very guilty, I effaced myself from her presence. Presently, Mother dressed me properly and I found my own level with some small girls who had come with their parents. The house was gaily decorated and overflowing with people, and as I was happily playing about with my little companions I was suddenly petrified to see Father coming towards me with a face like a thundercloud. He was in Jodhpur breeches, and from the whip in his hands I knew he had driven over in his 'tum tum', the name for gigs in those days. 'Well', he said, 'so your mother took you away?' I did not know what to say but to my great relief Pishima appeared.

'Ah, here you are Boku,' she began quite casually. 'You must have gone out of your mind to put the girl in a *firingi* boarding school. It's a good thing that Bou had enough sense to bring her away. Come this way now, and see the wedding gifts. The bridegroom will be coming after sundown so you must go home and change your clothes for I expect you to look after the guests who will be accompanying him. . . .' Father followed her in silence.

I learned afterwards that he had driven over to the boarding school to see how I was faring on my first day away from home, only to be told that the good nuns did not think it right or proper to keep me there since I was claimed by my mother. Later I discovered that he had made extensive arrangements for my comfort, including an Anglo-Indian girl to look after me and was deeply hurt when his arrangements were upset by Mother's 'unreasonable' behaviour.

She in turn was convinced that he had not acted in my real interests. She felt that my being a boarder would result in many complications, and make it difficult, if not impossible, to give me in marriage when the time came. This being so, she told Father if he desired to bring me up in an unorthodox fashion, she would not like to interfere since I was his daughter and he had every right to do so. But, at the same time, it was her duty, as a mother, to guard my interests. She pointed out the complications that would be certain to arise from my being led away from the normal life of a Bengali girl of the times. People would look askance at a girl brought up in a *firingi* boarding school, and marriage, which was then the only vocation possible for a woman, would be denied to me as no one in our society would be willing to welcome me into their family. What, then, would happen to me? To prevent me from becoming a permanent liability on the family, dependent on my brothers in my old age, she recommended that to ensure my economic independence it was of paramount importance to execute a deed beforehand in my favour, granting me the rights of a substantial portion of Father's real estate.

She was ever a realist and Father was not. He could not calculate or think so far into the future, nor could he visualize his restless daughter, now in pigtails and frock, as a staid old maid in economic distress. So, when all her arguments failed, Mother did what she thought would save me from disaster. It went against the grain for her to disobey her husband and court her own unhappiness, but it was just like Mother to adhere to her ideas of right and wrong, irrespective of the cost.

There was a rift between my parents, and I could sense the discord between them for many days. The money that had been deposited at the school for my boarding, was converted into clothes. It provided work for the needy Anglo-Indian women who lived in the Home and I wore the many frocks and petticoats they made for me till the time I was married, and then they had to be discarded altogether. I remember my eldest brother's wife using the last of my petticoats under her *sari* when she came to our home at the age of nine.

I was eleven at that time and my marriage took place the following year, 1911, when, to commemorate the visit of King George V, the capital of India was changed from Calcutta to Delhi and the partition of Bengal was annulled.

4

In the years before my marriage, I came to learn many new things about politics and religion, although I still enjoyed the games of childhood. My first introduction to politics was in 1905 when I was seven years old and Mother served us with *phal-ahar* [fruit meal] when it was neither a fast-day nor a *puja* day. It was not a holy day nor did I hear of any holy purpose, so I was somewhat puzzled to notice the unusual silence in the kitchen and find that no fires were burning at all. On enquiry I learnt it was associated with the *Swadeshi* movement.

When the Viceroy, Lord Curzon, decided to partition Bengal in 1905, a great wave of national consciousness swept over the country. It had started first in Bengal where, as a sign of mourning, kitchen fires were not lit on the 16th of October, 1905. People at this time took an oath to boycott foreign goods and pledged themselves to wear only *swadeshi* [of our own land] items of clothing.

It was also at this time that the *rakhi bandhan* ceremony was revived by the writer of many patriotic songs, Rabindranath Tagore. On the full moon day of Sravanna, a *rakhi* [strands of saffron homespun yarn] was tied by the girl on her brother's wrist. Even if the male was not her brother, with this bracelet on, he was honour-bound to protect her. It was a pledge taken by the courageous to shield the poor and weak.

With the passing of time, the small skein of yellow silk or cotton gained wider significance and became the symbol of unity. Thus it was, that under the impact of the emotion roused by the partition of Bengal, men embraced and bound themselves to each other using the *rakhi* as the symbol of unity and fraternity. Led by Tagore, high and low participated in it and used it to signify the unity of Bengal—nothing could tear them asunder, they were unaffected by the partition of Bengal, and would defend each other till death. To this day, even in the altered circumstances of modern times, this charming festival is observed all over India. The full moon, *purnima* in August is still known as *rakhi purnima* for it is at this time every year that the tying of *rakhis* take place, followed by feasting in an atmosphere of goodwill, fraternity and unity.

I became aware of other aspects of the movement three years later, but this time it was through a young cousin of mine. He was a tall and lanky youth who usually teased me, but that evening when he visited us he was unusually quiet. Mother had entertained him with freshly fried *loochis—loochis* seemed to be always ready to be served with a curry of seasonable vegetables, together with a sweetmeat, to anyone who happened to visit us in those days.

After partaking of these snacks he came to the veranda to wash his hands and rinse out his mouth. Drying his hands on the towel that I held out for him he looked at me gravely and said, 'Do you know what I have got with me?' patting his pocket. I shook my head. He held up a little paper pellet. 'The ashes of Khudiram!' he said,

I started. 'Yes,' he added with a smile, 'his body was cremated last evening.' 'Who was he?' I ventured. 'What! You do not know Khudiram? You seem to know nothing!' was his contemptuous reply. 'He worked for the *Swadeshi* movement and he gave his life for our country. He was hanged by the British at dawn.' And saying this, my cousin dramatically departed. This was on the 21st of July, 1908. Twenty-year old Khudiram was one of the earliest revolutionaries, and after his death, this song was on the lips of all young people:

O Mother for a while
Bid farewell to me,
I'll wear with a smile
The hangman's noose
For all the world to see!

Those two years, 1906 to 1908, were memorable for two other outstanding events. The first of these was a visit with my mother to her old paternal village home in Saidpore. I well remember the visit for it was the first time I spent nights away from my father's home.

My mother came from an old landowning family. Her father had been *zamindar* of the village of Taki Saidpore. He was no more, but her mother was living at that time and her six brothers still kept up the huge ancestral home and its many ceremonies. My aunts and uncles thought nothing too good for us and were lavish in their hospitality. Each day a different variety of fish was served and the courses were many.

One day some unexpected visitors arrived and stayed to dinner. My aunts worried amongst themselves that there were not enough fish for all. 'Never mind,' said an uncle, 'we shall soon get some from the *hapoth*.' And sure enough, that night we had tasty lobster curry and delicious prawns fried in butter. Strolling by the riverside with a cousin the next morning, I asked about the *hapoth*. The *hapoth* I was told, was a kind of wickerwork vat where fish were kept alive in storage in the river, to be used in emergencies.

My father's village, Sripur, in the district of Khulna, was on the other side of the river. Many were the stories I heard about the day he came to marry my mother, arriving in a procession of country boats ablaze with lights, each boat filled with wedding guests. What merry music there was, and what a grand feast! But I was more interested in my new surroundings than in food and weddings. To my unbounded delight I was allowed to roam about in absolute freedom unescorted by any adult. I heard from my cousins things new and strangely nice. They taught me to eat fruits and berries right off the trees and introduced me to new flowers and fruits. I learned how to climb trees, to bathe in ponds, and to improvise a fishing rod out of a twig, a piece of thread from my aunt's sewing box and a bent pin for a hook. I would bait this with an earthworm. Although I never caught any fish I always remained full of hope. I also learned a magical formula to ward off ghosts. 'They live there', said a small cousin one dark night, pointing to the tall trees that loomed in the distant orchard, 'But they can do no harm if you do not fear them, and this is what you have to say:

The ghost is my son
My daughter is the Sankhcurni [ghost]
When Rama and Lakshmana dwells in my heart,
What can they do to me?'

Here he snapped his little fingers in contempt. I was duly impressed and was told that these charmed words were most potent and kept all ghosts at bay.

My uncles had specially constructed a toilet for the benefit of their city-bred sister and niece who were, of course, unused to rural ways. But I followed the village practice of perching on a low branch of a tree in some solitary spot, and on my return to Calcutta I bragged about this to my brother. 'Oh, you didn't!' he cried, incredulous and green with envy. 'Yes, I did,' I replied smugly, feeling elated at his astonishment.

Fervently he begged to be taken along with Mother next time, but her visits to her father's village were few and far between. Only once more did she go before my marriage and that was during the wedding of a cousin, but my brother was not allowed to accompany us, because his exams were near and he had to study.

The other notable event in these years was more painful—I accidentally set myself on fire. My father disapproved of seeing me in *saris*, but there were special occasions when a *sari* was called for. Giving *bhai phota* to my brothers was one such occasion. That day in October the house was buzzing with numerous uncles who had come for their *phota* from their sister, my mother, and with cousins, big and small, who had come for their *phota* from my sister and myself. I simply could not wear a frock on this occasion.

The *bhai-phota*, a late autumn ceremony, is performed all over Bengal by women for the benefit of their brothers. The brother must receive a formal invitation from his sister, no matter how small she may happen to be and if she is married, he is the guest of honour in her home that morning. *Bhai* means brother and *phota* [dot], refers to the little ritual of placing a sandalwood paste dot on the brow of a brother. Placed just between the eyes, this dot is an auspicious sign and the sister performing the act thus wishes her brother health and a long life. If it is done by an elder sister, the brother receives this as her blessing, and if the sister is younger, it is given as a token of reverence and affection, and the brother blesses her for her loving act done for his welfare.

The little ritual is very simple. The sister spreads a small carpet and the brother sits on this before her. First she lights a small brass lamp fed by *ghee* and places this on a tall pedestal beside him. Then dipping the tip of the little finger of her left hand into the bowl of cool sandalwood paste, she lifts it to the centre of her brother's brow and murmurs in Bengali a verse that runs something like this:

With this *phota* I give on the brow of my brother
A barrier of thorns do I raise for Yama [the god of death]
Oh brother mine, with a sister's *phota*
You will never never come near Yama!

This is repeated three times and thrice the dot is made with the scented paste on the brow of the brother. Then the sister brings a bowl of *caru,* which consists of the water of the green coconut, a dash of fresh milk and a few drops of honey and the same amount of *ghee.* This is poured in his hand as she says in Sanskrit. 'O Brother I am your elder (or younger) sister; partake of this auspicious food I pray, for by this you will please King Yama and his sister Yamuna.' He cups the fluid in his hand and after inhaling the scent, allows it to run through his fingers into the bowl held out to him. He then washes his hands and sits down to a meal of several courses which concludes the ceremony.

I later learned that this little ritual had its origin in ancient times. According to the legend, Yama, the god of Death, and Yamuna his sister were the children of the Sun, and it was Yamuna who first performed this ceremony on the second day of the moon in the month of Kartick (mid-October to mid-November) for the long life of her dearly loved brother. As for the *caru,* it is said to symbolize *payasanna,* a preparation of rice cooked in milk and sugar which is served at weddings, birthdays and all such happy occasions. So this *caru*, with its health-giving ingredients, is symbolic of the food served by Yamuna in the very first ceremony.

After the ritual, the sister younger than her brother bows to touch his feet and receive his silent benediction while the elder sister is the one who blesses her brother. She serves him then with a plate of sweets and fruit and makes a gift of a new *dhoti*. Later there is an elaborate meal in his honour and this concludes the function.

My uncles took a keen interest in the ceremony and made it a point to come from their village home for the function. I remember one or two of them even told my mother what kind of *dhoti* they would prefer and the shade and width of the border. They must have had a strenuous time, my six uncles, in their efforts to be present before their two sisters who lived not very near each other in the great city of Calcutta. However, they divided their time quite harmoniously by lunching in one home and dining in another.

This particular *bhai-phota* day was a happy one for my mother. It was not always possible for her six brothers to assemble together, but this time they were all before her. They sat in a solemn line on their carpets, while, one by one, Mother gave them their *phota*. In another part of the veranda, Didi was doing the same to my brothers and cousins.

Although I had three silk *saris*, I did not possess a cotton one for day-wear in the home. Since it would have been inappropriate to wear anything other than cotton on this occasion I had borrowed one from my sister. This *sari*, being the full length of five and a half yards, proved much too large for me. Finding it difficult to manage, I had wound the unrequired length many times round my waist and attained a somewhat portly look.

Pleasant sounds and smells were emerging from Mother's kitchen where her Brahmin cook was busy preparing the *bhai-phota* feast. I was growing impatient for my turn, for not before I had given the *phota* would I be allowed to break my fast and the hot savouries and pastries were getting past their prime. When cold, they would not taste half so good, I ruminated, wishing my sister would hurry up with her ceremonies and allow me to finish mine.

Feeling important and grown-up in my voluminous *sari* I suddenly experienced a sense of great warmth. Turning round I saw my *sari* had caught fire from the lamp on the pedestal which was just as high as my waist. I saw the flames mounting before my eyes but found myself incapable of speech and all that I could do was to give a feeble pull at my sister's *sari.*

She was busy murmuring her formulas for the long life of her brothers and so was my mother. As for the brothers, they were all devoutly receiving their *photas* with lowered eyes and I stood there ablaze before them, without anyone knowing anything about it. The seconds seemed hours . . . it appeared to be ages before my eldest brother happened to raise his eyes . . . .

In the hue and cry that followed, all that I remember was my sister snatching at my *sari* and singeing her fingers in the process. By the time what remained of my *sari* was flung away, I was burnt quite a lot about my waist. I was put to bed and a medically qualified uncle told my mother to quickly bring some lime water and coconut oil. This was whipped into a frothy cream and when he applied it to my burns it felt wonderfully cool but was unable to prevent the blisters from appearing later. They were pretty bad when they burst and the soreness prevented me from wearing any undies. These used to be of the utility kind, tape-tied around one's waist, and their absence caused much embarrassment and made me miss school for many days.

Sometime during these years we all went for a change to Benares. Father stayed in the Hotel de Paris for greater comfort while the rest of us lived in a large unfurnished house in a remote area, called Shivalaya. Here there was a big enclosed garden where I loved to watch the goldfish in a little pool and was frightened by a giant chameleon changing its colours on a tree as it glared at me with baleful eyes.

Mother performed her Savitri *brata* here that year with great éclat and I wrote my first letter. It was in English to my brother, who had been left behind to finish his half-yearly examination. He joined us later for his summer holidays, and it was then I was told of the stir my letter had caused, as it was considered quite a feat to be able to express oneself in that foreign language.

It was at about this time that my father presented me with my first diary and a tiny notebook bound in red with 'Expenses' written on it in gold. Here I was to jot down what I spent out of the rupee he had given me as pocket money. He was very methodical and tried his best to inculcate good habits in his children but alas, for all his efforts, his sons never came near him in any manner, and as for me, well, I ought to have been much better than I turned out to be.

My father had great contempt for people who spent beyond their means and borrowed money to maintain their position. Incurring debts was a major crime to him, and he had a sad lack of respect for the ostentatious titled men of our country. Once he was advised to donate towards some worthy cause by a pandit who was somewhat worldly in spite of his vast learning. Mentioning a munificent sum which would certainly purchase a title for him the pandit went on to say, 'Many are doing this these days . . . Raja of Kidderpore! Come Tara Pada, wouldn't you like to be called by that name? It would suit you. And why not? Your income is far more than that of the Maharaja of——.' 'Bah!' replied Father with a scornful laugh, 'like him? Never if I can help it. Why, he is always begging his money lenders to pay his bills after he has entertained the Governor!' Then with a whimsical twinkle in his eyes, he opened his well thumbed volume and read aloud the lines of the Scottish poet . . .

Gie fools their silks and knaves their wine
A man's a man for a' that . . .
The man of independent mind
He looks and laughs at a' that . . . .

He loved the English poets and his copies of their works were copiously marked with his appreciation of particular lines. He had a good library and never failed to purchase the latest publications; on his visits to book shops he would allow me to choose my books and never raise an eyebrow over prices. I do not remember receiving any other gifts from him. In those days, children's literature in Bengali was limited and not very attractively presented, so it did not appeal to me as much as Grimm's fairy tales and the stories of Hans Christian Andersen.

They were the delight of my early years and I remember how fond I was of the entrancing annual, *Chatterbox*, with its colourful pictures and tales of adventure in strange lands. Possessing a voracious appetite, I read whatever came my way, skipping over passages I did not understand to get the gist of the story.

As I look back, I find my father was a man much ahead of his time and also full of contradictions. Although he felt the English way of life admirable and worthy of adoption, yet he never failed to don a *dhoti* during the Durga *puja* to pay his annual visit to Mother Kali in her temple at Kalighat. Once he had a dream, one never related to us, that inspired him to build a place for the musicians to play their devotional music within the temple.

My eldest brother, Bankim Chandra, named after the novelist Bankim Chandra Chatterjee, was married in July 1909. I have two memories about those days tucked away in the folds of my memory. One is of my father's illness and the subsequent events. The other is that I began to hear about my own marriage from this time.

Since my brother's wedding was the first in the family it was a rather elaborate affair. He went to the marriage ceremony in a coach drawn by eight horses and it was then I first became acquainted with the word 'postilion' and thought it rather funny. I was duly impressed with the dress and deportment of postilions not to speak of the shade of their skin (for they were either Europeans or very fair Anglo-Indians) and the manner in which they rode the spirited steeds. It seemed to me that all the world and his wife came to see my brother being married and every day was a feast day for ten days afterwards.

There is some ceremony or other connected with each of these ten days and it was within this time that my father suddenly fell ill. Always living in Olympian heights, aloof from normal household matters, he disappeared altogether from the scene and we saw only Mother. In those days women did not have separate banking accounts nor did they handle much money. The menfolk silently gave such funds as were needed to the servants when they presented the lists that had been made by the housewives.

Now, when it was known that Father was unwell no one had the courage to approach him for money, nor did Mother want to trouble him. The house was teeming with guests. Near and distant relations from the villages had all swarmed in with their children and some had brought their men and women servants to look after the little ones. The *amla* quarters were filled to overflowing with tenants and their families. They had come all the way from the remote Sunderbans to see their Master's eldest son being married and they remained for the post-marriage ceremonies. Fish and certain kinds of vegetables were constantly pouring in from the estates; rice, dal, flour, sugar, spices, *ghee* and oil had all been stored in large quantities in the store-room, but many daily requirements still had to be purchased. Whatever money Mother had had was quickly used up, and the clerks had also exhausted their spare cash. The day of the 'great feast', given on the fourth day after the wedding, drew near. My brother wore a worried look, the office staff was grave, but my Mother was as serene as ever, attending to the everlasting needs of her many guests, and Father's bedroom door remained closed. I had heard that many visitors would be coming to see the bride on the following evening, and I noticed more temporary hands in the kitchen.

Flitting about aimlessly, I came upon a downstairs room that was seldom used and, hearing suppressed voices, I became curious. I pushed open the door and entered. A strange sight met my eyes; Mother was making over some heavy gold ornaments to the lean and lanky uncle who was a resident of the *amla* quarters. With a serious face he was trying to judge the weight, then, nodding his head, he quickly wrapped the ornaments in a handkerchief, put the bundle in his pocket, and left the room. Mother frowned at me and asked me what I wanted.

I promptly disappeared. I never learnt whether those ornaments were redeemed or replaced later, but I knew they tided over the situation till such time as Father could be troubled with mundane matters.

I came to be very fond of my brother's little bride and she became my playmate and bosom friend. She was only nine years old when she came to our house and I remember we were very fond of playing a game called 'Crocodile! Crocodile!' We climbed on a bed which was supposed to be a boat and made the surrounding floor a deep river. One of us was the crocodile. Gingerly we bent down to see where the crocodile was, and when he was thought to be at a safe distance we stepped down and pretended to bathe in the river. One had to be swift about this or else one would be caught, and then, woe to the bather, become the crocodile doomed to remain in the water crawling about in search of prey. We had great fun playing this fascinating game with the little cousins who came with their mothers to stay with us for the marriage ceremony and the ten glorious days that followed, and it pleased us to have this game in a fresh room each day.

My two other brothers had been careful to lock their bedroom door to ensure privacy. They could ill afford to neglect their studies for that lengthy period of fun and festivity, and would stealthily retire to their room to study. When we had exhausted all other rooms, our roving eyes fell on this particular apartment; we longed to play here but, alas, it was locked. Diffident to approach the owners, we pondered long, and finally approached the little newcomer. 'You go and ask them,' we told her. 'If you request it, they cannot refuse.' My brothers were shy of this latest addition to the family, but she lay in wait for them. I can still see her going up to them, modestly pulling her sari over her head and lifting her large innocent black eyes. 'Listen, Listen,' she trilled, 'Could you kindly open your room? We want to play Crocodile! Crocodile! there!' Mejda [second eldest brother] grew red with embarrassment, then, taking the key from his pocket, he handed it to her and fled.

Bouthakrun, or Bouthan as we called her for short, literally 'Lady bride', came from a small town where her father was a lawyer. She was not uneducated for she had been to the

Mahakli Pathshala where the foundation of Bengali had been laid, but she knew no English. So to enlarge her education an Anglo-Indian lady of uncertain age, by the name of Mrs. Foster, was engaged. Solemnly Bouthan went every afternoon with her books under her arm to the room set apart for this purpose. 'Where are you going?' We would ask. 'To Foss Mister', she would lisp. She never could pronounce her teacher's name correctly, nor the word 'fish', which was always hissed as 'fiss' much to our amusement.

An elder brother is *dada* in Bengali, and this is what I called my eldest brother. He was religious-minded and inclined to be orthodox, but he was an ardent follower of Swami Vivekanada, who moulded the minds of many of that generation. After graduating, Dada passed his law examination. He was enrolled at the High Court, but he never practised, for to practise would mean twisting the truth to suit the case and the client, and he was very much averse to this. Or perhaps he did practise and I never knew anything about it, for my knowledge of him was limited to his interest in the Ramakrishna Mission. Once, soon after his marriage, he had a disagreement with Father and disappeared. Eventually he was found at the Belur Monastery where he had gone with the intention of renouncing the world and taking Holy Orders. Before this was carried out he was discovered by my uncle and persuaded to return home. Truthful to the extent of rudeness, forthright and quick tempered, he gave me my first lessons in the teachings of Sri Ramakrishna. But I was very young then and I did not know that they came from that great saint.

One evening, when we were at dinner and Mother was serving us with appetizing *loochis*, I asked him, 'Dada, how many gods are there and which is the true one?' Reading the Christian scriptures had raised doubts within my mind. 'Why, I thought you knew there was but one God,' was the reply. 'Yes, but at school . . . .' 'Oh, is that what is troubling you?' laughed Dada. 'Look it's just like this,' he said and here he raised his tumbler. 'We call this *jal*, Muslims call it *pani*, the French *l'eau* and the English *water*. All these many names mean just one thing. It is the same with God. He has many names but He is One.'

Once I was assailed with doubts about the Almighty. 'How are we to know that He *is*? We do not see *Him*,' I asked Dada, with much trepidation, for he was more than fifteen years older than myself and was usually stern and aloof. But I always went to him instead of to my other two brothers for he looked with understanding and affection on my questioning mind. 'I will tell you of a disciple who asked the same question of his teacher,' Dada replied with a smile. 'Oh did he?' I broke in breathlessly. 'Well, you must let me tell you the story, but I will spare you what the teacher did to his disciple.' 'What did he do?' I interrupted excitedly. 'He thrashed him soundly till the disciple yelled for mercy.' I gasped. 'The teacher then asked his disciple what was the matter', continued Dada. ' "Matter!" shouted the disciple in tears, "why you have beaten me and hurt me, and I am in such pain." "Hurt you? Pain? What is pain? I can't see the pain you mention," said the teacher. "It's here," moaned the disciple, pointing to his back. "Where?" the teacher asked bending over him. "I can't see anything." "I can't show it to you," wept the disciple, "but it is very real, I feel it!" "Ah," said the teacher, "that is just it! Now you understand—God, too, cannot be seen with mortal eyes, He manifests Himself only through His works and is realized only by His devotees." ' And with this story I had to be content.

The convent teachings raised a fresh conflict in my young mind and I came to him again one day with another problem. 'Which is the true religion?' I asked. 'All religions are true,' he replied. 'They are but so many roads that lead to God. Some roads are broad and some narrow, some are long and some are shorter ways to the same destination, that is the only difference,' was his reply. 'Then it doesn't matter much, does it, which road we take?' I asked, surprised at my own boldness. 'But it does matter,' he retorted. 'It all depends on how you look at it. You may reach your destination through a flower-filled garden, or through an unclean latrine, it is for you to choose which path you prefer.'

Dada was pious, but his language was not always polite nor was he inclined to be patient. He was rather blunt in speech.

and prided himself upon his ability to call a spade a spade. I am indebted to this brother of mine for a good bit of my early education. I am also indebted to him for arranging my marriage.

5

'When are you giving your daughter in marriage?' people frequently asked my mother after Dada's wedding had taken place. One day, in my presence, Young Grandmother raised her scanty eyebrows and asked the same question, adding a few more words in her own inimitable manner. 'Surely you are not going to wait for her to become an old woman before giving her in marriage? She is already ten years old. The honour of the Ghose family will certainly be tarnished if you delay much longer.' Mother murmured something about the indifference of Father, 'What does he know about such matters?' snapped the irascible old lady. 'If you need a man to help you, surely you can get Bankim, he is old enongh.' So, after this, whenever I noticed Dada and Mother conferring in the evening I tactfully kept my distance.

One afternoon I was told not to go to school. That day my elder sister took an unusual interest in my appearance. She rubbed a few drops of scented oil in my unruly hair, and then plaited, coiled, and pinned it back in a becoming manner and dressed me in a silk *sari.* I soon learned that some people had come to see me and was unwillingly led to meet them in Father's study. Here I found Father proudly handing round my school reports to two elderly gentlemen. I was given a chair beside them and heard one say to another in an undertone, 'Gracious! The girl knows French!' This apparently unnerved them for we never heard from them again! This was followed by a merciful lull in matrimonial arrangements and I was again allowed to go to school in peace. After this one effort by my father with this particular party, who must have been known to him for he was averse to strangers, he refused to be drawn into the matter again.

In the meantime I began to hear about horoscopes. In Hindu families the parents carefully consider every ingredient that contributes towards a happy union. Not only are birth and breeding, appearance, health, and education taken into account, but the horoscopes of the boy and girl must tally as well. My mother had much faith in horoscopes and they were consulted on all important occasions. When the talk of my marriage was in progress she called our family priest one day and gave him mine. He spread out the saffron-coloured roll, written in Sanskrit, and poring over it for a considerable time found certain unsavoury facts which greatly perturbed my mother. Didi had been taken into confidence and she became even more disturbed. I found her one day wiping her eyes and sniffing; when I asked what was the matter she shook her head and said it was not for my ears and told me to go and play. I was rather intrigued. What was it that made Mother look at me so sadly and Didi, always my arch critic, treat me so gently?

Gradually I learned the truth: an early widowhood had been foretold for me. This so disturbed my sister that she felt I would better remain unmarried all my life. I doubt if my father was made aware of all this, but his old Pandit, Nakuleswar Bhattacharya, was consulted. 'You must not eat anything tomorrow until Pandit has read your palm,' I was told one day. He came early next morning. Mother spread a carpet for him on the veranda in front of the *puja* room and gave him my horoscope. He nodded his head many times and following a long consultation between them, I was called. He took my hands in his and peered at my palms through his steelrimmed spectacles. 'Hmm . . . Hm . . . It can be . . .,' he muttered with puckered brows. Then he lifted my left hand and, smoothing out the skin of the palm, bent over it gravely. 'A good hand . . .,' he murmured. And turning to Mother he added, 'but—,' and left his sentence unfinished. With great compassion he looked at me and said that I could go. Mother's eyes told me that I was not to forget to make my *pronams* [obeisance] to the Pandit, so I bowed low and touched his feet in formal salutation, and ran off to have my breakfast.

Some time later, there was a simple ceremony one morning and I again had to miss School. After worship and prayers, Pandit Nakuleswar Bhattacharya unwrapped a shining heart-shaped locket with my name engraved on it, slipped it onto a thin gold chain and put over my neck. The locket was made of five metals—gold, silver, copper, iron, and lead—and held within it a sacred formula written on a piece of *bhurya patra* [bark of a tree]. This was the conclusion of an elaborate ritual performed by the Pandit according to certain directions given to him by his Guru who was adept in astronomy and palmistry. The Pandit had met this holy man in the remote Himalaya mountains and had been accepted as his disciple. He had been taught the formulas to ward off certain calamities and had also learned how to construct amulets that have the power to avert impending evil. But since the Pandit would lose his knowledge of this science if he were to use it for commercial purposes he was theoretically unable to accept any fee.

After this first ceremony for the long life of my future husband, a little ritual was performed for his welfare and longevity on a particular moonless night every month. The Pandit received a small fee from my mother for this service and he did it as long as he was alive; later his son carried on the good work.

When I received the locket I only thought it a pretty trinket. I did not know it was meant to shield my future husband from all harm, and had I known, I doubt if I would have worried over a husband I had never set eyes upon. My main concern at the time were the food restrictions placed on me by the Pandit. His parting injunction was, 'you must not eat crab, food that has been partaken of by another, or *akhadya* food. And, remember, you must wear this locket always and never part with it.' Now, the word *akhadya* has a double meaning, for it means food that ought not to be eaten, that is, unorthodox food; and it also means food unfit for consumption. Ever alert, my youngest brother at once accepted the former definition. 'Aha!' he cried, wagging an admonitory finger at me, 'from now on, chicken will be forbidden food for you. You can have nothing from Father's table!' 'But why?' I queried, the pleasure of possessing my shining trinket distinctly marred by this unwelcome information. 'Because that will be unorthodox food—food that ought not to be eaten!'

So, when on the following day I refused the chicken and told Father why I was unable to comply with his wishes, he flew into a temper and said I was not to listen to all that 'tommy rot'—a favourite expression of his when roused. Calling Mother, he took her to task for it. Referring to the Pandit, he was most irreverent and said he did not believe that such injunctions could be laid down in our holy books, since the Vedic Rishis [sages] performed rituals wherein it was compulsory to sacrifice animals. Since this was so, he reasoned, the flesh of mere fowl could not be held in such aversion. He then added that he would give the Pandit a piece of his mind when he met him next.

This perturbed Mother and the commotion took away my appetite altogether. That night as I lay beside Mother, she told me quietly that it was a sin to displease one's Father and that in future I was not to refuse anything from his table. She also told me I must conform to the Sanskrit *mantra*: *Pitha swarga, pitha dharma, pithahi paramantapa, pithri pritheema panne, prianthe sarva devata.* The Sanskrit words, roughly translated, mean some thing like this: 'Heaven is father, religion is father. The gods are pleased by pleasing father.' I was to learn these words and repeat them before partaking of the forbidden food. Thus peace was established, but it was not permanent!

Some time after my marriage, my husband was puzzled at my refusing a chicken curry that had been specially prepared for us. I told him about the amulet (but he never knew what it was for) and its restrictions. He was much amused. 'Well, don't you think your mother's method of overcoming the displeasure of your father may be applied to my case as well? If it is sinful to disobey a father, surely it is not a good thing to disappoint a husband. . . . So, since I would like you to share this with me, you had better insert "husband" in place of "father" in that Sanskrit *mantra* and come and finish this curry before it gets cold.' And so, except for observing the restrictions against left-over food and crab, which I was never addicted to, it was impossible for me to follow all the Pandit's orders in connection with my amulet.

Although Mother came from a family of landowners and was married to one, she disliked the class and was determined that her daughter should not marry a landowner. She had democratic ideas and set her heart upon a man who was capable of earning his living by some gainful occupation. She considered unearned wealth the harbinger of endless fads and foibles which could undo a man, wreck his life and bring disaster to the family. She was also adamant about birth, breeding, age, education and a healthy body and consequently turned down all prospective candidates who did not have the qualities which were essential for the happiness of her daughter. It was only after she had been satisfied on these points that the horoscopes would be compared to discover if the stars were propitious for a happy union.

One evening I overheard Dada comment caustically as Mother shook her head over a proposal, 'Nothing seems to satisfy you! I wonder if you are thinking of a *Shayambar* [bride's choice] ceremony for Shudha so she can choose her own bridegroom!' Perhaps this made Mother realize that it was time to make up her mind, for she again returned to serious consideration of the proposal. Then one night as I lay beside her listening to one of my favourite legends she interrupted the story and quite casually asked my opinion about the matter weighing on her mind.

'Which would you perfer? The boy of one proposal is very good-looking but not at all well educated. He is just a matriculate without a university degree; but he comes from a wealthy *zamindari* family of east Bengal. Their home is in Barisal where they have vast estates . . . but I did not approve of *zamindars*. . . .'

'The other boy is not so good-looking but has a splendid physique and he has had a good education. His home is in Murshidabad where he has just been appointed a Deputy Magistrate. The family is an old one and known to your

Dada's father-in-law who has brought this proposal. The boy's father is the private secretary to the Nawab Bahadur of Murshidabad. But I hear that a Deputy Magistrate does not stay in one station, he gets transferred and works in many places.'

The word 'Nawab' had romantic connotations and a roving magistrate sounded more interesting than a dull landowner planted in a remote part of East Bengal. And as for looks, why, only a few days ago I had learnt from my Bengali primer about the flamboyant *palash* flower that no one loves because it has no scent. It had been explained to me that men were prized for their merits, and that good looks without good qualities had no value, for the flame-red *palash*, because it has no perfume, can never be used for any *puja*. All this was fresh in my memory, while the idea of travelling to new places, being always on the move, and living without any fixed abode, seemed absolutely fascinating. But how was I to voice my thoughts?

'Murshidabad is only five hours by train from Calcutta . . .,' Mother was talking to herself now, and this gave me the desired clue. 'Barisal is across the Padma river . . . so very far away . . .,' I said in a small voice and then fell asleep.

One fine day in November of 1910 I was preparing for my annual examination when I was told that I would not have to go to school any more for my marriage had been arranged. It was with the Murshidabad boy, but now I found little pleasure at the prospect of my nomadic life with him. No school! Never to see my schoolmates and the good nuns any more! A gloom descended on my spirits and I moped about the house not at all happy about the idea of marriage.

Soon after I received the news of my impending marriage Mother took me to bathe in the river Ganges. The river on which Calcutta stands is known as the Hooghly, but since it is a branch of the Ganges it is often referred to as the Ganges. I always enjoyed the crowd, the atmosphere, the dip in the water and the adventure of changing my wet clothes inside the closed carriage. Finally the priest from Orissa would stamp my forehead with cool sandalwood paste in a design I myself had chosen from his collection. This rotund priest with shaven head and neatly tied top-knot did this to all the bathers, although it is an optional ritual. He sat under a tree beside the river, ringing a bell to attract attention and making his living by collecting the coins that bathers he had attended cast at the shrine beneath his tree.

We were particularly early that morning, as the bath was a ceremonial one in connection with the eclipse of the sun or moon. I drew my *sari* modestly over my shoulders and dipped in the cool waters. Closing my eyes, I held my nostrils with both my forefingers, plugged my ears with both my thumbs, dipped under, and came up panting for breath. Opening my eyes I saw my school bus filled with my schoolmates going over the bridge. My heart sank. I felt left out and forlorn and my eyes smarted with tears.

As we were returning home, Mother noticed the look on my face and asked me what was the matter. I burst into tears and begged her to allow me to go to school. I did not want to get married I told her between sobs, I only wanted to go to school. But my opinion did not count and matters proceeded.

One day Dada pointed out a serious-looking young man in a group photograph of students and said this was my bridegroom-to-be. Shortly after this I was once again dressed by Didi and sent to Father's study. Here Dada was in Father's chair and with him was a grey-haired man with kindly eyes. He looked at me and smiled. 'Where is your Father?' he asked me. 'He has gone to the settlement,' I replied, and that was all. He was my future father-in-law.

Afterwards I learnt that he had taken a fancy to me and said he found 'something' in my face that was lacking in all the other faces he had seen. Goodness knows what he saw in me then; I had not completed my twelfth year and was gawky and graceless and had little to commend me.

In March 1911 I began my thirteenth year. A few weeks later there took place what is known as my *ashirbad,* literally 'blessing', but the ceremony is actually a betrothal. In this betrothal it is the parents and elders, who by a little ceremony of 'blessing' held separately in their respective homes, formally announce that the marriage has been arranged. The next step is 'blessing the bride' and 'blessing the bridegroom', although this too is done in the respective homes.

On an auspicious day, the boy's friends and relations assemble at the home of the girl. The future father-in-law or elder who is arranging the marriage and standing in his place, blesses the bride-to-be and makes a gift to her in token of his approval and good wishes. After the ceremony there is an elaborate feast to celebrate the occasion. Later a similar ceremony is held in the home of the bridegroom. At this time the date of the wedding is decided and the exact auspicious moment announced.

Thus it was that one evening late in April, I was 'blessed' by my future father-in-law and presented with a heavy silver box of an ornate pattern in which to keep vermilion. It contained a small packet of vermilion and two old gold coins from the time of Emperor Akbar. My father-in-law came with a few friends and relations and in token of the happy event had sent to our home many dishes of sweetmeats, bowls of curds, baskets of *pan* and many kinds of spices. Our family priest and Pandit Nakuleswar Bhattacharya began the ceremony by blessing me with Sanskrit *mantras* as they sprinkled over my head a few grains of golden paddy and blades of *durva* grass betokening wealth and prosperity. Then my father and a few elderly relatives did the same.

Some days later, Dada and a few relations went to Murshidabad to perform the same ceremony for the bridegroom. Dada was accompanied by servants carrying similar courtesy gifts to the people of the bridegroom-to-be, who was also 'blessed' with golden coins. On their return the next day, Mother questioned them at length about her daughter's future home, son-in-law and relatives. Dada and our relatives had been feasted and feted, and all were unanimous about the desirability of the match. They felt that the relationship with this Murshidabad family would be a happy one.

The wedding had been fixed for the 7th of July. As the days passed many interesting things began to happen and I found myself becoming interested in my marriage. Measurements were taken for my ornaments and clothes. The weaver women came with their merchandise and Mother chose *saris* while I hovered around, fascinated by the colours and patterns. The local goldsmith brought glittering gold ornaments and

Dada brought more modish ones from fashionable shops. I was thrilled with the gold wrist-watch on a Milanese bracelet, but Mother did not approve of the bracelet as it was not made of guinea gold but merely 18ct English gold. Then there were fancy soaps and perfumed oils, creams and powder, combs and pins, ribbons of gold and silver, and so many other novel and exciting things that I was completely captivated and ceased to mourn for school.

My comments were loud and candid and never failed to amuse Dada. But one day an aunt came on a visit and I was reprimanded by my old nurse for being so voluble. 'Shh! you must not pass opinions so loudly in front of everybody.' 'But why?' I demanded. 'Because people will speak ill of you. It is immodest to display so much interest in your own wedding. You must learn to be silent.'

This old maid-servant had come to our house many years before when my second brother was an infant. She had been employed as his nurse and was therefore known as Khokar-jhi, the 'boy baby's maid'. Later she nursed my youngest brother and when I made my appearance, her services were transferred to me but her name remained unchanged. Having being entrusted with the care of three children of the family she held a position of her own and it had been decided that she should accompany me as my personal maid to my father-in-law's home. As she had become old, Mother felt she might not be able to care for me in a proper manner, so she decided that Parvati, a younger maid, would go too, much to the disgust of power-loving Khokar-jhi.

I was pleased with the prospect of having Parvati for she held me in respect, whereas Khokar-jhi was forever finding fault with whatever I did. I realize now how dearly she loved me but, in those days, I fiercely resented her and much wordy warfare was waged between us. Mother had told me very firmly that I was to listen to her when I went to live in my father-in-law's house and that she was to see that I behaved myself properly there. All this rather clouded the golden days preceding my marriage, for whenever I thought of leaving the old familiar house of my father, my heart became heavy and the glamorous wedding gifts lost their allure.

One morning I awoke to the sweet moving strains of the *shehnai* [an Indian oboe]. The haunting music made my heart ache. Tears pricked my eyes and I was filled with a sense of sorrow at the prospect of leaving the known and a vague fear of meeting the unknown. I turned over and buried my face in my pillow. 'Wake up! Wake up!' called Khokar-jhi. 'It is your wedding day!'

I had enjoyed myself immensely the day before . . . the day of my *ayurbriddhi-anna*, 'rice of longevity' ceremony. This was an elaborate meal ceremoniously prepared for the bride and the groom each in their respective homes. Rice simmered in sweetened milk with raisins, cooked into a thick creamy mixture flavoured with rose water and sprinkled with thinly-sliced pistachio nuts, and almonds, is *payes*, the last but most important item on the menu. For this ceremony it must be cooked by a happy wife. Fish, said to be auspicious in Bengal, was served in a variety of ways. Fish spicy hot; fish fried in oil; fish lathered with mustard, wrapped in banana leaves and steamed in boiling rice; fish swimming in sweet-sour sauce; fish cooked in coconut milk; fish cooked with curds, cardamoms, cloves, and cinnamon; were served with plain or spiced rice. No meat or eggs are permissible on these occasions, but *dal* (savoury lentil soup), various vegetable dishes and a lengthy desert of curds and thick cream followed by numerous sweet-meats conclude this ceremonial meal which was permeated with the blessings of parents and elders to endow the bride and the groom with health and long life.

Women and children had flooded the house, and gifts of *saris* accompanied by huge plates of sweetmeats had come pouring in as my wedding gifts. In those days, only close relations gave ornaments or jewels on this occasion, and other types of gifts were not given. Amidst much merriment, I was led to a rice lunch of many courses served in silver plates and bowls. Dressed in a sea-green Benares *sari*, flecked with silver and wearing my new gold ornaments, I sat down to my *ai-bura-bhat*, as the *ayurbriddha-anna* was called colloquially and blithely bade farewell to my maiden days.

'Eat well', whispered a cousin with gay laughter, 'you will

have to fast tomorrow. No more cooked meals till the ceremony is over.' Since marriage is considered a serious undertaking great care is taken to prepare body and mind for the sacred rites. The wedding day is an austere one for both the bride and the bridegroom. The only permissible foods are fruit, curds, and sweets taken after the wedding at night. During the day one is allowed only cool drinks of fruit juice—sherbet. I remember I felt very hungry and demanded to know from Mother why, instead of feasting as English people do on this day, I should be made to fast. Turning a sad face to me she gently smiled, and tried to convince me that it was advisable to conform to our own customs. Giving me another glass of sherbet, she comforted me by saying that the time of the ceremony was fast approaching and as soon as it were over I would be given my favourite fruits and sweets.

The *gaye-halud* is a ceremonial bath which is usually held with much pomp and circumstance on the *ai-bura-bhat* day. But, for some reason or other, in my case it was not done that day, and the ceremony was observed very simply on the day of my wedding.

Gaye-halud means 'turmeric on the body' and since turmeric possesses antiseptic properties, it was an important toilet item in the olden days, used much as soap is in the present times. To both cleanse and beautify, turmeric paste was rubbed on the body followed by a bath performed with rituals. This was done to both the bride and bridegroom in their own homes. At present this turmeric bath is only taken symbolically. A token quantity of turmeric paste is smeared on the forehead with some ceremony and much merriment, for the younger generation mercilessly tease the victim. The elders keep a safe distance, pretending not to hear the hilarity, but keeping a watchful eye on the rites which if improperly performed, could imperil the future bliss and welfare of the one about to be married.

As I was having my argument with Mother, an elderly cousin appeared on the scene. 'Come! Come!' she laughed. 'It's nearly time for your *gaye-halud*.' I did not care over much for this cousin, Jushi-di, as she was rather domineering and I was annoyed with Didi for selecting this time for having a baby. Just when she was needed most she remained incarcerated in the accouchement chamber. The new mother and her new-born babe were confined there for a whole month in order to recoup her health. I failed to see this in its proper perspective then, and inwardly seethed against what I considered Didi's unreasonable action. I gave myself up to Cousin Jushi-di with ill grace.

She marched me off and made me change my *sari*, then led me to the quadrangle before the *puja* room. Here four banana trees had been planted on the four sides of a small square which was enclosed with long lengths of handspun cotton yarn. Within this square was a beautiful *alpana*-painted *piri*, which is a flat piece of polished wood on which to sit cross-legged. I stood on this decorated *piri* in my new white red-bordered *sari* while five young married women, also in new *saris* presented to them by Mother for this particular function, chattered and laughed as they touched my brows with the auspicious turmeric paste. This paste had arrived in a little silver bowl accompanied by other gifts from the bridegroom's people. A gaily painted winnowing fan was touched to my brow while I stood surrounded by articles meant to bring good fortune to me. The air was filled with the sound of conch shells and verbal instructions from the elder women to these five young ones, who appeared to be taking their duties very lightly. It was all much ado about nothing as far as I remember and when it was finished I was led to the *puja* room where I found Dada busy performing what was called the *Abhuti* ceremony.

Orthodox Hindu weddings are performed according to the Vedic rites that have been maintained for countless years. From very ancient times the responsibility of the ceremony belonged to the father, or other elder of the family and was shared in varying measures by other relations and kinsmen, friends, and neighbours. Every attempt is made to assure the material and spiritual welfare of the girl and boy about to be married, and hence these many ceremonies performed by the families of both the bride and the groom. A vital interest is taken in all the proceedings and as there is no marriage document, family and friends are essential as witnesses to the marriage ceremony.

Abhuti is an abbreviation of the word *abhyudayika* which means 'that which brings prosperity'. There are actually three rituals in this ceremony. It commences with the worship of the goddess Shashti and the sage Markandya. Shashti is the deity who presides over children, whom she shields from all evil. In the *dhyan-murthi* [image to be meditated upon] she is holding a child in her arms. The elder entrusted with performing this ceremony (always someone from the paternal side) prays that the progeny of the bride, or of the groom as the case may be, might be blessed with health and long life, and by Shashti's grace reach a high plane of mental, moral, and spiritual elevation. Markandya was a great ascetic who by severe penance and austerity achieved immortality. His spirit is invoked and his grace sought in the same manner.

After the invocations of Shashti and Markandya, certain aspects of Shakti, the divine force or power, and the cosmic feminine principle, are invoked. The different aspects of Shakti are referred to as the sixteen Mothers. These include Gouri, the beautiful daughter of the Himalayas who gained Shiva by the force of her austerities; Padma, another name for the goddess of wealth and prosperity; Sachi, the consort of Indra and goddess of enjoyment; Savitri, the consort of Brahma and goddess of creation; Jaya, the goddess of victory; and Vijaya, goddess of unvanquishable might and power. The other Mothers represent the power of peace, sustenance, endurance, contentment, memory and many others. When all these beneficent forces have been invoked, they are symbolized in the 'cords of good fortune' which are worn on the wrists of the bride and the bridegroom as a token of the benedictions of the sixteen Mothers.

The cords are placed on a winnowing fan which is used as a tray to hold symbolic articles that promote the health and happiness of the person for whom the rites are performed. These include Ganges silt, symbolic of purity; a piece of rock for a stable material life; grains of paddy for existence; ghee for energy; a swastika for good fortune; vermilion for vital strength; white mustard seed to disperse unseen hostile forces; gold, silver and copper for prosperity; a mirror for correct judgement of self; and a small lighted lamp to symbolize the aspiration of the soul. The cords themselves are seven strands of handspun yarn within which all the elements of grace from the sixteen Mothers are confined.

The yarn is rubbed with the turmeric paste till tinted with its rich golden hue, then seven blades of *durva* grass are securely knotted in the centre of the skein. The priest ties this on the left wrist of the bride, but on the right wrist of the bridegroom. He then outlines in vermilion a sacred symbol on the walls of the room where this ceremony has been performed. This is to signify that the beneficial forces have been invoked and established in the home for the welfare and happiness of the young member who is about to begin a new life.

The final rite is the *shraddha* which means 'that which is offered in respect'. This ritual is in remembrance of revered ancestors and consists of prayers and almsgiving for the peace of their souls. But first there is a special ceremony for all those unfortunate ones who have died friendless and unmourned and for whom no rites have been performed. It is after their spirits have been helped to gain beatitude that three generations of the family are remembered. The Sanskrit *mantras* are meaningful and melodious and the offerings are in the form of flowers and fruit, grain, sweets, and cloth. During the naming rite of a child this tribute is also paid to the ancestors for their blessings are considered necessary for the descendants' future welfare. This concludes the rites of the *abhuti* ceremony.

So, on my left wrist the priest tied the 'Cords of Good Fortune'. I was told that this was to remain for ten days and at the conclusion of the post-marriage ceremonials my bridegroom would untie mine and I his.

Sometime later, Cousin Jushi-di led me to the quadrangle again. I was told that I was to have my ceremonial bath, and once more I was surrounded by the five frivolous young women. This time each of them carried a small terra-cotta jar decorated with the auspicious *alpana* designs. The previous evening these young women had gone to fill these jars with water from the Ganges and had returned home with much merriment. Now accompanied by the long-drawn sound of a conch shell they circled me three times. Then, laughing and jesting, they sprinkled me with what they said were the 'waters of endearment' while women relatives of all ages watched appraisingly and called out different instruction. At the same time some giddy girls edged up to me to make facetious remarks about the efficacy of the charmed waters to win over my bridegroom-to-be.

Following the ceremonial bath I was allowed to retire for a proper bath. The *sari* I had used during my bath was claimed by the barberwoman who had spent a busy day with her pedicure work. All the maidens and wives who were our invited guests that morning had their feet conditioned and beautified by her. Producing a tiny brass bowl from the little bundle she always carried, she filled it with water. Moistening a piece of porous stone she scrubbed and cleaned the soles of the feet then pared the toe-nails and washed the feet very thoroughly. Drying them with her red-checked towel, she painted a slim red line over the edge of each foot. This was done with a disc of cotton wool that had been conditioned with lac. Dipping this *alta* [red cosmetic] into her bowl, she squeezed out the crimson colour with thumb and fore-finger and made the outline with the tip of her thumb. This was all done with meticulous care and good humour as a part of the auspicious event. As the women were barefoot, making the feet beautiful was an important part of a married woman's toilette and the hostess extends this courtesy towards all the maidens and wives who are her guests on the festive day.

Together with my *sari* the barberwoman was given a large new brass dish filled with sweetmeats and silver rupee. Our washerwoman was also given similar gifts. In fact, all the men and women servants received new *saris* and *dhotis* that had been dyed a light yellow for the auspicious occasion, and my old nurse had received the additional present of a gold armlet that she wore with much pride.

The shadows were lengthening. 'It is time to dress the

bride,' said Cousin Jushi-di placing her hand on my shoulder and leading me away from my friends. 'Oh let us come too!' they pleaded, but Jushi-di was firm in her refusal. 'No, you will see her later,' was all she said as she closed the doors.

6

Jushi-di was renowned as the 'bride's decorator' and she took her work seriously. First she cleaned my face with a home made cream, freshly prepared every day with the thick soft skin of milk that had been boiled and allowed to cool, mixed with a liberal amount of orange peel paste and a sprinkling of flour. The cream rolled off like putty, carrying away all impurities. She combed out my hair and worked with a fine comb till my scalp tingled and then burned under its sharp teeth, then pursing her lips she made a centre parting with meticulous care.

'Now be careful', she warned 'always keep to this line and never make a crooked one. The parting is most important. Your bridegroom will place his vermilion mark on this and you must renew it everyday, for it is the sign of a happy wife. Now lift up your head . . . .'

With a splash of rose water and the help of a wet towel, she deftly set my front hair in waves of the modish 'leaf cut' of those days. A broad ribbon was placed over it and tied under my chin to keep the 'leaves' in order while she did my *khonpa* [chignon]. After the hair had been firmly tied at the nape of my neck, it was divided into two portions. Then each length was given a twist, covered with gold ribbon, knotted at the ends and coiled around a gold-mounted comb that fitted snugly at the back of my head. Securing this gleaming circle with golden pins, she pinned two gold roses on both sides and a lovely butterfly whose ruby eyes and quivering antennae had quite enchanted me. Finally she encircled her creation with a fragrant string of jasmine. Given a mirror to admire her handiwork, I could hardly recognize myself. She appeared pleased at my reaction, but when I timidly enquired whether she could loosen the *khonpa* a little for comfort, she was shocked. 'What! . . . and leave the *khonpa* to fall off with the first pull of your veil? Oh no, that is how you will have to do your hair now and also cover your head.'

I had become accustomed to frocks and flying plaits and my heart sank at the bleak prospect of always wearing a veil and elaborate coiffure. 'Come don't look so woeful,' she said smilingly 'you will soon be used to them.' Dipping the end of a thin silver stick in the little bowl of sandalwood paste, she very carefully dotted a pattern on my forehead and placed a dot of vermilion in the centre.

'Can we come in now?' begged my friends from without. 'Yes, but not all. You are most distracting!' growled Jushi-di allowing only two girls to enter. 'Now, apply the *alta* and mind you don't mess her feet,' snapped Jushi-di to one. The other was told not to stand and gape but untie the big cardboard box holding my wedding garments. I was carefully dressed in the rose-coloured Benares *sari* with its matching jacket, both shimmering as the light caught their gold thread.

There was a knock at the door and Mother entered carrying the jewel box. She was followed by her sister, our Mashima who had gained popularity by always bringing us sweets. My friends had entered with Mother and now stood in silence, awestruck at my transformation. As Mother had other work to do, she left Mashima with the jewellery. A jewelled tiara and pair of earrings added to the weight I already carried on my head, and a pearl collar and ruby necklace further increased my discomfort. From above my elbows down to my fingers I was covered with ornaments of many kinds. Finally a pair of *hat-padma* [hand-lotus] were clasped on my wrists. These are elaborate bracelets with chains which reach to a jewelled lotus on the back of the hand and jewelled rings for each finger.

My feet, already outlined with *alta* were adorned with a similar pair of ornaments in silver, as gold is never worn on the feet. To these *charan-padma* [feet-lotus] were added the traditional silver anklets with tiny bells that tinkled with every movement. All this made me immobile although they drew long drawn sighs from my friends.

Jushi-di also tinged my lips with the rosy *alta* and rubbed it discreetly on my cheeks. After touching the tips of my fingers with it, she washed her hands and darkened my eyes with *kajal* [collyrium]. This was very simply prepared in its own metal container. A smudge of clarified butter is placed inside the container which is then held over the flame of a clay lamp fed by mustard oil. This produces the black substance which is good for the eyes. The last touch was a fine pink and gold Benares silk *orna* [scarf] which covered my head and was kept in place by jewelled pins. With repeated injunctions to me not to fidget and ruin her handiwork, Jushi-di left in a blaze of glory.

Surrounded by my admirers I vaguely wondered what my school friends and the good nuns of the Convent would think if they saw me now. Suddenly there was a commotion . . . . Voices raised in excitement could be heard from without. . . . A distant band could be heard playing an English tune. . . . It came nearer and nearer. 'The bridegroom! The bridegroom! The bridegroom is coming!' cried everyone. Old and young ran out to look upon the bridegroom who was coming in procession with music and lights and I found myself alone. . . .

In accordance with tradition the bridegroom has with him a pith helmet fancifully made with touches of tinsel and a small sword made of either silver or steel. On his neck he wears a garland of white tuberose, jasmine and *bael* and his brow has a minute pattern dotted with sandalwood paste. Thus perfumed and decorated, the bridegroom, followed by friends, relations and the family priest, starts at an auspicious moment of the wedding evening for the home of his bride. Preceded by a procession carrying gas lights and the band of musicians, it was usual for him to travel in a landau drawn by as many horses as were fancied. He is received in ceremony, heralded by long-drawn sounds of conch shells and led to a seat of honour that has been festooned with flowers. The guests are first greeted with floral garlands and then escorted to an elaborate feast. In the meantime the bridegroom is entertained by the people of his bride's family while they all await the auspicious time for the ceremony.

When the auspicious moment arrives, the bridegroom is led to the place that has been prepared for the rites. Here the father, uncle, or brother of the bride who is to give her away, performs a brief ceremony of formal welcome. A new carpet is first offered for a seat on the floor, then water from the river Ganges, fresh flowers, silken apparel and a ring of gold. The names of three generations of ancestors are recited with the announcement that their offspring are now to be united by marriage.

When this has been done, the bridegroom is escorted to the inner courtyard for *stri-achar*, the rites of the women. He stands in the centre of a floor, decorated with *alpana* paintings, ready to receive the formal welcome of the wives and maidens of the bride's family. Dressed in gleaming Benares brocades and silks, covered with gold ornaments and jewels, a glittering group of women, each bearing some auspicious symbol, circle him thrice. When the last round is made, the winnowing fan that holds the little lamps and each of the other articles meant to symbolize aspects of good fortune, is touched on the brow and an offering of flowers and sweets is made by the senior-most lady. Usually it is only the elder ladies who participate in this rite while the younger women blow on the conch shell and raise joyous cries to proclaim the happy event.

The bridegroom then retires with his valet to change into the white Benares silk *dhoti* with red and gold border that had been presented to him. After dressing with meticulous care, a broad scarf is placed over his shoulders and a fresh garland of flowers around his neck. Returning to the place prepared for the marriage rites the bridegroom stands on an *alpana*-decorated *piri* as the sound of conch shells proclaim the entry of his bejewelled bride. Seven times she circles round him before she sits facing him on another decorated *piri*, and now he too takes his seat.

Between them is the auspicious jar of water which had been sanctified by the invocations made that morning. The bridegroom places his hand on this and the bride places her hand over his. Then the priest who conducts the ceremony ties their hands together with a garland of flowers. He also places before them a small stone symbol of Narayana—another name of Vishnu, the preserver. The bride's guardian sits beside them and performs what is called the *Sampradan* or 'giving away' ceremony. This is said in Sanskrit, prompted by the priest, and includes the presentation of further gifts. When this is over the priest releases the hands from their bondage of flowers.

There is now a ceremony that is purely custom and not part of the prescribed rites. This is called the 'auspicious gaze' when the bride and bridegroom are supposed to look upon each other for the first time. Sitting face to face, a piece of fine material is placed over them and beneath this veil they look at each other in silence and exchange their floral garlands amidst happy laughter of friends who shower them with flowers. This concludes the ceremonies of that evening, and they are led away to an inner chamber.

In ancient times perhaps the couple did play dice with their friends, but now a token game is played. Young girls take sides, some supporting the bridegroom and some the bride. The 'dice' of small sea-shells is tossed with the object of knocking over clay containers filled with unhusked rice stained with turmeric. The rules of the game are simple and it is played with much laughter and badinage between the bridegroom and the young women.

When this game is over the elders who have not participated in the game enter and the bridegroom is introduced to them. He makes his salutations and receives their blessings in the form of gifts, and only then are the bride and bridegroom allowed to break their fast. The night is spent in a flower-filled chamber where they sit surrounded by their bantering friends and entertained by music and song.

Next morning the bridegroom has to make a money gift to the young women before they allow him to leave the room. Later, there is a ceremonial bath when there is some more fun and frivolity for the young people. After this comes the final rite when once more the couple are escorted to the marriage place.

Here, an altar has been prepared and all arrangements

made for what is called the *kushandika* ceremony. While some families complete all rites on the previous night, it had been the custom in both my father and father-in-law's family to defer these until the next morning. Once again the symbol of Narayana is installed in the marriage place but now it is the bridegroom's priest who conducts the ceremony. He lights the altar fire with a torch and soon the fragrant wood springs a tongue of flame. With melodious Sanskrit *mantras*, the priest pours out *ghee* and the flames rise higher. The bridegroom now stands with his bride behind him; her hands go round to join his and together they pour the puffed-rice and clarified butter on the sacred fire. Both the symbol of Narayana and the fire are witnesses to their marriage ceremony. Then, hand in hand, they go round the altar flames seven times, completing what is called the 'seven steps'. After this, the bridegroom touches his bride over the heart and says in Sanskrit:

> In all that I dedicate myself, offer thou thy heart
> May thy mind in all consciousness follow mine.
> May thy speech be ever one with mine.
> May the Lord of Creation keep thee
> Ever dedicated to me.

To this the bride replies in one word only and that is 'barhom', meaning, 'I shall try my utmost'.

After the priest blesses the bridegroom by saying, 'May there never be any discord between you and your wife', he addresses them both. 'In body, mind and speech, may thou be one. Towards the four paths of life, *dharma, artha, kama, moksha,* . . . may you proceed together in a harmonious manner.' To this both the bride and the bridegroom answer 'barhom'.

The bridegroom is given a ring and the bride also receives one, but it is not compulsory to wear it. It is the vermilion with which he touches the centre parting of her hair that is important. This she will daily renew as a sign of her wifehood till she is in that happy state no more. And this concludes the marriage rites.

The bridegroom's people who had left the previous evening

had now returned to witness this last and most important ceremony. This is followed by another feast. In the late afternoon they escort the bride and her bridegroom to her 'father-in-law's house', for that is how her new home is termed. Both the bride and her groom again wear their wedding clothes but now one end of the lengthy silk scarf that is draped over her head is knotted to an end of the one that mantles his shoulders and the little finger of her left hand is locked in his right forefinger. They bow low before the *Pujaghar* [family chapel] and touch the feet of the elders to receive their blessings . . . the conch shells blow to proclaim their departure. The farewell ceremony is a tense affair filled with tears and heartache for it is then that the bride leaves the house of her father for that of her father-in-law.

When the bride reaches her new house she is greeted much in the same manner as the bridegroom was received by the women of her family. Wedding *shehnais* and conch shells blown loud and long signal her arrival as a young girl hastens to lay down the long length of a new red-bordered *sari* for her to step upon as she enters the threshold. Usually a young sister-in-law takes her hand and lovingly leads her to the *alpana*-painted place where she stands beside her bridegroom to receive the ceremonial welcome. The bride is thought to be Lakshmi, the goddess of Fortune, and she is honoured accordingly. Milk, tinted pale rose with *alta*, is made available to wash her feet and in token of acceptance she dips her toes into the basin. Gaily dressed maidens and wives gather round to greet her with gifts, but it is her mother-in-law, bearing the lucky symbols on the winnowing fan, who comes forward first. She is very precious, her son's wife, for she is his 'other half'.

The mother-in-law's gift is generally a pair of gold bracelets and a smooth reed-thin iron bangle that is worn on the left wrist. Like the vermilion, this bangle is the symbol of her wifehood and is only taken off when she has the misfortune to become a widow. The newly married couple is then led to the 'worship room' where both pay their homage and receive the benedictions of the men of the family and gifts from other relations and friends. The night is an inauspicious one called the *kal-ratri* [dark night] and for their future welfare the newly married couple must not set eyes on each other after nightfall.

The next morning the bride must be hostess to her bridegroom's people in the *bou-bhat* or 'bride's rice' ceremony. In former days she received the freedom of the kitchen where she cooked the rice and other dishes to be offered to her new relations. But that custom has disappeared and now an elaborate feast is prepared by many cooks. At the commencement of the meal the bride serves kinsmen and friends with a spoonful of rice mixed with spinach.

There is another small rite that morning. The bride and bridegroom stand face to face; a lamp is lighted and a conch shell blown, and the bridegroom makes a ceremonial gift to the bride. The gift includes cooked food served in a new set of silver or bell-metal dishes and a new *sari*, which pledge the bridegroom to always provide food and rainment for his wife.

The evening is full of excitement. First, servants from the bride's home arrive bearing the wedding gifts and baskets of flowers for the *phul shajya* [bed-of-flowers]. There is also new rainment for both as well as fragrant sandalwood paste and an entire set of floral ornaments for the bride. On the 'auspicious night' she wears bracelets, armlets, neckchains, rings and a crown all skilfully created with bright flowers. The walls of the bridal chamber are festooned with flowers and the bed is strewn with them, and it is into this room that the bride is led to meet her bridegroom.

I well remember my first arrival at my father-in-law's house for I almost died within the gilded palanquin which carried me to my husband's ancestral home. We were very much in *purdah* in those days, and nice women were neither seen nor heard, especially new brides. I had all this well explained to me by Jushi-di and others who were anxious that I do the right things among my new relations. Feeling rather sick and forlorn I looked at Mother. She seemed to have a cold; she cleared her throat several times and then nodded and said in a low voice that I should always listen to Khokar-jhi. When my eyes fell on Father, I noticed he was blinking with a frown on his face. 'They will miss the train if there is any more delay . . .,' said someone and I was led to the landau. In the midst of all these strangers I derived comfort from the thought that Khokar-jhi, formidable though she was, followed in a hired carriage. 'Your Dada will come and see you soon and your Sripur uncle will come to fetch you when the 'ten days' are over,' were Mother's parting words and that was also another comfort.

My father-in-law had reserved the entire compartment for myself and my husband and my maids. The train started from Sealdah sometime after 2 p.m., and ambled along in a leisurely fashion till five hours later it reached the small town of Murshidabad. Khokar-jhi had rearranged my veil and given me a reminder to behave properly, but neither she nor I had noticed that my *sari* had rucked up a little in front, so both of us were adequately ashamed when someone pulled down my *sari* as I stood uncertainly at the open door. As I wondered how I would descend, someone held out a hand from below and helped me to alight. No sooner had I done so, than the train gave a piercing whistle and started to move . . . fervently I prayed that Khokar-jhi and Parvati were not borne away with it. From beneath my veil I recognized the person who had so kindly made me presentable and assisted me to dismount as my father-in-law. Aware of a large crowd and much commotion I felt safe as I followed him to the gorgeous red and gold palanquin. Although I had never been in a palanquin before I was thankful for its shelter and to see Khokar-jhi.

It was a spacious palanquin, made comfortable with silken quilts and velvet cushions. Khokar-jhi leaned back on a fat gold-embroidered bolster and beamed approval at the manner of my reception, but I felt suffocated as the sliding doors closed. We were hoisted on to many shoulders and the bearers commenced a plaintive chant that kept time with their pace. No light filtered through the chinks as it had been draped with a piece of heavy gold brocade. I could hear a brass band playing selections of English music, and the clamour of crowded streets and I felt I could not breathe. Pushing aside my veil I gasped, 'I'll die . . . oh Khokar-jhi, what shall I do now? I'll surely die!' 'Hush child, this is only for a little while,' was all she said and I felt I could weep aloud in my agony . . . . The moments passed like hours . . . I clenched my hands, my breath came short and fast . . . suddenly the bearers stopped, the palanquin rested on the ground. . . . The doors opened and a whiff of God's blessed air cooled my face. I drew a long breath, Khokar-jhi quickly pulled down my veil, someone reached for my hand and helped me out.

Lights dazzled my eyes. Before me was a great gate flanked by the auspicious water jars crowned with green coconuts. I heard the high notes of the wedding oboes, the sonorous sound of the conch shell and the traditional cries that women raised when they ceremoniously welcome the new bride. As I entered the threshold I became aware I was not alone. Beside me walked my husband and though I did not know him then and had hardly seen his face I found comfort in his presence.

Once again he took my hand and the scent of his jasmine garland was borne to me by a passing breeze. The silver anklets tinkled on my feet as I walked with him to his home but first we bowed low before the grave of an old *faqir* [Muslim mendicant] at the entrance where a little earthen lamp cast its flickering light. No one knew exactly when he lived and died and why he was buried here, but it was said the blessings of this Muslim saint rested on the old house and his spirit guarded it ever since it was acquired by Rai Udai Chand Mazumdar in 1825.

7

The family I had now become a part of could trace their history for many generations. Their caste was Kayastha. Chitra Gupta of *swarga* [the heavenly sphere], is said to be the original ancestor of all Kayasthas. He emerged from the body of Brahma the creator to transcribe the deeds, both good and evil, of mankind. It is according to these deeds that judgment is meted out to them by Yama, the god of Death. As the Brahmin was born from the head of Brahma and the Kshatriya from his arms, the Kayastha, coming from his body, is said to be endowed with the wisdom of the learned Brahmin and the strength and courage of the Kshatriya race. Traditionally, the Kayasthas have been civil servants and administrators and the Mazumdars conformed to this pattern.

Sometime between the ninth and the eleventh centuries, the King of Bengal invited five Kayasthas from North India to make their home in Bengal. During the beginning of the rule of Raja Ballal Sen (1119-1169), the title 'Kulin' was conferred on administrators possessing intelligence and high moral virtues. One such family chosen was that of Dasarth Guha, the great-grandson of Birat Guha who had come as one of the five original Kayasthas.

There is nothing notable in the ancestors who followed until we come to the three brothers, Bhavananda, Gunananda, and Shivananda. The sons of Bhavananda made their mark in the Moghul court. They were given landed property in Sunderbans and Jessore and invested with the title of 'raja'. They became Raja Vikramaditya and Raja Basanta Roy. Vikramaditya's son became Maharaja Pratapaditya who refused to recognize the Moghul conqueror as his sovereign. Many are the tales told about his bold fight and victory in 1605, and defeat and capture later by the Moghul army.

Shivananda earned merit and fame by serving the Moghuls but later came to Jessore where he was of great help to Pratapaditya. Shivananda had expected much from his nephews in return for his assistance but finding his hopes frustrated, left Jessore a disappointed man. He migrated to a remote place in East Bengal with his family and arranged a good match for his son Haridas who received land and property in the village of Aghoid.

Shivananda's great grandson Rajnarayan Guha, went forth to seek his fortune. He became a highly respected officer in the Moghul Secretariat and in the year 1685 was awarded the title 'Mazumdar'. To this day it is only during religious ceremonies that the family is referred to as 'Guha'.

Rajnarayan's great-grandson, Udai Chand, was born on the 17th of June 1792. As a young man he left Aghoid and came to Murshidabad, then the capital city of Nawab Nazim Humayun Jah, Governor of Bengal, Bihar and Orissa. Udai Chand's talents attracted the Nawab's attention and he was made Naib Dewan, Deputy Chief Minister of Revenue, and decorated with the honourable titles Rai Saheb and Rai Rayan. Udai Chand then purchased land and property in Murshidabad. He was a man of singular virtue, and gave most of his great wealth to charity. His son, Umesh Chandra, lived for only twenty-three years and left an infant son of four months. Born in 1856, Purna Chandra grew up to be a brilliant scholar. He passed his law examination with credit, but refused the British Government's offer of a magisterial post, preferring to practice law in his home-town. Dedicated to public service, he was held in high regard. Of a literary bent, he wrote the *Musnad of Murshidabad.* In addition to his other work he became the legal advisor and later private secretary to the Nawab Bahadur of Murshidabad. He was my father-in-law and I was sorely grieved when he died in January, 1912.

The recollections I have of the first ten days at my father-in-law's house seem mostly to be connected with the difficulty of managing my veil, silver anklets and *sari,* and my desire to speak out. I had repeatedly been told that it was most improper for a new bride to speak in anything but monosyllables. Accustomed to the freedom of short frocks and the hoydenish life in my father's home all these restrictions were irksome. Then there was the food affair . . . new brides are supposed to be shy, so during meal-times and in between, food is pressed on her in case she is left hungry.

Never a large eater, all the excitement had killed my appetite completely. Although I shook my head most emphatically (a new bride is never heard) my plate was heaped with food of alarming proportions. 'You must eat it all up,' whispered a young sister-in-law, 'Otherwise you will earn ill-fame as a wasteful bride.' The food had new flavours, the curries were too hot and spicy, and the amount served could have nourished me for a fortnight. I remember gazing at them in despair, picking and sampling some, leaving the rest, and then hearing, 'The new bride has eaten nothing at all!' Some commiserated saying, 'The poor dear is shy', others were quite certain I went with a hungry stomach all through the day. Overcome by the coaxing that is extended to a new bride, I would be very near tears at meal-times.

I was always dressed in many gold ornaments and the finest *saris* for people seemed to be continually dropping in to see the bride, but what embarrassed me most were the silver anklets which never left my feet. I had been briefed by a slightly older cousin about the length of veil to be lowered before people—the proper measurement varied according to the degree of intimacy established. One of her injunctions was to be always bashful, for bashfulness is the indispensable ornament of the new bride. I was to be very bashful before my husband she warned, and was on no account to be seen in his presence before elders. Every time he happened to pass through the veranda (and this seemed very often) I would dash to the adjoining room in a most unbridelike manner with my anklets raising a frightful din. 'You had better sit still with your veil lowered a little more instead of leaping away like that,' said a young sister-in-law with a sly smile and that is what I did afterwards. When I told my knowledgeable cousin about my predicament and the contrary advice, she pursed her lips, nodded and said that that too was in order for it was another method of showing how bashful I was.

She had also told me how to behave on the 'auspicious night'. 'Be quite still and wait for him to speak, for yours must never be the first words, also, be sure to speak in whispers for there will be many people lying in wait to learn what you say to each other and you will be teased to death by the watchers.' It is usually the young sisters-in-law who enjoy this game and when they have spied for awhile, they announce, amidst much hilarity, that all is well with the newly married ones.

'But, what do you think he will say?' I had asked perplexed. 'Oh he'll ask your name perhaps', was the airy reply 'for that is what most of them do.' I giggled. 'But why?' was my query, 'He surely knows already for isn't it printed in all the invitation letters?' 'He must say something, you silly, and mind don't you go and laugh on your *phul shajya* night, you'll be thought to be very shameless.' I covered my face with my frock and giggled more than ever. She eyed me with disgust. 'What do you find so funny? I really don't know what you are going to do at your father-in-law's. I am sure you will return covered with ill-fame and that will serve you right. I am not going to tell you anything more,' and saying this she flounced away. I was sobered, for like all Bengalee girls I had grown up with the knowledge that a father-in-law's home was a place of high standards.

The day after I came to my father-in-law's house was the *bou-bhat* ceremony and I was thankful indeed that I did not make any *faux pas* or upset the dish of spinach and rice when I was serving the family. Early in the afternoon I had been dressed with care in a gold and green Benares *sari* and gold and jewelled ornaments. People from far and near had been invited to 'see the face of the bride', and they were to be feasted afterwards. I sat on the carpet beside a young sister-in-law who lifted up my veil and tilted up my face so it could be seen. My head had been bowed bashfully but even after it was tilted up I was unable to see the guests for I had been told to close my eyes to indicate my bashfulness.

I could only hear their approbative 'Bah!' (exclamation of praise and wonder) accompanied by a 'a beautiful bride', or 'She has a lovely face'.

As I had never been told I was good-looking I was happy to hear all this and enjoyed being on display. I had been very conscious of my lack of beauty and bemoaned the fact that my brothers were given fairer skins than mine by inconsiderate Fate. Mejda, second brother, had often been mistaken for a European. I was just a pale beige and my hair did not ripple down to my knees as did Rani-di's who was my ideal. She was Mashima's daughter and was blessed with abundant glossy black hair, a pink and white complexion and graceful movements. I thought her perfectly ravishing and remember making two petitions in my nightly prayers: one to be transformed into another Rani-di and the other to have my sums correct the next day at school.

At first I had been quite pleased to hear all these flattering words, but as time passed and afternoon slipped into evening and evening into night, I lost interest and became very weary. The large silver plate in front of me overflowed with silver coins and other gifts that I had been 'blessed' with by those who had 'seen my face'. Even my father-in-law's tenants had been invited and presented me with small coins. Later, every woman who had made a gift received a new *sari* as a souvenir of the wedding.

I was so tired and sleepy that I have no recollection of what followed later except that I was led to a room that seemed to be filled with flowers and I too was wearing flower ornaments. It must have been quite late at night for the house was very quiet. 'Now close the door', I heard amidst a gale of laughter, 'and sleep well!' I pulled my soft cotton *sari* over my face and lay on a corner of the bed strewn with the petals of red roses. My floral ornaments pricked me and although most uncomfortable I dozed off. With my heart aflutter I became aware that someone was softly unhooking my floral wristlet and slipping the floral rings from my fingers . . .by the dim night light I came to know it was my husband.

'Now you can sleep in comfort,' he said in a low voice,

then holding up a bracelet asked, 'What is this called, a *sinthi-pati*?' I suppressed a giggle. 'What an amusing man, he does not know a *sinthi-pati* from a bracelet!' was my thought for I was wide awake now. *Sinthi* means the centre parting of the hair, and the ornament laid over the parting is the *sinthi-pati*. I was highly amused and enlightened him accordingly. It began to rain, the July rain fell heavily and soon the wind began blowing it in through the open windows. He rose to close them and as I watched him, I vaguely decided he was not only amusing but nice. Seeing Dada ask Bouthan to do small things like this, I was pleasantly surprised to see my husband closing the window. But I was soon drowsy again and relieved of the prickly flowers promptly fell asleep. Next morning I was cross-examined by some giddy girls . . . 'What did he say?' I was believed when I swore I had slept all through the night and neither spoke nor heard a word.

There were so many house guests and meals were so elaborate that the cooks could not possibly serve everyone at the same time, so again it was very late when I was taken by a bevy of laughing young sisters and cousins-in-law to my bedroom. After some hilarity and many injunctions to my husband not to keep me awake for long as I had had no rest in the day, they left. 'Are you really tired?' I was asked in a whisper. 'No,' I whispered back, then lifting my veil I giggled and told him how I had foiled the inquisitive 'in-laws'. I was quite pleased at my feat and gave him a vivid description of their questions and my replies. Both of us were shaking with muffled laughter when there was a noise within the room.

Promptly, I pulled the veil over my face and covered myself with the sheet waiting anxiously to find out who the intruder was. Soon, I heard my husband cry out in surprise. . . 'Boudi!' [elder brother's wife]. Instantly voices from without demanded entrance . . . the door was flung open and about half a dozen girls flowed in. Amidst much merriment 'Boudi' explained how the mosquitoes had driven her from her hiding place—a rolled up mat which stood in the corner. 'And' said she pointing at me, 'if I had not heard with my own ears, I could never have believed that she was such a liar.' I nearly died of shame.

There were no more 'watching episodes' and we were able to talk at length when we met at night. I told him about my school and home life, of my games with my brothers, what a great tease the youngest one was, how I thought I was better than him at the kite contests, and could bowl quite well at cricket. My husband, in his turn, would regale me with stories of his escapades at school and college, the idiosyncracies of his teachers, and the foibles of fellow officers. I was most interested in all he said, for he was a good raconteur, and when we laughed at the same things, I found it hard to remember that he was eleven years older than I.

When he told me that his friend had asked him whether he found me beautiful, I squirmed with delight and whispered, 'And what did you say?' The answer took me aback. He had said he could not tell as he had had no opportunity as yet to see my face properly. Reflecting on his words I found I could not remember what he looked like either; we only met at night by the dim light of an oil lamp. Since it was highly improper for a new bride to be found in the same room with her husband in broad daylight, I always left while it was still dark and went to sleep beside my mother-in-law in the next room.

During those first few days as a new bride I was never allowed to do anything more strenuous than help make the *pan*. Many little packets of this edible leaf were prepared daily by a group of young women who gossiped and laughed and made gentle jests at my expense. One morning as I was helping to prepare pan, a young sister-in-law came and said, 'Boudi, Dada's friends want to see your English handwriting, so do write a few words for them.' With this I was handed pencil and paper. I never heard what my husband's friends thought of my calligraphy but they must have been somewhat bewildered by the words I wrote.

Vital spark of heavenly flame
Quit Oh quit this mortal frame,

....
Oh the pain and bliss of dying.

I have forgotten the third line and really cannot think to this day what made me quote those grim words of Alexander Pope. I remember I had learned them and jotted them down in my note-book along with other obtuse lines which caught my fancy. The alliterations held a special appeal and I loved to get the lilting words by heart never knowing how disastrous this could be.

When the ten days were over I rejoiced to see my Sripur uncle come to fetch me at last. The acquaintance with my husband had been forged into good friendship and we promised to write to each other till we met again. I told him that both my Bengali spelling and handwriting were appalling, but he only laughed and said, 'Never mind, write in English'.

In that year of 1911, the months that followed found me deeply engrossed in our correspondence. I was initiated in the art of letter writing: the Bengali words and phraseology were supplied by the knowledgeable cousin, and the correct English terms were dictated by my two elder brothers. As I recall the past I cannot but think that my father-in-law was somewhat unusual for at that time I knew of no one amongst us who corresponded with a new daughter-in-law in English. I still cherish those letters written in his neat precise hand and giving me news of my new relations at Murshidabad and of his son. He always addressed me as his 'Dear Daughter' and ended giving his affection and full signature.

As for his son, he affixed 'My dear' before my name, chatted about nothing in particular and ended decorously with his full name. In one, he gave me the addresses of my new sisters and cousins-in-law and said they expected me to write to them too. And, of course, I was to write to his mother and young brother, and well remember my predicament. In my first letter to the eight-year old brother-in-law, I had blithely used the trite Bengali phrase of 'not being able to write earlier for lack of time'. His reply in a better hand than mine ran as follws: 'You say you could not write sooner because you did not have the time, but don't I know about the letter you wrote to Dada as soon as you reached Calcutta? How did you have the time then? Do you think you can dodge and throw dust in my eyes? Oh no, I understand everything!'

I was quite shaken and became chary of phraseology after this episode. Data dictated my dutiful letters to my father-in-law, and Mejda, the stilted ones beginning with 'My dear husband'. Sucking my pencil, I would make laborious drafts, then laying on my stomach, spend whole afternoons copying them out in my neatest hand and finally give them to the office boy to post personally, beseeching him to bring the replies straight to me when they arrived.

My brothers read all my letters and I gave them without demur but on the day I found my husband had added, 'est' to the usual 'dear', and 'your' before just his first name, I decided this was to be kept most secret. So, when I was asked to show the letter I flatly refused and was chased all over the veranda by the youngest of my brothers until I rushed into Dada's study. Tearful and breathless I complained about his behaviour. But Dada only laughed and said it was undoubtedly wrong of Chorda to try to wrest the letter from me, but there also should not be anything in it that could not be seen by others. Devoted to Swami Vivekananda and Vedanta philosophy Dada was austere in his ideas about material matters.

In Autumn that year, my father-in-law sent a lovely light green gauzy Benares silk *sari* strewn with silver roses for me to wear during the Durga *puja* festival. Gifts of Murshidabad silk *saris* and *dhotis* were also sent for all the family, together with two enormous tins of luscious curdled milk balls fried a golden brown in deep *ghee* and steeped in syrup. I felt quite proud when everybody praised my father-in-law's good taste in making presents. Similar gifts for the Murshidabad family were sent by Mother, with appropriate ones for my husband.

When the cold weather came, my father-in-law sent a pink velvet jacket to wear with a soft warm Kashmiri *sari*. Among other gifts was a basket of fresh oranges, apricots, walnuts, raisins and almonds. These gifts were sent just before he left with the Nawab to the Delhi Durbar. We had heard that several compartments were reserved in a special train for the Nawab's retinue and were excited that my husband was going as their guest.

King George V was holding a *durbar* [formal reception] that December in Delhi and all the elite were invited to participate in the ceremony. Being the premier nobleman of Bengal, His Highness the Nawab Bahadur of Murshidabad would be there to pay his homage, along with other ruling princes, to the King Emperor of India.

Calcutta was *en fete*; the roads that he would pass through were bedecked with flags, the Union Jack flew everywhere and tier upon tier of seats were constructed for the citizens to see their sovereign as he passed in state in an open carriage. People talked of nothing else and we watched all these preparations being made and longed to be in a front seat on the great day. But Mother was revolted at the price. 'Ten rupees for a seat? Why its perfectly preposterous! Money doesn't grow on trees . . . besides, what is there to see?' We pleaded, my brothers and I, that so and so was going, but she replied in scorn they were the *nouveau riche* and easy money went easily, and that our ancestors did not leave their hard-earned wealth to be squandered in seeing Kings but to be devoted to a more worthy cause. She took us, however, on the day of the dress rehearsal and we watched the whole procession as it would be on the day the King would arrive.

'There,' she said, waving her hand at the gleaming barouche with prancing horses bearing some high official. 'Instead of that white face would be another white face so, what do we miss? Nothing. What would we gain by having a fleeting glimpse of the face we see so well in every newspaper?' Calcutta, she said, was a city of hectic scenes and if one was not careful one's coffers would soon be empty. Her arguments were irrefutable and her decisions irrevocable so we had to abide by them. Father, of course, had a front seat in some prominent place reserved for the members of the Bengal Landholders' Association and went fully dressed in frock coat and top hat.

The coming of King George V is linked in my mind with the anguish of losing a most loving father-in-law. He had been overworked in Delhi; shortly afterwards he caught a cold in Calcutta that developed into pneumonia and he died, alas, early in January 1912. I remember praying fervently for his recovery and wept bitter tears to hear he was no more. Mother made me follow the austere rules of mourning but I did not mind having the one dish of boiled rice and vegetables for my midday meal. It had to be done in a new earthen pot everyday and should the vessel crack during cooking there would be no cooked meal that day for the mourner. So Mother would first tap and test the clay pot and cook carefully over a slow fire fed with jute sticks. With a lump of butter and sprinkling of rock salt I thought this was a delicious meal. Served on a fresh green banana leaf, the meal was concluded with a small marble bowl of thick creamy milk and a banana. In the evening there was a cup of hot milk, fruit and a small lump of *chana* [curdled milk sprinkled with brown sugar.

This was my food for the mourning month; my mourning clothes consisted of two cotton *saris* and a warm jacket, for it was very cold at that time of the year. I was even colder at Murshidabad, where I went, before the month was over, to be present for the *shraddha*, the ceremonial rites for the peace of the departed one's soul.

8

As I stepped within the house that had previously welcomed me so gaily I was greeted by wailing cries that made me shudder. I slept that night with my mother-in-law and awoke early at the sound of a long-drawn wail. 'Oh Baba, my Baba where are you?' cried my poor grandmother-in-law, who had lost her only child. My mother-in-law joined in wordless wails while the sisters-in-law crooned in grief. There were a few house guests and they too wailed aloud till the whole house was filled with mourning cries. I shivered anew in the cold grey dawn.

This was the first time I had come in contact with such grief. Mother had never taken me to a house of mourning and all that I remembered of my grandmother's death was a penetrating silence pervading our house. Each morning and evening the house was rent by these heart-rending cries until the *shraddha* was over. I felt lost and miserable. My grandmother-in-law forbade rigid observance of mourning rules regarding my food, saying it was inauspicious to do so within the wedding year. She herself cooked many kinds of vegetable curries and tried her best to induce me to eat, but I could hardly touch my food. I shall never forget her kindness at this time, although over seventy and herself in mourning she never failed to serve my mother-in-law with her mourning meals as well as the rest of the family. She was undemonstrative and austere, but I could feel her affection for me and later learnt to hold her in love and veneration.

I never saw my husband during those days, for he slept with his friends and kinsmen in another part of the house. It is the privilege of the eldest son to perform the *shraddha* ceremony and this was duly performed by him, officially ending the mourning period. This was followed by a ceremonial meal with friends and relatives. I stayed on for a few more weeks and then returned to Calcutta.

After returning, I went to Benares with my parents, for my father was to perform a *shraddha* ceremony there. This was for a great-grandmother who had retired to Benares in her declining years and desired her *shraddha* ceremony to be performed in that holy city. Once again all of us stayed in a rented house in the city while Father remained in the Hotel de Paris. Elaborate preparations were made after consultation with a great many learned Pandits, but at the last minute Father was debarred from performing the rites because he happened to meet with a slight accident the evening before. The Pandits insisted that this was a *badha*, an omen of obstruction, indicating that Father was not meant to undertake this task. According to the rules of religious observances, the body of the person who is to perform a sacred ceremony must be in good order, and Father had gone and burnt his hand and acquired a blister. That was sufficient to make him unsuitable for the ceremony. So, it was Dada who devoutly performed the last rites of the old lady.

We remained for some time longer; all that I remember is the bitter March wind that chapped my skin and made it bleed, the mischievous monkeys who would disappear with the washing, and my dips in the Ganges. When bathing in the holy river I would pray that the merit derived might devolve on my husband, who was then taking his settlement training at Mymensingh. My first *darshan* [auspicious viewing] of Viswanath's *arati*, the ritual of evening prayer, is still in my memory. The waving lights, clanging bells, colourful flowers, fragrant incense and melodious voices of the chanting priests combined with the surging crowd's full throated cries of 'Viswanathji ki jai'—'Hail to the Lord of the Universe!' influenced me strangely and I found myself praying for his grace with the tears streaming down my face.

In this year of 1912, my education was enlarged by Didi who took me to the Bengalee theatre I had heard so much about. Dada held strict views and thought it a den of vice and

Father was not interested in the Bengalee stage, so neither Mother nor I had ever been inside a theatre. I envied Didi who could do as she liked at Howrah. Her husband, an easy-going person whom she twisted around her little finger, was also addicted to the theatre.

As Didi could not come with us to Benares, Mother went to see her on our return with some Viswanath *prasad*—a delicious hard creamy sweet called *pyanra* that had first been offered to Viswanath, the Lord of the Universe. I and Didi's eldest son, Sisir, who stayed with us to go to St. Teresa's Convent, accompanied Mother. Both of us looked forward to these visits, for the long drive to Howrah in the closed carriage was full of excitement and Didi always had some little gift for us. We stood at each door, clutching the handles to keep our balance as Jim, our big brown horse, trotted along the Strand Road and over the Howrah bridge, neighing and snorting according to his mood. On our return journey, which was always late in the evening, I curled up and slept with my head on Mother's lap while Sisir would be stretched out full length on the opposite seat.

Didi had a small house with a handkerchief of a garden which seemed very cosy in comparison to our big home at Kidderpore. An added attraction was a tiny toy train that could give a piercing whistle as it puffed its way to and from one station to another. Sisir always wanted to do what I did and created a frightful row when Didi suggested I remain so she could show me something I had never seen before. Even though he was told that no one of his years ever went to a theatre, he clung to the veranda railings and refused to return to Kidderpore.

All this disturbed Mother who began to doubt the wisdom of leaving me behind. Father would not like my spending a night out—a thing that had never been done before—nor would Dada approve of my introduction to the Bengalee stage. She brought these arguments forward, but Didi merely laughed and told her not to worry. 'Don't say anything to Dada', she said, 'and Father will surely not mind if Khuki, (to them I was still *khuki*—baby girl) spends a night with her own sister. All of you seem to forget she is married now!' Thus persuaded,

Mother agreed, but my nephew deeply resented the treatment meted out to him. 'Wait till you come to Kidderpore then you'll see what'll happen . . . I'll tell . . .' Before he could finish he was bundled into the carriage and with many injunctions to Didi about my safety and care, Mother closed the doors.

The coachman flicked his whip and Jim broke into a brisk trot leaving me standing at the gate with mixed feelings. I was elated but a little uneasy at the prospect of facing Dada's displeasure. But my misgivings evaporated when Jamai Babu, elder sister's husband, squeezed my arm and chuckled to hear what Didi had done. 'Yes, let's go to the Minerva theatre,' he said. We had a hasty meal and scrambled into the hired carriage. 'We have a long way to go so you can sleep a little if you want,' he said looking at me with amusement. I indignantly replied that I didn't feel like sleep, but he only laughed and said, 'You had better, for we won't be back before tomorrow morning.' I gasped, 'What about your office?' 'O—h we'll manage,' he replied with twinkling eyes as he pinched my cheek. The steady beat of the horse's hooves within the semi-darkness created by closed doors had a soporific effect and I did fall asleep against my will. Awakening with a start when the carriage gave a jolt and stopped, I hastily covered my head with my *sari*.

When the sliding doors opened I could see a large building, brilliant lights and many people. We dismounted and I followed Didi up a narrow staircase to a broad balcony overflowing with women and children. There did not seem to be an inch of space anywhere and I wondered where we were to sit. But Didi clutched my hand and miraculously found us a seat right in the front. Immediately in front of us hung a net curtain which kept us respectfully concealed. None of the women cared for this and I could hear much grumbling; luckily we sat between a gap and had a good view of the stage.

When I voiced my dislike, Didi said this was much better than the split bamboo affair of former days. They were called 'chicks' and nothing much could be seen through the narrow chinks. 'Yes', said Didi, selecting a *pan* from her small silver *pan* box and popping it into her mouth, 'Things are much better now. Do you know how strict people were before?' I shook my head as I could not conceive of how things could be any worse. Chewing her *pan* with relish, Didi continued, 'Well, I have been told our great-grandmother used to be dipped into the Ganges, palanquin and all.' 'My goodness,' I exclaimed in a horrified whisper, 'But why?' 'Not to give anyone a chance to see her at all! It is meritorious to have a bath in the Ganges and she naturally liked to have one now and then and this was the only way to have them. We only have to cover ourselves properly and lower our veils to have a real bath in the Ganges.' I had to agree that we were better off.

The play commenced. I followed every word with my eyes glued on the players. During the long intervals when scenes were being changed, I became impatient at the delay and asked Didi frequently when the curtain would rise. I shed copious tears at the sorrow of the lovelorn hero and heroine and harboured a bitter hatred for the heartless father of the girl. Her husband was of noble birth but alas impoverished and unable to provide for her in an adequate manner, so her father refused to send her to his humble home. Ah, the cruel insulting words he had for his son-in-law! Then, hearing of her husband's illness, she stole away in secret only to find him on his death-bed. Only then was the hard heart of the father touched but it was too late! 'Alas! Alas!' wept the women around me. 'Alas!' I sighed with an aching heart, 'why could she not have come to him before?' I was quite certain no one could keep me from my husband no matter how he lived. 'What is the name of this play?' I asked Didi wiping her eyes. '*Kaal Parinay*—The Deadly Wedding. It is sad, but all these "social" plays are like this. Never mind,' she laughed looking at my doleful face, 'the next one will be amusing. Now let's go. You must be hungry, your Jamai Babu will be waiting for us.'

The interval bell rang and from the hall below came strident cries of 'Pan Biri!' and 'Garam Chaa!' as the hawkers went around with the little folded leaves, country-made cigarettes and hot tea in a kettle. Every one crowded to the door where the menfolk were waiting with big cone-shaped leaf packages filled with steaming hot savouries. Each one had brought some food from the restaurant for the women of his party and there was Jamai Babu holding out a package for us. It was good to see his familiar face amongst all those strange ones. 'Well, how did you like *Kaal Parinay*?' he asked. 'It's too terribly sad,' I replied with a sniff. 'Never mind, the other play will be a farce.' 'What's the time?' asked Didi with a yawn. 'Past midnight, and the next play will take another hour or more. You had better hurry to your seats or you'll lose them.' And sure enough on our return we found them already occupied and had to be content with the next best ones. 'What is a farce, Didi?' I asked. 'Something funny that makes you laugh,' she replied. The woman beside us looked at me with curiosity in her eyes, 'Are you sisters-in-law?' she queried. 'No,' was my indignant reply, 'she is my own sister.'

The curtain was still down. Everyone talked and laughed as they chewed their *pan*, but the children had become fretful. A maid-servant of the theatre went round requesting mothers to pacify their children. Some infants in arms raised their voices loudly and I began to wonder how on earth we were to hear anything. At that moment the bell rang and the curtain began to rise and I caught my breath when I heard, 'Oh Mothers, do give your breasts to the babies!' shouted in stentorian voices from below. I cast bewildered eyes on Didi, but she continued to chew her *pan* and told me in a placid whisper that the injunction came from the rowdy section of the audience downstairs.

Transferring my gaze to the stage I received another shock. Three tall angular women, heavily made up and dressed in the oddest clothes, bounced towards the footlights and began to behave in the strangest fashion. Waving handkerchiefs they twirled round and round singing falsetto something that sounded like . . . 'We are of the Habshi (Abyssinian) band . . . .' They fluttered their eyelids, pirouetted, posed and pranced about from one end of the stage to the other, flinging their legs and arms about with wild abandon. Never in all my years had I beheld any woman behaving in such a shameless fashion. I felt all the shame was mine . . . I wondered if I was asleep and seeing a nightmare. I could not understand why this was considered to be funny and why the audience was tittering at these performers. Whether they were trying to give some imitation of the French can-can dancers I do not know, but I remember being so utterly sick that I tried to shut out the terrible sight. 'Oh Didi', I wailed, 'I don't want to see any more. How can they do this? Don't they feel any shame? Let's go away . . . .' The woman beside straightened her spectacles and looked at me severely as she said, 'Have you never been to a theatre before?' I shook my head miserably. Her scornful comment still rings in my ears: 'Child, are you *ashikshita*?' This word can mean 'illiterate' or 'uneducated'—perhaps she meant both.

I slept most of the morning and was still yawning in the afternoon when I heard the carriage arrive. Khokar-jhi appeared with a grim smile and informed us that Sisir had 'told' and Dada was furious. My heart sank, but remembering Didi's words, I tossed my head and told her, 'I am married now, so he can't do anything to me!'

Nothing did happen and I remember no unpleasant consequences. Time has changed the Minerva theatre and its audience beyond recognition, but that night's entertainment and the contempt I earned from the votary of the theatre has not been forgotten.

My husband was still at Mymensingh but my mother-in-law wanted me at Murshidabad. My presence would help to comfort them, she said, so I was sent there along with Khokar-jhi. The old house had a dreary air which was enlivened only by my brother-in-law and his many small friends. Thakurpo, my younger brother-in-law, became my good friend and companion. He was eight, four years younger than I but inordinately solemn. I would eagerly wait for him to return from school and give me news of the great world beyond the four walls.

I came to know about Thakurpo's teachers, his friends and the adventures which happened on the road he travelled every day to school. He brought books for me from the school library and introduced me to Robert Blake, the wizard English detective whose adventures were published in Bengali. Although sometimes needing assistance when I found the Bengali too high-flown, I avidly devoured the whole series.

Thakurpo was greatly distressed at my weakness in Bengali and had given me some very large homemade exercise books in which he had drawn lines an inch or more apart. 'The larger you write, the better; and be sure to write with the reed pen to get the thick and thin lines clear. You must improve. Your handwriting is awful now,' he lamented, 'whatever will your father-in-law's people say?' Every afternoon I secretly practised writing in Bengali.

Thakurpo had also smuggled in the literature of Panch Cowrie Dey whose murder mysteries had alluring titles like *Nil Basana Sundari* [The Beautiful Woman Dressed in Blue]. I, in turn, would regale him with English fairy tales. The winter evenings were long and cold in Murshidabad. Since women never wore any footwear, my feet felt like lumps of ice after walking about on the cold stone floors. When my mother-in-law asked, after dusk, if I would like to sit on the bed beside her, I was grateful for the opportunity to warm my feet under the quilt. I would try to read something by the dim light of the hurricane lantern as I waited for Thakurpo to appear.

He had a private tutor after school hours who coached him in special subjects. When this was over, he would come upstairs and join us under the quilt. This was story-telling time and we heard tales from Thakurpo and my mother-in-law until the maid came to announce dinner.

At that time we had a temperamental cook from Orissa whose knowledge of the culinary art left much to be desired. He was so passionately fond of flavouring his dishes with chillies that they drew tears from eyes. 'Since you do not eat anything,' said Thakurpo 'why do you sit down to dinner?' His tongue was caustic beyond his years, but I knew it was his way of showing concern. We had our evening meal together, and I had the midday one by myself unless it was Sunday.

My grandmother and mother-in-law ate in what was called the 'vegetarian room', eating food prepared by an ancient woman whom we called Deeda. She had become a widow while still very young and had been in the home very since.

They followed the strict food rules of orthodox widowhood, rigidly abstaining from fish, meat, eggs, onions and certain other vegetables and lentils. The cook from Orissa, helped by a maid of all work, presided over the 'fish kitchen'. I doled out the daily rations from the store-room according to instructions from my mother-in-law, but the maid, Kelor-Ma [Mother of Kelo], filched the grain and spices and complained that I had not given the right measure. I could swear I did, but being a new bride had made me tongue-tied. A long time afterwards I found the biscuit tin in which she hoarded them and could finally tell my mother-in-law about it.

Meals were usually late at night, for the cook would not turn up in time and if reprimanded would threaten to resign. Brahmin cooks were few in Murshidabad and since none but Brahmins were allowed entry into the kitchen in those days, they were in great demand. While we waited for our meals, my mother-in-law would at times drowsily call out for 'Snow White', a special favourite of hers. She commiserated deeply with the vicissitudes of Snow White and rejoiced to hear about the downfall of the Queen.

She told us abbreviated versions of the historical romances of Bankim Chandra Chatterjee and one of them fired my imagination to such an extent that I begged the book from her and with Thakurpo made a valiant attempt to translate it into English. We poured over the book on Sunday afternoons and fondly hoped for fame and fortune. Before we had finished the book I left for Calcutta.

Thakurpo's knowledge of Sanskrit fascinated me and so I persuaded him to teach me in return for English lessons. But I refused to memorize uninteresting grammar and wanted to begin immediately with the story of the 'Swan that walked with the crow', but I have no recollection of anything else. At other times, I would fly kites with him, changing into the meek daughter-in-law when anyone appeared. And we played *golok-dham*, a game in which you went to heaven on a paper board if you played your cowries right, or else straight to hell, or a tavern, if you failed. This game held great allure for me and I was forever jingling the little sea-shells, cowries, which were the dice, and dying to test my luck in our spare time. It was with these devoted friends and my grandmother and mother-in-law that my days passed placidly.

Daily I would come to the apartments of my grandmother-in-law to arrange for her Shiva *puja.* I sorted the flowers and *bael* leaves, rubbed the sandalwood paste into the little bowl and washed the fruit and rice for the food offering. All this I did with effortless ease but when it came to moulding the symbol of Shiva, I trembled and prayed it might come out right. It seldom did. Since her very young years, my grandmother-in-law had been a skilful maker of the symbol and was intolerant of the least flaw. 'Look', she would say, taking a fistful of the soft silt from the Ganges, 'you do it like this.' First rolling a small ball, she would create a perfect little symbol with only four movements. Indeed, her sculpturing was so immaculate that before her marriage, a *ghatak,* or marriage broker, saw her handiwork and thought her to be a mature woman. She must have been very beautiful once for traces of great beauty could be seen in her still. She had a slight figure, very small hands and feet and skin that was soft and the colour of old ivory. All this I remember well for I massaged her with oil before her daily bath.

In his letters my husband wrote : 'Try to be near grandmother at times. It might assuage her grief to have you with her.' No servant was allowed within her apartment which was cleaned by Deeda early in the morning before I came to prepare for her *puja.* In the afternoon I would take the broom and sweep it once again. I did not hear my grandmother-in-law cry aloud any more, nor did I ever see her smile, and when she spoke, it was only to ask me whether I had had my food. Her face never lost its grief-stricken look as she sat silently turning the rosary in her hands.

I had overheard someone say to Mother that my husband's people would be prone to think that the death of my father-in-law was because I, the new bride, had brought ill-luck to the family. This had made me feel guilty, fearful and ashamed, but to my intense relief it was just the reverse. I was made to understand that since my father-in-law had chosen and brought me to the house, I was of special value. Because he had been fond of me, I was looked upon with favour. In spite of his many pre-occupations at the Delhi Durbar, he had found time to purchase some souvenirs for me. The large ivory inlaid box, ivory book marks, lovely sandalwood fan together with some colourful picture postcards of Delhi and Agra were handed over to me later by my mother-in-law. 'Aha,' she sighed, 'it was his cherished desire to see the face of his son's wife and he had his wish fulfilled before he left. You were very dear to him Bouma.'

In those quiet afternoons she would sit and tell me stories about the family in bygone days. She had heard these tales from the 'Thakruns,' the ladies who had had the ill-fortune to be widowed at an early age, and being more or less destitute, had received sanctuary in the home of the Rai Saheb. Many of them were very young when they had first arrived and they lived the austere life of the Hindu widow. Each made her own particular contribution towards the house and its inmates, where they were held in honour and considered to be the 'aunts' of my father-in-law. When his children arrived, they became 'grandmothers' and vied with each other in spoiling the grandchildren.

From what I could gather, my mother-in-law had a comparatively easy time with little or no responsibility. To the ladies she had remained the 'Bou', the bride, and had never appeared before them without a lowered veil. And it was from them that she had learnt about the grandeur of the house during the days of the Rai Saheb and the vicissitudes of the family.

The Rai Saheb's three young sons were given in marriage to exquisitely beautiful brides. Within only ten days of the wedding one was widowed and a few weeks later another became a widow. The two girls, not yet in their teens, were taken away by their parents. The father of one, influenced by the advanced ideas prevalent at that time, became a 'Brahmo' and joined that monotheistic group, which had broken away from orthodox Hinduism. Both women's education and widow remarriage were advocated by the Brahmo Samaj, so he sent his daughter to school, and when she came of age, gave her in marriage to a worthy man. It was a successful marriage and she bore him two sons.

'What happened to the other widow?' I asked. 'She lived the usual life of widows of the times. When she grew up, she divided her time between her father's and her husband's home, where she held an honoured place. But I must tell you now about the third bride, my mother-in-law,' she said with twinkling eyes, 'But for her—neither you nor I would have been here today.' The Rai Saheb, heartbroken at the loss of his two sons, centred all his hopes on his third son who was then still a student. Thinking it not wise to let the young man become preoccupied with his lovely bride, the Rai Saheb had kept them apart. The son slept in the outer building while his bride lived with the 'ladies' who occupied another portion of the house. Some of them were tender-hearted and took pity on the young husband and wife so cruelly separated. One night they secretly led the heavily veiled girl to his room and left her there, with whispered instructions that she be returned to them before daybreak. It was they who saved the family from extinction. . .for the Rai Saheb's son died when his little grandson was but four months old.

The Rai Saheb did not live long and this infant remained the only male in the family. The decline of the family fortunes compelled most of the dependants to leave, and only a few 'ladies' stayed on with the sixteen-year-old girl widow and her babe. An old family retainer, the *Shikdar*, looked after the little family and guarded the house but it was beyond his powers to provide for them. Though the Rai Saheb had earned much wealth, his extensive charities allowed him to leave only the old house, a few pieces of silver in the family chest, and an honourable name. In a remote East Bengal district there were estates, but who was there to realize the rents?

When most of the silver had been mortgaged or sold, the girl widow emerged from her sheltered life and, accompanied by the *Shikdar*, made the long journey by train and steamer to the estates. Since the holdings were water-logged for most of the year, she travelled in a country boat to collect the tithes herself. As it was not the custom for women in her position to either speak or be seen, the *shikdar* explained all to the tenants. When they saw the young widow with covered face holding their infant landlord in her arms, they hastened to make their salutations and to pay all their dues. Periodically she went like this and appeared before them veiled and silent and never returned empty-handed. The remainder of the time she lived in seclusion with the 'ladies,' observing the rigid rules of widowhood.

The child did well at the Murshidabad school. He was the apple of her eye, but when she was advised to send him to Calcutta for higher education, she did not hesitate to mortgage a portion of the estates to raise the required funds. Her sacrifice was well rewarded as he did equally well at college. When she realized that the time had come when the boy would need guidance other than hers and the old *Shikdar's*, she gave him in marriage to the only child of a good and worthy lawyer. He released the mortgages, took over the management of the estates and saw his son-in-law through the perils of college life in Calcutta. Finally, the son returned to become a successful lawyer in Murshidabad.

'Yes,' said Ma, 'My father was a good man and paid us many visits here before he became a Brahmo.' 'Why, what happened then?' 'Nothing,' she replied, 'but my mother-in-law did not quite approve of his action and felt he had lost his caste. He was very fond of my baby son, and we went to see him sometimes in our village home in Mymensingh.' My husband was still 'the baby boy' to her. Before him she had borne three daughters who had all died in their infancy so after his birth she had prayed to Mother Kali that his life might be spared. And when he was a month old, the goddess had been worshipped with much pomp and circumstance; and this practice was repeated when he ate his first rice, before his naming ceremony and after his marriage ceremony. Two daughters and a son had come after him but the eldest still remained the 'baby boy'. 'Ah,' she sighed, 'as I see my mother-in-law mourn for her son, I tremble with dread, for who knows what fate has destined for me? The span of life allotted to the sons of this family does not seem to be very long. . . .'A cold chill swept over me as I remembered what had been foretold in my horoscope and clutching the heart-shaped amulet that hung from the gold chain on my neck, I fervently hoped that the evil had been averted.

When I went to Calcutta again, Mother came one day with an earthen plate containing some sweets and cut fruit sprinkled with a few vermilion stained flowers. She touched this on my brow and passing her finger over the smudge of vermilion on a *bael* leaf, touched the centre parting of my hair. She then placed a bright dot on my forehead, not forgetting to touch the iron bracelet I wore as a sign of my wifehood with this auspicious mark. She said Pandit Nakuleśwar Bhattacharya had sent his *prasad* from the ritual he had performed for the welfare of my husband and I was to take something from the plate. 'He still does this every month! How long has he to do this?' I asked as I selected a sweet and touching it on my brow in respect, popped it into my mouth. I felt my face burn as I heard her say, 'Till you have a baby.' What a ridiculous idea: I was aghast and quite angry with the Pandit. Just then my youngest brother happened to pass and catching sight of the *prasad* unceremoniously helped himself. 'Ah the Pandit!' he said with a mouthful of fruit, 'I am sure there is not a word of truth in what he says and this is just a method of getting some money each month from Mother. . . .' Here he reflected for a moment, 'I know, he is just like Rasputin!' Mother was shocked at his levity. She did not know who Rasputin was, neither did I then, but for once I was thankful to Chorda for he helped to lighten my heart and look at things from a different angle.

9

Sometime late in 1913 my husband was posted to Faridpore. My heart leapt with joy when I learnt that I should be going with him. Accompanied by Khokar-jhi, an old Brahmin cook called Pandey, and a considerable amount of luggage, we left for the distant station in East Bengal.

In those days, brick and mortar buildings were rather rare in that part of the world so we were considered fortunate to have found one consisting of three small rooms with a veranda and kitchen. In the open courtyard there was a well and an enclosed square with a tin roof to serve as a bathroom. Beyond this was the main road, and by it was a room I rarely entered for it was here my husband entertained his visitors. We slept on two *taktaposhs*, divan beds with wooden planks. I arranged my beloved books on a small bookshelf on the wall and thought myself very clever to have contrived a dressing-table out of a window sill beside which I hung a length of mirror. The only other furniture we possessed were two folding tables and four chairs with hard wooden seats, but we were supremely happy.

At the back of the house lay a piece of fallow land and beyond that was a jute field where the jackals howled hideously at night. As they prowled through the night and raised their shrill cries, my blood curdled in terror. 'Listen,' I would whisper shaking my husband by the shoulder, 'I am frightened', and he would awaken and gently attempt to assuage my fears.

At first we ate our meals separately as we had in Murshidabad, but as time passed we grew bolder. One day my husband ordered the cook to serve our food in the same room and then leave, for we were too shy to eat together before the servants.

'Do you think he will tell the Murshidabad people about this?' I asked in an excited whisper as he closed the door.

I had no fear of Khokar-jhi, but it took some time before I was at ease before Pandey, who had been provided 'from the home of my father-in-law'. I feared he might carry tales of our improper doings. Khokar-jhi ruled both he and I with an iron hand, constantly reminding me what I should and should not do. As soon as my husband returned from office I would regale him with some of her injunctions.

He, in turn, would tell me about fellow officers and the interesting cases he had dealt with. Sometimes we talked nearly all night, much to the disgust of Khokar-jhi. The 'son-in-law boy,' she remarked, 'talks so much, that if he had a wooden mouth it certainly would have cracked, and as for you,' here she glared at me, 'you are just a *mayna* (small green parrot) repeating whatever you happen to have heard as soon as he comes home.'

Time hung heavy on my hands when he was away and reading palled after a time, so I was delighted when my husband suggested I write an essay. 'What's that?' I asked for I had not reached the essay stage in my school. 'You write on any subject you choose,' he answered. At this moment, a cow mooed in the field, 'Why,' he smiled, 'you could write an essay on a cow.' 'But what do I write?' I said miserably, feeling quite lost. 'Oh, all you know about it, what it looks like and what it does,' and with this he hurried away to court. I remember writing with great pains about the cow possessing four legs, two horns and a tail and nobly giving her milk to nourish mankind. My husband praised this and I went on to write another essay on the river Ganges.

At first we meekly submitted to whatever Pandey and Khokar-jhi thought best for us, but with the passing of time we began to have our own ideas. Even though I had no knowledge of housekeeping I did not think that Pandey should use the silver milk jug to hold chillies. 'Can't we have our tea in the silver service?' I asked my husband. Since that was the only wedding present we had brought with us we decided to enjoy it. When the cook was away I retrieved the service from the kitchen shelf and cleaned and polished it. Then my husband gave Pandey directions to put away the china set and serve our tèa in the silver set. And I was joyful when Pandey did not object!

The neighbours who came to call on us were very kind and helpful. 'But, you are surely not going to visit in what you have been wearing at home?' gasped Khokar-jhi, shocked at the informal dress in which I was about to leave the house. Holding out a gold embroidered sari and with tears in her eyes she begged me to change, but I only laughed and ran off to pay my visit. Formal dress was unnecessary as we had become intimate with two families and I regarded the wives as my 'didis'.

One day my husband came home from a dinner-party full of praise for the culinary powers displayed by his hostess. This piqued me and I suddenly became interested in cooking. 'Didi,' I asked when visited next day, 'may I watch you in the kitchen?' 'Certainly', she laughed and thus began my visual lessons in the art. When I was not there, I was poring over *Pak-pranali* [cooking recipes] in chaste Bengali or *Mrs. Beeton's Cookery Book* with its exotic dishes and exciting illustrations. One day Pandey fell ill and I was thrilled to have the freedom of the kitchen. 'What are you cooking?' asked my husband, entering in his slippers. 'Let me help; it must be done like this,' and taking the *khunti* [paddle] from my hands, he deftly turned over the fish in the frying pan. I was full of admiration but Khokar-jhi was shocked. 'He entered the kitchen with his leather foot-wear!' she said, for by entering the room wearing shoes he had polluted it. Then she chastised me for wasting two days oil and *ghee*; I only laughed, knowing she was powerless before my husband. 'It's written in the book that so much would be needed,' I replied, but she snorted in contempt and thought it all very crazy. 'The Master', entering a kitchen and me culling knowledge of the culinary arts from books! Later, she loudly proclaimed that these were things she had never seen in all her days.

Didi, our next-door neighbour, was not only a good cook but also clever with her needle and from her I learned how to sew with neatness and precision. When her children were away at school she would entertain me by reading aloud from famous Bengali novels. In the evenings I would relate these stories to my husband who was pleased that I was learning to love our own literature. So far my taste for reading had been confined to English books and my latest fancy had been *The Three Musketeers*. Dumas was at that time a special favourite of mine and though I adored his *Count of Monte Cristo*, I had to put it away one day when Chorda, returning from college, informed me that reading novels would lead me directly to hell. Seeing my incredulous look he graphically repeated the words of a Christian preacher to a College Square audience. For a long time I believed him, but as time passed my terror of the nether regions subsided and I returned avidly to my novels.

It was also Didi who taught me to love Tagore and his music. Tagore had become the vogue and Didi, playing on her box harmonium, would softly sing his songs. The melodies haunted me and I yearned to learn how to handle the instrument. 'Didn't they teach you any music at school?' she queried for she thought that anyone brought up in the great city of Calcutta was without a doubt endowed with all accomplishments. I had to confess my musical education was limited to a few scales and 'The Blue Bells of Scotland'. 'That's foreign music. You surely must know some Bengali songs!' she exclaimed, refusing to believe in my abysmal ignorance. Once she realized I was earnest in my desire to learn, she wholeheartedly co-operated in the venture. Finally the day came when I could pick out the notes with one finger and hum the words of 'Tomari geyhey. . . .' and I was overjoyed. One by one she taught me his lovely songs with their lilting tunes.

This was my first glimpse of Tagore and I was thrilled by the magic of his words and tunes. Didi introduced me to his patriotic songs and I felt exalted as if new vistas had opened before me. One particularly moving song was 'Amar Sonar Bangla', the first verse ran as follows:

My Golden Bengal I love thee;
My heart echoes to the music of thy skies and thy breeze
My mother, the sweet fragrance of your mango blossoms maddens me

In the plenty of you cornfields,
Mother, what a honeyed smile I see.

When Didi and I sung this together would be very near tears. The love songs also stirred me although some of the metaphors were quite beyond my comprehension. Borrowing Didi's *Gitanjali* (the Song Offering) that had won Tagore a Nobel prize, I laboriously copied the words. Pacing back and forth, I would try time and again to reproduce the melodies. As my lessons were all by ear, I found it hard to practice without the help of Didi's little music box.

One day I was surprised to see that a very large parcel had arrived from a reputable English firm that sold musical instruments in Calcutta. I could not believe my eyes when I opened the case and found a beautiful folding organ! As I raised the lid I caught my breath to find on an engraved plate an inscription from my husband saying 'with love'. 'Ooh,' I gasped, 'whatever will people say when they see this inscription? Don't you think it's a bit too shameless?' 'Not at all,' he laughed pinching my arm, 'I hope you like it. And now you can practice your songs by yourself at home.' Didi came later to test the volume and tone and teased me about the inscription. The neighbourhood was now constantly regaled with the notes of the organ and my husband and I spent many happy evenings with it.

Then followed a period of life that was cloudless and carefree but marred very often when a dark shadow seemed to fall and blot out the brightness of my days. The memory of our Pandit's prophecy was never completely absent from my mind. I had heard my misfortune would be averted with the advent of a baby and I found myself desperately longing for one.

'You don't look too well these days,' said Didi looking at me with searching eyes. 'Its just because I always feel sick in the morning, something I eat must be disagreeing with me,' I answered. Didi was concerned and asked questions. My replies confirmed what she had suspected and taking me under her wing, she gave much sage advice about diet and mode of life for the future. I was acutely embarrassed when I came to know about my condition but gradually this passed and gave place to a sense of relief and shy wonder. Khokar-jhi become jubilant as she now had more responsibility than ever. She urged Didi to write to Mother immediately. 'Don't you see, the Murshidabad people must be told through Mother,' she said. 'Oh no', I implored, 'not just yet. . . .' for I feared I would be snatched away from this new home and separated from my husband.

Sometime in early 1914 Mother wrote to say that Father was planning to go to Europe and if he did, I should come to Calcutta before he left. As I could not delay my departure much longer, one day Khokar-jhi became frantic and the fateful letter was despatched. Soon after, my mother-in-law arrived from Murshidabad with the family priest to perform the Panchamrita ceremony. For the necessary rites I was to wear an auspicious *sari*—a handwoven red-bordered one given to me by my mother-in-law which was presented with its two ends still intact as when it was taken from the loom. I was terribly embarrassed to have my condition made public by the ritual for the welfare of the unborn child and emphatically told my husband I had absolutely no faith in such ceremonies. Although he was of the same opinion we had to give in where family custom was concerned. At the conclusion of the ceremony I had to uncover one of the two covered receptacles so that the sex of the child be predicted. The symbol foretold a boy. 'What nonsense!' I told my husband later, 'I don't believe it at all.' Both of us were of the opinion that it would be very nice to have a little girl.

My mother-in-law left soon after, but not without many injunctions to Khokar-jhi to look after me in a proper manner. Mother wrote reams of sage advice and one of Father's clerks arrived carrying gifts of food and clothing. One basket contained some carefully packed venison which Mother had taken great pains to procure. It was accompanied by detailed instructions as to how it should be cooked since it was this meat, she wrote, that would make my child 'have the large lustrous eyes of a deer'.

Sometime later, one of my father's old clerks was sent to escort me to Calcutta. My heart sank when I saw him and I grew sick at the thought of leaving my husband. But the auspicious day for travelling dawned, and accompanied by Khokar-jhi, I left Faridpore with bitter tears in my eyes. For a long time after I came to Kidderpore I would cry in secret and many were the letters we wrote each other during the time I was there.

Dark clouds were hovering over Europe and soon the world was to be plunged into the vortex of the First World War. Oblivious to all this, Father sailed for Marseilles with Mejda and Pir Mohammed to act as his valet. Pir Mohammed had his language difficulties in France but in England became popular at a certain Kensington Hotel when he prepared a delicious chicken curry for the dinner party that Father gave for his friends. War was soon after declared in London and we were all concerned about Father's return home.

All around me were comments about my unborn child. When I became addicted to eating ice-cream Chorda teased, 'What a greedy creature she has become, it it's a boy we'll call him Koolfi [Ice Cream].' I shuddered at the prospect. Mother made me put away my English books and read the *Ramayana* and the *Mahabharata*, which she said would exert a beneficial influence over my unborn child.

Soon after I sat down with a few closely related young married women to eat my *shadh* [fancy]—an elaborate midday meal of many courses which includes all the dishes the prospective mother fancies. Held a short time before the birth of child, the *shadh* was heralded by the sound of the conch shell. In front of me was a *pradip* [small lamp], and on either side were two little children—a boy and a girl—meant to symbolize good fortune for the coming event. All efforts are made for the contentment of the future mother, whose frame of mind is important for the well-being of her babe. My father's absence and the war news cast a gloom over the family so my *shadh* ceremony was performed very quietly. A few days later, on the morning of the 12th September, a son was born to me after much travail.

I had been entrusted to the care of a midwife called Khiroda who was reputed to be good. She had a kindly pock-marked face, wore a spotless white *sari*, spoke very little and seemed to know her work. She had come the day before and when she found her services would not be required immediately she promptly started to sew some small garments out of my old *saris.*

Layettes were not looked upon with favour in those days as it was thought they might help foster expectations that might never be realized. So many untoward events might occur to shatter one's hopes, how could one dare to set store on what the future might bring? Whether one's lot would be laughter or tears only time could reveal. 'Let the child come by God's grace' it was said, 'and there will be plenty of time for coddling it with new clothes.' The main concern was over the safe arrival of the infant.

I had two maid servants to look after me and my baby, but the precautions that were taken for our well-being were traditional rather than scientific. I remember being tormented by thirst as it was thought water might be injurious for my health. Nor was fresh air considered beneficial so the windows were closed to prevent my baby and myself from catching cold. A great fetish was made about 'touch'. I was not permitted to emerge from the room nor were visitors allowed to pick up the baby or touch me. Except for the midwife and the maids, no one was allowed entry into the accouchement chamber. I did not know then that these were the hygienic measures of olden days meant to protect mother and child from infectious germs that they were susceptible to at that critical time. Unaware of the cause of all these precautions, I was full of resentment and labelled them silly superstitions.

The maids were treated with great consideration by Mother and were served with special food, for on their health and goodwill depended my comfort and the care of the child. She would make them wash and change into fresh garments after they came out of the room, and they had to be in clean clothes when they entered it again.

The sixth day was devoted to the goddess of children, Mother Shashti. Before the open doors of the accouchement chamber, the priest performed a simple ritual of worship and prayer asking that the blessings of Mother Shashti be bestowed on the child. Then a new slate and piece of chalk were placed beside the infant. This was for Bidhata Purush, the god of Fate, who it is said visits the child in secret this night and writes the fate of the child across his forehead in invisible yet indelible letters. His destiny would be determined by his *Karma*, the acts of his previous life. That night my maids observed the custom of holding the child in their arms as they kept vigil to know what his fate would be. I slept heavily that night and woke only once when the baby cried. By the flickering light of the *pradip* on its pedestal I could see the maid trying to rock him to sleep and heard her drowsily murmur, 'He must have felt the presence of the Bidhata Purush.'

On the eighth day the house was gay with the laughter of little children who had been invited, according to custom, to see the baby and play a particular game. Solemnly they trooped past the open doors of the accouchement chamber to gaze at the sleeping infant and then they marched down to the open quadrangle before the *puja* room. Here, four of them held an ancient winnowing fan and the rest, each holding a stick in their pudgy little hands, frantically struck at the fan with all their might as they cried:

Eight cowries,
O eight cowries,
The baby,—is he well?
Lighting up the Mother's lap
The baby's very well!

In shrill joyous voices these words were repeated with great gusto as they battered the winnowing fan beyond recognition. The remnants of it were flung away and it was believed that with these pieces went all the ills of the newborn child and its mother. Later the children were treated to sweets, and each was given a souvenir of the occasion. This was a large terracotta bowl decorated with *alpana* paintings and filled to the brim with freshly made crunchy cereals that had been sizzled on hot sand and tossed in molasses. It had a sprinkling of salted fried gram and puffed-rice and on the top of this were placed eight little sea shells (cowries) and a silver coin. A gaily painted terracotta dish covered the receptacle which each happy child returned home with, and news went round the neighbourhood that all was well with the mother and her new-born babe.

I had set my heart on a daughter and had chosen the name Roma, 'the beautiful one'. When I learnt it was a boy I was obstinate in my decision to retain this name. 'Don't call him Khoka (baby boy),' I snapped at Khokar-jhi who was crooning over her charge, 'his name is Roma.' She pursed her lips and shook her head. 'Oh dear, how can that be?' she wheezed 'why the old man who sells mustard oil in our village is named Roma Nath.'

I became furious with her but more determined to have my way and wrote at length about this to my husband. 'There is nothing to hinder us from giving the child this name, but since pet names usually end with a 'oo' or 'ee', we could call him Romu,' he wrote back, and Romu it has remained, although he was given a proper name according to his natal star at the naming ceremony performed when he was eight months old.

I was confined in the accouchement chamber for a full month. It was a hard time with its many restrictions, but youth is resilient in body and spirit and I survived the ordeal. After my Shashti *puja*, when the Mother was ceremoniously worshipped on the thirtieth day, I was allowed to cross the threshold of the room to resume a normal life once more.

Father returned home safely in October by the P & O boat, 'Persia', which was torpedoed and sunk on its next voyage. Shortly after, my husband took me back to Faridpore, much against Mother's will. She thought it was too early and that all manner of mishaps would befall me and the child. Blithely ignorant of the rudiments of mothercraft, I left Calcutta one cold December night accompanied only by my husband and Khokar-jhi. We had a reserved compartment that the railway authorities were to detach and then attach to the Faridpore train to save us from changing trains in the middle of the night.

We had slept heavily after the excitement of the day and woke to find the bright sunlight steaming in. Through the window we could see a field but not a soul in sight. My husband walked some distance till he came to the station and here he was told the railway people had forgotten to attach the carriage to the Faridpore train. He insisted on his right to be taken to his destination without further delay and after much argument and despatch of messages there arrived a special engine to draw our carriage to Faridpore. 'A special train? Someone important is arriving by special train!' said people at the station. 'The son will surely be a most important man someday since he has been given a special train to travel in, for his very first journey!' When I arrived with my baby son he was the talk of the town, but with all the excitement we had been through, I was too worn out to enjoy the situation.

Mother had given a small *neyar charpoy* [tape-woven cot] for the baby and he slept in it on the sunny veranda most of the day. My neighbours would come and advise me how to feed and handle him and I carried on accordingly. I enjoyed cutting out and sewing his little garments and Khokar-jhi would dandle him as she crooned her village lullabys. In a cracked voice she would sing:

> O bird with drooping tail so long,
> Come play with baby and sing your song,
> Milk and bananas for you I keep
> To lull my baby boy to sleep.

I well remember the commotion there was in the house when he laughed for the first time. Didi had gone to Calcutta for the Christmas holidays and had brought him a large rattle festooned with little bells. When this was shaken before him it struck him as so amusing that he broke into a silvery peal of laughter which both my husband and myself thought to be the most beautiful sound we had ever heard. News went round of the wonderful event and it became the usual thing for a visitor to test the truth of our words by shaking the rattle before the baby.

In February 1915 the baby was six months old. It was time for him to be weaned, introduced to his rice meal, and given a name, all with due ceremony. Since his father could not obtain leave at this time this had to be postponed until the eighth month. Even then, leave was denied, so the family priest came from Murshidabad to fetch us. My grandmother-in-law had come to pay us a visit and to meet her great-grandson with whom she appeared to be very pleased. Her silent disposition did not permit her to be effusive, but she would look at him with benediction in her eyes as she fingered her rosary. I was on my best behaviour and tried my utmost to please her. In spite of the difference in age I was unaccountably drawn towards her and could sense her affection towards me.

It was a memorable day in my life when she passed a complimentary remark about the way I kept the house, stressing the cleanliness. This was perhaps due to the eagle eye with which I watched over the onion peels, fish scales and egg shells, to which she objected as an orthodox Hindu widow. A kitchen had been improvised for her in the corner of the veranda adjoining ours and she was very appreciative of the fact that these objectionable things never came her way.

I travelled with her, the baby, the family priest, and Khokarjhi to Murshidabad and was utterly worn out at the end of the tedious journey. Trains had to be changed in the middle of the night and the priest was of little help to us. He got so badly tied up with the luggage that we nearly missed the corresponding train. The baby became fretful and I did not know what to do to soothe him.

My sisters-in-law had foregathered with their families in the old home at Murshidabad to witness the *annaprashan* [first rice meal ceremony] of their brother's child. My husband came the day before, but after receiving an urgent message from the District Magistrate of Faridpore he had to catch the night train after the ceremony was over. Chorda had come with gifts for the child including a set of silver bowls and plates from which to eat his first rice. Mother had also sent a gold chain, bangles and armlets, for such was the custom even though the baby was a boy. My mother-in-law's gift to her grandson was a necklet of beaten gold engraved with roses. Every guest who arrived blessed him with silver coins and he was fed with his first rice in the form of *payes*, a milk pudding ceremonially cooked. In the silver utensils were also served a rich *pullao* sprinkled with almonds and raisins; and many kinds of curries. All this was touched on the baby's lips with a spoon, as he sat on the lap of his uncle, dressed in his new red silk garments and gold ornaments. Beside him on a pedestal was lighted the small boat-shaped lamp, the *pradip* fed by *ghee*, while conch shells were blown to proclaim the happy event.

That morning, according to age old custom, the ancestors had been remembered by the *abhyudayika* ceremony—the ritual that is also performed on the marriage morning. Gifts of grain, cloth and money had been made in hallowed memory of the forefathers. When this was over the baby was ceremonially given a name in accordance with his natal star. The world was at war so the name was a martial one—Ranesh, 'Foremost in war'. The other name was the usual 'Chandra', meaning 'moon', that is affixed after the names of the men of my husband's family.

There was feasting and much merriment in the house, but I carried a heavy heart because of my husband's sudden departure, and for once was thankful for the veil. It was the proper thing for a young daughter-in-law to lower it to an appropriate length in her 'father-in-law's home', specially when it was so full of guests. It hid my doleful face and saved me from being teased by my sisters-in-law for not being able to conceal my feelings. In those times, it was highly improper to exhibit interest or affection for one's husband or wife. Young married people only met late at night in the privacy of their bedroom when everyone else had retired and where their voices were never heard.

10

One day I learnt with dismay that my husband had been transferred to Madaripore. He wrote to say no accommodation was available there and he did not know when he would be able to secure a place for myself and the child.

Meanwhile, I had been hearing of marriage plans for Mejda and Mother wrote to my mother-in-law asking for permission to take me to Calcutta. As there was no objection, the old clerk came to fetch me.

The first proposal was with a girl named Basanti. We met her by appointment near the aviary in the zoological gardens one afternoon, the men of both families discreetly keeping their distance. Left to ourselves, we became friendly and the topic of our conversation was mostly about the war in Europe and the German warship the 'Emden', that had become front-page news. The 'Emden' was haunting the Indian Ocean near the Bombay coast and the Captain had become a legendary figure reputed for his knowledge of Sanskrit. I found Basanti quite a sweet girl but for some reason Father, who had not met the girl, did not approve of the match and we saw her no more.

The next proposal was with a daughter of an East Bengal landowner who had received the title 'Raja' from the British Government. The Pandits of his village home were very orthodox and raised objections to the marriage on the ground that Father and Mejda had crossed the oceans and gone to Europe. In those times, the orthodox section of Hindu Society did not look favourably on visits to foreign lands. Father held liberal views and had so far lived according to his own ideas. Naturally he recoiled from this mode of thought and decided to drop this marriage proposal altogether. But the Raja was anxious to have Mejda for his son-in-law and urged Father to perform the *prayaschitta* [atonement] ceremony to placate the Pandits. This would involve a small ritual where Father would publically proclaim his repentance for committing the sin of foreign travel and the distribution of largesse to learned Pandits and needy Brahmins. Indignant, Father refused to do this.

The Raja now sought the help of a Maharaja who was the premier nobleman of Bengal and the accredited leader of orthodox Hindu society in Calcutta. The Maharaja knew Father well. The Raja also approached another estimable man, the first Indian to be placed on the Viceroy's Executive Council, who was held in high regard by Father. These two friends approached my father and asked him to reconsider his decision. The Maharaja assured him that the ritual would be merely a matter of form but that it was a necessary procedure in order to live in harmony with one's own group of people. Long discussions ensued and eventually they succeeded in altering Father's point of view. The matter was finally decided at a large dinner-party held in our house. Amongst the guests were the two mediators as well as the Raja, and Father was formally approached by them at the function and he agreed to perform the ceremony.

The meaning of *prayaschitta* is repentance, and this ceremony, which my father had been assured was of 'little consequence', stirred me to the very depths. I was then deep in the books of Marie Corelli and was contemptuous of all things that were false. I made no attempt to conceal my sentiments and was jeered at by Mejda who called me a 'suffragette'. The much discussed ritual was quietly performed and I was filled with indignation to see Father's signature on a scroll which said he had repented of crossing the ocean to a *mleccha* [non-Hindu, foreign] land where he had partaken of *mleccha* food cooked by *mleccha* hands. This paper was perhaps meant for the East Bengal Pandits but I remember how ridiculous it all seemed when the very same evening of the recantation Father and the invited guests were enjoying chicken curry, a recognized *mleccha* dish, prepared by his Muslim cook, Pir Mohammed.

I was pained to the core by this farce but no one seemed to look at it with my eyes. It was regarded as a formal affair to conciliate the orthodox section of society and as such dismissed very lightly. The marriage was arranged and performed in due course and I left for Madaripore soon after.

It was the height of the rainy season and this was the first time I had travelled by steamer over the great river Padma. I sat on the deck, captivated by the many coloured sails of the fishing boats tossing on the swollen, tawny waters. They looked like so many gay butterflies sporting in the breeze. At times we could faintly hear the folk songs sung by the fishermen as they plied their boats. The words were mystic and the tunes haunting. At times we could see distant hamlets but more often it was just a vast expanse of water that stretched before us unendingly. It was all very new and strange and I was entranced by the beauty of the changing hues of cloud and water and the play of light and shadow at dusk.

On the second day, we left the steamer to travel by a small country boat to our destination. My husband had succeeded in securing an obliging landlord who had built a place for us to live. The walls and roof were composed of corrugated iron which made a house partitioned into two rooms and a veranda. The floors were cemented but to my dismay, I found the corrugated iron walls finished several inches above the floor. Consequently, the rooms became flooded when it rained and all manner of crawling life sought shelter through this opening. I remember how I shrieked with horror and loathing when I happened to squash a frog with my bare foot one evening while reaching for the pedal of the organ. There was a pond on either side and the torrential rains caused the water to rise so that the house was almost surrounded by water. When I arrived by country boat, I had to walk over stepping-stones till I reached dry land on the veranda.

My husband became very popular with the young men of the town and was elected president of their club. A junior doctor who was our neighbour, became the Secretary and between them they organized many games and theatrical performances for the benefit of the members. But one day there came a letter from the District Magistrate warning my husband to be careful and to refrain from mixing too freely with these young men who were known to be involved in the *Swadeshi* movement. This was a great blow to my husband who had enjoyed the company of these young people but he had to resign.

Gradually I became aware of how the career of a Government officer could be adversely affected by any connection with people who held patriotic views. The Government took many precautions and posted spies nearly everywhere. I had become friendly with the wife of a leading pleader and later learnt with dismay that her husband was a paid informer of the Government. It was an open secret, and people looked on his activities with loathing and scorn. Before long his life was in danger, and both he and his house were under constant protection. The more I came to know about this state of affairs, the more unhappy I felt, and a cold shiver ran down my spine when I discovered a man in black clothes eavesdropping under our windows. From that time I began to realize that all was not well with our country. We had always to be on the alert for unseen dangers that lurked in the most unsuspected places. My husband told me not to unbosom myself too freely with my neighbourly 'Didis' . . . as I was only seventeen and absolutely ignorant of the art of holding my tongue or concealing my thoughts. My carefree days seemed to be at an end, unconsciously I found I had begun to watch my speech and behaviour and observe that of others. Mercifully we were not in Madaripore for very long.

After a few months we were moved to a small station close to the Garo hills in Mymensingh named Netrakona, 'tear drop'. And I was very near tears myself as we made our painful way by train, steamer, country boat and finally spent twenty-four hours in a closed hackney carriage in order to cover the last sixty miles of our journey.

At first, we were the guests of my husband's superior officer. Every effort was made to secure some sort of accommodation for us but when absolutely nothing was available my husband decided in despair that I should return to Calcutta while he would move to the ramshackle traveller's bungalow meant for touring officers. This did not appeal to me at all and when our hostess, an old friend from Faridpore days, insisted that we share a portion of their roomy bungalow, we thankfully accepted her kind offer.

The extreme cold told on the baby and he suffered from many ailments. It was here I experienced the sorrow of parting forever with my faithful old Khokar-jhi when it was discovered that the scar on her finger was due to leprosy. We sent her to Calcutta with an escort and I gazed after her retreating figure as long as my eyes could follow. When the dear familiar figure could be seen no more I groped my way to my bed and sobbed out my heart. Chorda, then studying medicine at the Medical College, had her properly examined but since in those days it was not easy to have the disease treated, Khokar-jhi was sent to her native village with a small pension. Mercifully she died soon after this, from another cause.

This tragic incident cast a gloom over me and, to add to my unhappiness, our hostess fell ill and went to Calcutta. I was now left alone in the big lonely bungalow across the narrow road from a large empty house said to be haunted by a headless figure that stalked at night. At Netrakona, although I was spared the tension caused by political movements, my blood would run cold to learn of crimes peculiar to that part of the country. One case of revenge shook me badly. A poisonous snake had been shot through a length of bamboo to land on the bed of the sleeping enemy and deal him a terrible death. Nothing lasts forever and before long my nightmare days at Netrakona came to an end; it was with much relief we learnt that we were being transferred to a West Bengal station nearer home and our people.

Sometime at the end of 1916 we came to Suri in the district of Birbhum, only night's journey from Calcutta. We were at Suri for three years and I learnt much while I was there. It was at this place I became interested in what is now called 'social work,' but I do not remember hearing this phrase in those days. Saroj Nalini Dutt, the wife of the District Magistrate, called on me and a few other officials' wives and proposed that we form a *mahila samiti* [women's society]. She explained that this would be a social organization to provide an opportunity for the townswomen to come out of their homes and meet and know each other. This would help foster a better understanding between them and break the monotony of their secluded lives. As women in those days rarely visited each other except on formal occasions such as births, deaths, marriages or when invited to religious ceremonies, social life was confined to these events mainly amongst one's own relations. Women of gentle birth rarely stirred out of their homes for any other purpose, and no matter how near their destination, they travelled in closed vehicles.

To propagate this idea of the *mahila samiti*, I would accompany her to call on the wives of the leading men of the town. I remember how we waited for the best part of an hour in the home of a well-known pleader, a worthy man of wealth and influence, before we could see his wife. She had taken great pains to wear one of her best *saris* and most of her ornaments and treated us to enormous quantities of sweets and fruit on silver plates. She was all smiles, kind and hospitable, gave a patient hearing but said she could not commit herself in any manner without consulting her husband.

Later, Mrs. Dutt met the gentleman and although he was obviously overwhelmed by her visit—for the District Magistrate and his consort were held in awe by all the people—he flatly refused to allow his wife to be associated with this new movement. 'But why?' she had asked. 'What objection can you have?' and hastened to add that the token subscription would be only one rupee a year. But he only shook his head and said the addition of his wife's name to the membership list would be sufficient to damage their reputation. Mrs. Dutt was pained but his resolution remained unshaken.

Most of the local gentlemen held the same view. They felt this new movement would be the death-knell of family life, and that it foretold nothing but discord and disruption in their homes. They were firmly convinced that the women would abandon their household duties, neglect husband and children, break away from the seclusion of their homes, and eventually compete with them in their spheres of work. In fact, they were convinced that their women would become thoroughly immodest and unwomanly and lost to them forever. But, the Government officers and their wives, junior pleaders, and such people were flattered by the visits of the District Magistrate's wife, and they promised to co-operate in the venture. Eventually the much discussed *mahila samiti* was formed and Mrs. Dutt became its president.

The inauguration meeting was a grand affair. No men were allowed as almost all the women there were in *purdah.* The carriages hired for the occasion began to arrive in the early afternoon and the elite of the town alighted wearing their best *saris* and jewelled ornaments.

Mrs. Dutt gave her full attention to the guests and we, the junior officers' wives, helped her in entertaining them. The orthodox ladies whose menfolk had stoutly opposed this newfangled movement had nevertheless come in response to Mrs. Dutt's personal invitation to come to her home for the function, as her honoured guests. The senior orthodox ladies smilingly declined refreshments but Mrs. Dutt had been prepared for this and had planned accordingly. She gently led them to a tent in a corner of the spacious ground. Here her husband's head clerk, an orthodox Brahmin, had arranged sliced fruit and sweets and cool sherbet all served in terracotta dishes. When they were convinced that the food had not been touched and thus contaminated either by Mrs. Dutt or her Muslim servants, and that the Brahmin clerk had observed all orthodox rules of cleanliness they no longer hesitated to accept the hospitality provided, and loudly extolled the merits of their hostess in so thoughtfully providing for them. Those who were not so orthodox enjoyed other delicacies in the form of savoury snacks and sweetmeats. The function was a great success and Mrs. Dutt rejoiced in the victory scored over the orthodox section of the town.

The next meeting was held in the commodious bungalow of an officer of the judiciary who was blessed with a sociable wife and a bevy of good-looking daughters. Mrs. Dutt tried to put all assembled at their ease by asking those members who were known to be musical to entertain the others. But we shyly declined until Mrs. Dutt, herself very accomplished, opened the proceedings with a popular song by Tagore. Soon others agreed to display whatever talents they happened to possess. Tongues were loosened and there was gossip and laughter with the elaborate tea provided by our amiable hostess.

Subsequent meetings took place in different homes with more or less the same items on the agenda. These became occasions for the display and discussion of *saris* and ornaments and indulgence in feminine gossip, but gradually the membership dwindled. The cause was mostly financial. For some reason or other, the meeting happened to fall towards the end of the month when all housewives have to struggle to make both ends meet. At this crucial time, the cost of hiring hackney carriages became a luxury most could ill afford. Yet this was a necessity since the gentlewomen of Suri, like their sisters in other urban areas, never moved through the streets on foot. Then, there was the added problem of providing a very high tea when one's turn came to be hostess. Concerned because attendance was declining, the president raised funds for the *samiti* and transport was provided for the members. But once again personal visits had to be made to plead the cause and only then would members consent to use the vehicle that would call for them at the appointed time.

When the *samiti* had been firmly established, Mrs. Dutt proposed that we help in the war effort by working for the Red Cross. There was no opposition and soon large boxes of cut-out garments arrived from Calcutta. These were to be sewn for the Indian troops who were engaged in the war on the Western Front. We met regularly and the garments were distributed by Mrs. Dutt. If we were unable to sew ourselves we could have them made by the local *durzi* [tailor] but for this of course we would have to bear the cost. Although it was an expense many could ill-afford, this was what most did as very few possessed sewing machines. By this time, the novelty of freely mixing with the District Magistrate's wife had worn off and, in spite of the free transport, membership had again dwindled. But a small faithful group continued to attend and make our contribution to the war effort. We also made countless little bundles of *nim* twigs to be used as tooth brushes by our troops. Each night a fresh twig is soaked in water and in the morning one end is chewed to a soft pulp. This makes an excellent brush for cleaning the teeth since the *nim* tree has special properties which have a beneficial effect on dental hygiene. For the recreation of our men we made multi-coloured patchwork squares on which to play their game of *pachisi*.

During the crucial stage of World War I, Britain and her allies were sorely pressed for resources of men and money. At that time the British Government in India began to encourage the youth of the country to enroll. Indian soldiers were already fighting in France, Gallipoli and other places. After the Lucknow Pact of 1916, some of the leaders of the Indian National Congress and of the Muslim League actively assisted in this recruitment drive. Surendra Nath Banerjee, the great patriot and orator, helped in the movement at that time. My husband, then also serving as District Recruitment Officer, invited him to come to Suri. His wonderful eloquence was the talk of the town. He called upon the young men to come forward and join the Bengali Regiment and the Indian Defence Force, explaining that if we wanted the privileges of imperial citizenship we must fight to defend the Empire.

I deeply regretted not being able to see and hear him and asked many questions about the affair. I was told he wore a white beard and was quite mild when not giving his fiery speeches. My husband expressed his surprise that Surendranath could live at the pace he did and be so full of vitality at his age.

Amongst the candidates for enrolment was a very young boy who was bitterly disappointed when he was told he was under age. He told the recruiting officer he had the main requisite—courage—and since this was so he should not be disqualified. Seeing he was not taken seriously, he whipped out a knife. 'Now you will see whether or not I have courage,' and saying this, he chopped off his thumb!

At this time there was a good deal of excitement in the *mahila samiti* over a batch of Bengalee boys who had volunteered for the army. Members became tearful and felt they were the mothers sending off their brave sons to battle. The boys were feasted and feted by the townspeople and our *samiti* decided to give them a sumptuous lunch. Each member was made responsible for one item of the elaborate menu and I well remember how nervous I was over the preparation of innumerable potato rolls. The president had been assured there was no need for her to cook any dish so she arrived with an enormous terracotta pot filled with the favourite Bengali sweet, *rasogollas*, which she served personally.

The Birbhum Mahila Samiti continued its good work on behalf of the Indian troops in conjunction with the Red Cross. When the King's Birthday Honours list came out in 1918, it was found that the President, Mrs. Saroj Nalini Dutt, had been made a 'Member of the British Empire'. A reception was held at our house and despite the wet afternoon the members all attended. It was I who had to read the painstakingly prepared paper of congratulation, even though my knees trembled terribly.

It was only a few days later that I made my maiden speech. Miss Lees, the sister of the Divisional Commissioner, had been invited to a Samiti meeting and in spite of the difference in years, we had become good friends. She was sympathetic, warm-hearted and gifted with that inestimable quality of putting people at their ease. There was a party in her honour and Mrs. Dutt pressed me to make an impromptu speech. 'But, what do I say?' I moaned, not far from tears. 'Just a few words of welcome—.' And I found myself stuttering: 'We—we—are all so happy to have you with us today, and—,' here I looked around wildly, gulped hard and added with a pitious look at Miss Lees, 'I—I—am sure you understand all I would like to say, but—but—cannot—'and with my face on fire and heart going like a sledge hammer I sat down on my chair. Although I was quite crushed by my own performance, Miss Lees told me afterwards she understood how dreadful it was to speak in public and I loved her for her understanding heart.

I was greatly indebted to her in the following year for helping me maintain my courage during the awful ordeal of coming out of *purdah*. When women do not emerge from the seclusion of their homes they are said to be in *purdah*, which means 'screened'. We hardly ever appeared at public functions and on those rare occasions when we did there would be a special place provided where we sat behind a net curtain or split bamboo screen, able to see but not to be seen.

In February 1919, there was an important function organized by the Government for the education and entertainment of the people of the district. It was an annual affair and called the *mela* or 'fair.' Health and industrial exhibitions, cattle-shows, and open air amusements would continue for a whole month. On this occasion, Mr. Cumming, a high Government official, came from Calcutta and Mr. and Mrs. Guru Saday Dutt gave a garden party in his honour. The elite of the town, including Government officials, were invited but as the women were all in *purdah* Mrs. Dutt found it difficult to find any of them to be her guest.

She came to visit me one evening and insisted that I come to her party. 'Oh no!' I gasped. 'But why?' she queried. 'Because there will be so many men present and I shall feel terribly shy—.' She reminded me of my convent education and brought forth many arguments why I should not be so bashful about appearing before men, but I remained unconvinced. Then, with twinkling eyes, she said that there was a way out of this predicament of shyness and that was by looking straight into the eyes of the man I would be confronted with. I shuddered and held my peace, quite certain I would never be able to accomplish the feat and determined to keep away from the function.

But alas for my resolutions! Persuaded by my husband, I yielded, and the fateful day found me accompanying him to the garden party. To my horror I found that except for the headmistress of the local girls' school, who had never been in *purdah*, I was the only Bengalee woman in that vast gathering. But my heart leapt with joy when I saw Miss Lees; she greeted me with a kindly smile and straightway took me under her wing. Both my host and hostess did all they could to put me at ease and, except for Mr. Cumming and two or three other European officials, I was spared the ordeal of further introductions and shaking of hands. Mrs. Dutt pressed a piece of cake on me with my cup of tea but I was so miserably self-conscious that I felt sick at the mere sight of food. It must have been very obvious, for Miss Lees suggested that I drop the cake between her chair and mine and she would spread the folds of her flowing frock to conceal it from view. This little incident lifted my spirits and I began to take an intelligent interest in my surroundings. Miss Lees knew my fondness for books and before long I told her all about my love for Marie Corelli and my latest interest in Jerome K. Jerome. By the time I returned home I found to my surprise that, thanks to her, I had managed to enjoy the novel experiences of that memorable afternoon.

11

Our son was not yet five years old, the age to begin one's formal education, but he was eager to learn. Kindergarten classes were not available so I taught him whatever I could at home and then persuaded the headmistress of the Girls' School to give him some private lessons after school hours. He was fond of English and the learning of new words gave him much pleasure. I found him one day with a solemn face repeating, 'Matha—is "head", Matha is "head", "Head Mistress", "Matha Mistress", "Head Mistress"—"Matha Mistress".' As he memorized the translation of the Bengali 'Matha' into the English 'head', he tapped his own little poll with his fingers.

Being an only child he was rather lonely, so I played with him and joined in his games and we seemed to grow up together. He had an ear for music and refused to fall asleep unless I crooned two particular songs of Tagore and patted him to keep time to the tunes.

Amongst my husband's books I had found a copy of Edwin Arnold's *Song Celestial*. When he returned from office that day, I excitedly told him how much I liked the book although much of its meaning was beyond comprehension. Amused at my outburst, he smilingly said, 'Of course it is too early for you to understand the meaning of this book—it is the *Bhagavad Gita*.' Sometime later I was given an edition in three volumes, with the verses in Sanskrit, English and Bengali, and these I treasured.

Another book that made a deep impression on me was Trine's *In Tune with the Infinite*. I read a good deal and my daily chores did not seem so dull when I enlivened them by memorizing my favourite poems. Many were the vegetables I peeled on the veranda with Sarojini Naidu's *Golden Threshold* and *Bird of Time* open beside me. As I repeated the lilting lines my mind would escape from the tedium of work to dwell on the beautiful themes conjured by the music of her words. But no matter how much I read I found the early afternoons rather wearisome, so I was delighted when my husband suggested that I take music lessons.

The ancient *ustad* [music master] who came to teach me could not boast of birth nor breeding nor formal education. In his youth he had lived in Benares and learned music from his *guru*. On the first page of my note-book he painstakingly wrote in large irregular letters a few words. He explained these words as the four-fold path referred to in our scriptures, of *Dharma*, *Artha*, *Kama* and *Moksha* that could be attained through music—harmonious sound—which was *Sabda*—Brahman, God Himself, as sound. He stressed that music was a spiritual art and must be approached with reverence. He spoke with great love of the various *ragas* and their wives the *raginis*—the legendary spirits of music. According to the ancient theory of Indian music there were six principal *ragas* and each had six *raginis* as wives. Each of these *ragas* personified one of the six seasons, each season representing six different moods of the human mind. The *ragas* had their special names and were to be invoked during different parts of the day and night. Each tune is said to embody one of these *ragas* or *raginis* who are endowed with god-like beauty and grace.

The modern science of music has deleted the *raginis* altogether installing a total number of ten modes called *thatas*, and all *ragas* are conceived out of these. My old teacher was passionately fond of every one of them, and when played he closed his eyes and a beatific smile appeared on his face. After it was ended he would tell me in a confidential whisper the name of the particular *ragini* he had been in communion with, and murmur ecstatically, 'Isn't she beautiful? Now, she must be adorned with ornaments.' Then he would begin to embroider on the tune, striking gently at first, then faster and faster making the strings resound with the metal ring on his first finger till the sound rose to a crescendo so unbearably beautiful that I always held my breath when he arrived at this stage.

Only when the last vibrations of the music could be heard no more, would he reverently lay aside his instrument, join his palms and raise them to his brows in salutation to the Spirit of Music that he had invoked.

Once while I was being taught the sweet haunting 'Behag Ragini' and failed to finish the tune he wrung his hands and cried out in agony, 'A-ha! What have you done? How could you leave her in mid-air? Return her to her chamber at once.' And it was not until I had gathered my wits together and brought the high notes down in the correct manner that the pained expression left his face. He was a dear soul, but apt to fly into a temper when he heard a wrong note.

At my first lessons he taught me how to hold the unwieldly *sitar*. At one time he was in despair at my awkward attempts and sadly shook his head saying I had lost all grace and flexibility by the pernicious habit of sitting on chairs. Times without number he made me balance the instrument in the approved manner. One end had to rest on the floor and the other remain poised properly on my shoulder for both hands to be free to play on the *sitar*. Weeks passed before I learnt to hold it in the correct position and only when I had achieved this feat did he show me how and where to press for the notes. Slipping the plectrum ring on my finger he showed me how to pluck out a tune and how to draw the bow tenderly over the strings and sing some very old hymns and devotional songs to its accompaniment. I was also given violin lessons but I never became proficient in any of the instruments. Yet the hours I spent with him were not without value, for he inculcated in me a love and reverence for music that I never could have acquired otherwise.

Being left much to myself I was blessed with leisure to read and reflect. I was then nineteen and had somehow turned towards serious literature and developed religious tendencies, not in consonance with my years. My acquaintance with the *Bhagavad Gita* had ripened into love and I found myself greatly drawn towards Sri Krishna and his wonderful teachings in the *Gita*.

There was a small spare room and this I converted into a retreat for meditation and prayer. I read a fixed number of verses each morning and mused long over the commentaries and tried my best to grasp their purport. I became painfully aware of my failings, yearned to improve myself, aspired to live a spiritual life, and ventilated my thoughts in a diary. I had read much but apparently digested little, for as I look back I find I was obsessed with a good deal of self pity and was something of a prig. My discovery of the ephemeral quality of the things of the world tinged my thoughts making me less interested in my home and surroundings. I prayed long, fasted occasionally and all this rather worried my husband, but he didn't interfere.

I remember having strange dreams at this time about flying through space and would awake unrefreshed and weary as if I had actually flown over long distances. One dream is still deeply etched in my memory: I was flying with a feeling of great exhilaration towards the south-west, when all of a sudden the clouds parted before me and I beheld Goddess Kali representing time and death. The awesome towering figure rose from the earth to the skies and was so terrible to behold that I covered my face with both hands and turned aside. When I opened my eyes, the dread image was no more and the sky was bright and blue. . . . Then a rosy glow appeared and again the clouds were rent asunder and from within appeared a most radiantly beautiful figure clad in crimson. She too seemed to have the earth for her footstool and her shining diadem touched the skies. She looked at me with benediction in her eyes and with a smile held out a rose coloured lotus. I stretched forth my hands. . . . The flower fell on the earth and lay with its petals scattered around, its white heart with the golden centre revealed the tips of the little seeds embedded within. . . . 'Tuley ney, Tuley ney!', 'Pick it up. . .pick it up!' The indescribably sweet tones of the divine voice echoed in my ears as I awoke with the rays of the newly risen sun on my face. At the time this seemed no more than a beautiful dream, but many years later I realized the significance of this vision that was vouchsafed to me.

In April 1919 the shooting of unarmed citizens of Amritsar at Jallianwalla Bagh created a great stir. Strict censorship had at first prevented news of these outrageous events in the Punjab from leaking to other parts of India. But nevertheless news of the atrocities spread and a mighty wave of horror and indignation swept over the country.

One morning in June I opened the *statesman* and was thrilled to find the historic letter, addressed to the Viceroy Lord Chemsford, in which Sir Rabindranath Tagore renounced his knighthood. With breathless interest I read through it again and, like countless others, saluted his valiant spirit with reverence and love.

My heart beat rapidly as I read, '. . .the least that I can do for my country is to take all consequences upon myself by giving voice to the protest of millions of my countrymen surprised into a dumb anguish of terror. The time has come when badges of honour make our shame glaring in the incongruous context of humiliation and I for my part wish to stand shorn of all special distinctions by the side of those of my countrymen who for their so-called insignificance are liable to suffer degradation not fit for human beings.'

'Robi Babu' as we call Tagore in Bengal was dear to me before, but now, this glimpse of his flaming spirit and the beauty of his noble gesture completely captivated me and I longed to set my eyes on him. The opportunity came sometime in September that year when Santosh Babu, the Rector of the Santineketan School, invited us for the *sharadotsab* [autumn festival].

Santineketan was but a few hours journey by train from Suri. The song festival would commence at sundown, so dinner was served at an early hour. My husband dined with our host in a separate apartment, but as I never appeared before Santosh Babu, my food was sent to me in my room. Afterwards, when it was dark, I was escorted to the enclosure reserved for women and from here avidly enjoyed the feast of Tagore's melodious songs, so exquisitely rendered by the students of Santineketan. Later I had the joy of seeing the poet himself on the stage. We returned to Suri at 3 o'clock in the morning and although I had a splitting headache my heart overflowed with happiness at having beheld Tagore at last.

My husband's term at Suri was nearing its end and we discussed at length the possibilities of being transferred to this or that station. He was due to receive charge of a sub-division and we fervently hoped this would materialize, not only in recognition of meritorious work but also for financial reasons.

The pay and prospects of his service were not too good, and yet the ICS was considered one of the honourable occupations open to the young men of the times. A junior officer generally had a hard time trying to make ends meet after the usual deductions had been made by the Government. From the slender remains a monthly contribution was first sent to Murshidabad for my husband's mother and younger brother. The periodical family rituals were also faithfully maintained in the ancestral home and after meeting all these obligations there was very little left to tide us through the month.

My personal needs, however, were supplied by Mother. This seemed to her the right and proper thing to do as I came from a landowning family of some prestige. When I went on my periodical visits to our Kidderpore home she would replenish my wardrobe sufficiently to see me through the year; whenever I was ill I would go there and my medical expenses would be met and I also received a small allowance each month from Father. This eased our financial situation to a certain extent but nevertheless we always seemed to live on the edge of our income.

My husband had a little patrimony to fall back upon and this too helped to balance our budget somewhat. We were not particularly down-hearted over monetary difficulties nor did they tend to make us morbid, for we never forgot we were better off than many. Nor did being perennially short of funds prevent us from building castles in the air!

We dreamed of the time when our young son would be of age and we would send him abroad for his higher education. 'We could go too, couldn't we?' I would say excitedly in soaring spirits, seeing rosy visions of the future and then be deflated as the question of the funds arose. 'No,' I sighed. 'Besides, hardly any Hindu women from orthodox homes that I know have crossed the seas, and the few who have are those who have broken away from the Hindu fold. So, I suppose it will not be possible for me to go.' Although I said this, deep within me I had a feeling that some day, somehow, I would be given the opportunity to visit foreign lands and to see the sights and places described in the books I had read.

By the end of September 1919 our financial position became rather precarious. Three months house rent was overdue, the bill for the gifts of *puja* clothing remained unpaid and we were beginning to take a gloomy view of things. I would be seized with a sense of guilt when I used a scented soap or hair oil, feeling they were luxuries we could ill afford, and consequently lengthened my time of prayer. At this critical time an invitation came from Mr. and Mrs. Dutt for tea and tennis.

After I had broken *purdah* at the memorable garden party, they had asked us to dinner. It was another ordeal for me and I tried hard to escape but Mrs. Dutt would not take no for an answer and pressed me to tell her why I felt so shy. 'How am I to open my mouth to eat before Mr. Dutt?' I had wailed. She promised me I should be spared that trying experience. When I followed her to the dinner table I saw that she had placed the overflowing flower bowl between me and her husband so that he would not see me eat. I had been taught it was highly improper to eat before a man, but with flower bowl in front I was not afraid to eat in the company of Mr. Dutt.

On the day of the 'tea and tennis' my husband played well. I had watched the game with another guest and when we were having tea I nearly choked over the cake that I was eating when Mr. Dutt said we would soon be leaving Suri. Orders had just come for my husband's transfer to Tamluk as Sub-divisional Officer. This was near Calcutta and considered to be a 'prize post'. We were deliriously happy for it seemed we had arrived at the promised land at last. We kept awake till the early hours of the morning discussing our good fortune.

We bade farewell to Suri without much regret and blithely disposed of a few belongings to square up our accounts. My husband went to Tamluk first, leaving me with my parents at Kidderpore.

Here I found Chorda using a planchette board to assist his communication with spirits. 'Don't you believe in it,' scoffed Mejda, 'but the name of the board is appropriate—it's "plain cheat".' Mejda was afflicted with an irreverent tongue so one day the spirit of an English business magnate, who had died recently in Calcutta, was asked how Mejda could be cured of his use of profane language. 'Not even the rods of the Romans can cure him,' was the prompt reply. This was quite an entertaining spirit and we enjoyed his visits. At that time I was rather worried over the condition of my hair and thought it a good idea to ask him why it was falling out and what could be done. His only reply was: 'Why do the leaves of the tree fall off?' Everyone laughed.

Sisir, my 15 year-old nephew, appeared to be a marvellous medium. He had only to place his hands on the board and it would commence to write. He was in great demand but had to be coaxed to join us for he was bored with the whole game. My husband neither believed in, nor approved of the planchette, yet he frankly confessed he could not account for the strange words that came from it. They were nearly all in English and the idioms far beyond Sisir, whose knowledge of the language was poor.

One peculiar incident almost made Chorda give up calling spirits. The talk of the town right then was a well-known English dentist who had committed suicide after discovering his wife's unfaithfulness. Mother, accompanied by Chorda, had gone to him for dental treatment and he had become somewhat friendly with Chorda. 'Hullo Young Ghose!' was scrawled on the paper one evening. 'Who are you?' stammered Chorda for this was the late dentist's mode of addressing him. Giving the name he was known by, the spirit, in moving words, said he was in great agony, deeply regretted his action and urged Chorda to 'ever walk in the path of righteousness'.

Mother was greatly perturbed on hearing this and said since the dentist had died an unnatural death, prayers and offerings should be made for the peace of his suffering soul. But none of us knew how this could be arranged. At that time an Anglo-Indian lady was giving piano lessons to my sister-in-law, Ava. She advised us that a mass could be performed for him by a priest in Church. Accordingly Mother gave the lady a sum of money for the ritual and we ceased to hear from the erstwhile dentist.

Another strange incident took place at one of these sittings.

One evening we found Chorda had specially cleaned his room, placed some white tube-roses in a vase, and was burning some incense sticks in a stand. In solemn tones he instructed us to leave out footwear outside the room and observe silence. The chairs had been drawn aside and we sat around on the cool marble floor. The lights inside the room were dim on this full-moon night. Who was the spirit to be invoked, we asked in a hushed whisper. My brother startled us by replying that it would be that of the great eighth century sage Sankaracharya.

Sisir squirmed and I could see he was longing to get away to his play-fellows. Chorda ordered us to become reverent. When the board began to move we held our breaths not knowing what to say. . . . The pencil made illegible marks on the paper. . .till at last Chorda stammered we were grateful for the advent of the sage and would he very kindly give us some spiritual instruction. The pencil scrawled rapidly, then it trailed away and in large sprawling Bengali script was written, 'In your father's library you will find my *Moha-Mudgar*', and there were a few more words to say that we were not to disturb him again. This had a chastening effect on Chorda who was not inclined to any further communications with spirits that evening. We knew little about Sri Sankaracharya except that he had been instrumental in reviving the Hindu faith after the Buddhist era. His own austere philosophy advocated renunciation of the world. But we had no idea whatsoever about the *Moha-Mudgar* that was mentioned. Chorda began to hunt through Father's library for the book. He hunted for days and was about to give up the search when he came across a small booklet of ten pages wedged in between two substantial volumes. This was the *Moha-Mudgar*—'The Mace that shattered all illusions'.

The discovery of the *Moha-Mudgar* created a stir and even Father came to know about it. He now took a special interest in the subtle humour and caustic philosophy of its beautiful verses and sought the aid of Pandit Nakuleswar Bhattacharya to elucidate their underlying wisdom. He would call me to him in the evenings, making me repeat the verses after him until I mastered the correct accent and intonation. I found myself fascinated by them and before long had all the seventeen verses by heart. My young son would sit quietly by me during these sessions and one day I heard him solemnly recite one of them to himself:

Who to thee is thy wife and who thy son?
This temporal world is so changeful.
To whom dost thou belong?
From where hast thou come?
Ponder over this mystery, my brother.

The challenging quality of the *Moha-Mudgar* was rather disconcerting. When I happened to lose my temper it was awkward to be confronted with:

In me, in thee, and in all creation
Pervades the One Vishnu,
Why then dost thou to no purpose
Become angry and impatient with me?
In thine own Self, see the All Pervading Self
And abandon all differentiation between thyself and others.

In November 1919, Mother, Ava and her children, and I went to Madhupur. This little up-country station was noted for its salubrious climate and it was thought it would be good for my health. Here we lived in a small bungalow with a flowering garden and were able to enjoy long walks in the countryside. In this remote rustic area *purdah* was not strictly observed, so in the early mornings and late afternoons groups of women of all ages walked about unescorted and free.

Our nearest neighbours were extremely orthodox people, goldsmiths by caste but belonging to a wealthy and well-known family from North Calcutta. The women of the family were elaborately dressed when they went out for their constitutionals but wore white cotton stockings without any shoes on the rough roads. On enquiry we were told that for a woman to use leather footwear was a sacrilege and disapproving glances were cast at our sturdy walking shoes. They were firmly convinced that we never could be respectable Hindus and had drifted away to Christianity—the faith of the ruling race whose habits we had adopted. In fact we heard that they had circulated the news that we were new converts, because Mother still persisted in performing *pujas*. Ava and I tried our best to sustain this belief by sprinkling English words in our Bengali speech and pretending we were addicted to still more outlandish things when we were in Calcutta.

The days passed pleasantly enough at Madhupur and my young son who had learnt the 'Charge of the Light Brigade' entertained us by 'charging' Mother's maid 'Pinkie' at all times of the day. She had a mutilated nose, the result of a jealous husband's knife, and an impediment in her speech. 'Now now,' she would mumble, raising her hands in protest, 'don't do that. Go on with your Haplee! Haplee! There's a good boy....' And he would burst out into boisterous laughter calling for us to hear Pinkie's pronunciation of 'Half a league! Half a league!'

Though I was unrestricted and carefree in this charming place I grew unaccountably restless. Deeply conscious of my many failings, I yearned for an ideal state which I vaguely glimpsed and understood as beautiful, but elusive and hard to attain. The nights were long and I would sit up late with Marcus Aurelius, another find from Father's library. His wise words were of great help and I would read them aloud, but for some inexplicable reason this distressed my six year-old son, who would implore me to stop. Perhaps it was my serious face and voice that disturbed him, for he said his 'mind became clouded with sadness,' when I read.

My husband came for the Christmas holidays and we all made a short train journey to the temple of Vaidyanath. This shrine is a very ancient one dedicated to Shiva as the 'Divine Physician' and many came here to be healed in body and mind. It had a reputation for its rapacious *pandas* [temple priests] and we were told to beware of them. They were guides of olden times and had contrived an intricate system of keeping track of families for generations through the names and addresses recorded by the pilgrims.

When a visitor arrived he was immediately surrounded by these guides and assailed with questions. Searching enquiries were made about his home district, profession, names of his father and grandfather and names of mother and grandmother. With the information received, they would consult their ledgers and call out the names of those who had been their clients and insist on their claim to serve the descendants in like manner. Mejda and my husband were determined to do without a *panda* and gave misleading answers much to the distress of poor Mother who thought this improper at a holy place. But the men had no inhibitions and felt they were perfectly justified in keeping the belligerent hordes at bay by bantering replies and refusing to say clearly where we came from.

The crowd was great, the babel of voices deafening, yet strangely enough none of this affected me in the least. I seemed to be all alone and yet not quite, for I felt an unseen presence . . . I found myself trembling and with tears streaming down my face as I silently prayed for divine grace. Hand in hand with my husband I walked out of the darkness of the inner shrine into the brightness of the sunlit courtyard. I felt my tears had cleansed me and my restless mind became calm and serene. My faults and failings had been understood and pardoned. The past was dead and I was born anew in a fresh world that held promise and fulfilment.

Clamorous hands were held out for alms; raucous voices of the *pandas* haggled with clients over their dues; and noisy priests pointed out minor shrines to the pilgrims. Despite all this, my heart rejoiced over that which had been vouchsafed to me and my spirit was at peace.

12

In January 1920 I came to Tamluk and was enchanted. This little town was at one time a flourishing river port, famous for its temple dedicated to Bhima Devi—another aspect of Durga. Our bungalow had a wide veranda which looked out over a spacious lawn and the gleaming waters of the Rupnarayan River.

In February, Chorda came to fetch me to join the family party that was to meet his intended bride and her people. Our relatives were very excited about this match because her family was from West Bengal and we had originally came from the east. It was thought best not to inter-marry since the two groups had different customs and different values.

Accompanied by her mother and sisters, the girl had been brought to the Zoological gardens to meet us. This informal place had been chosen because people would be more at ease here and it also dispensed with the difficulty of extending and accepting hospitality. It is awkward, to say the least, for the bridegroom's party to partake of a sumptuous meal and then find that the girl is not up to their expectations. But this match had been more or less decided and our meeting was a mere formality. Her father was a distinguished barrister who had been knighted by the King. He frequently visited Great Britain and regularly went to take the waters at Vichy. Despite all this, the family maintained its old-world traditions and the wedding was performed in April with the usual orthodox Hindu rites.

Nevertheless, Young Grandmother did not approve of the marriage and she and her family were conspicuous by their absence. So great was her displeasure over the alliance with a

West Bengal family that she returned the silk piece and the plate of sweets that had been sent to her as the bride's gift.

Mother's relations had also raised objections but most of them capitulated in the end. Mejda, an adorer of pomp and ceremony, had taken charge of all matters pertaining to the marriage and plunged into expenditure on a lavish scale. He far exceeded the allotted budget to the dismay and displeasure of our parents who were both by nature unostentatious and averse to spectacular display. There was feasting and merriment for days and Chorda and his bride received innumerable presents from their parents, in-laws and friends. All agreed that the last child of the Ghose family had had a splendid wedding. Six weeks later, Chorda, leaving his bride behind, sailed for London to take his medical degree.

Soon after my arrival at Tamluk I received a visit from Miss Matheson, a Canadian lady of the Methodist Mission. My heart went pit-a-pat when I learnt she had come to request me to give away prizes at the Mission Girls' School. Feeling quite ill I was on the verge of making some lame excuse when my husband accepted on my behalf.

'I'm sure I'll make a scene and disgrace you,' I moaned when we were alone. 'You won't,' he replied with a burst of laughter, 'All you have to do is to hand over the prizes with a bright smile and leave the rest to me.' Although it was a comfort to know he would be there to preside over the function, my heart was heavy and full of misgivings when the fateful day dawned. It was the first time I had sat beside him in public and I could hardly lift my eyes.

The prize distribution passed off smoothly and mercifully the audience was not large. Apart from the children and their guardians they seemed to be mostly local converts who were employees of the Mission.

Only a few days later we were invited to a double wedding in the Methodist Church, a long low thatched hut with lime-washed walls. One of the bridegrooms was the Mission House *mali* [gardener] and his bride, an orphan, was the kitchen maid; the other couple were also on the Mission staff. The District Magistrate and Collector of Midnapore, Mr. Cook had come to Tamluk on tour with his wife and they too had been invited.

After the ceremony, tea was served in the garden and I was introduced to them.

Before coming to Tamluk my husband had been congratulated on his posting but friends had also commiserated over his having Mr. Cook as his superior officer. I had heard he was rude and ruthless and had dreaded meeting this ogre. But both he and his wife were so friendly and courteous that I was soon put at my ease. I enjoyed that tea party and lost my heart to the beautiful blonde English girl who accompanied the Cooks. I was thrilled to learn she had driven ambulances full of wounded soldiers during the war. I still cherish the memory of that brief encounter in my impressionable years when she appeared to represent all that was beautiful and best in an English girl during the First World War and the early post-war period.

My husband's predecessor was a senior officer whose wife had been elderly and wordly wise. When the local ladies extended the usual courtesy of calling on new-comers, to me they made no attempt to conceal their surprise at what a callow creature had been installed in her place. One of them even made tactful enquiries to ascertain whether my husband was an aged widower and I his second wife. I was only twenty-two and in those days prone to be moved to quick laughter at the slightest provocation. But I had been warned to beware of exhibiting any signs of levity and instructed to act more serious and dignified. I began to realize my husband's onerous administrative duties and tried hard not to jeopardize his position by injudicious behaviour. All this weighed heavily on me.

My visitors were nearly all elderly ladies and their conversation centered on the vagaries of the weather, shocking bazar prices, knaveries of serving-men and maids, and the illnesses of children. They arrived at sundown and remained late. As I found it difficult to be always palpitating over the price of potatoes, the visits left me rather exhausted. One day when I was sighing over the dullness of my life, my husband smiled and said, 'Why don't you attempt to organize a *Mahila Samiti* here? I am sure that will make things more lively for you.'

I turned the subject over in my mind, was a trifle scared at first and then became excited at the prospect. I had soon mustered up enough courage to talk to my visitors about this idea. To my delight it was favourably received, particularly among the wives of the young officers.

None of us knew how to proceed or had any concrete idea of the programme of work to be undertaken, but all were unanimous in their decision that the rate of subscription should remain the same as that in Suri—one rupee. After lengthy discussions we decided to arrange social gatherings with music and subscribe to a couple of popular periodicals for circulation amongst members. With these modest aims in view and the firm intention of expanding our activities later, the Tamluk Mahila Samiti was launched on an auspicious day in April 1920; forty ladies attended the inauguration meeting at our bungalow and the function was considered a great success.

When I found myself the 'President' I realized with a sinking heart how much was expected of me and how ill-equipped I was for my task. 'The first thing you have to do now is to prepare a set of rules for the Samiti,' was my husband's cheerful comment. I was rather taken aback at his words for the Suri Mahila Samiti, as far as I was aware, had no formalities of this kind. We met at stated times and everything else was done by Mrs. Dutt. But he laid stress on a 'democratic' manner of work. The word was new to me. The implications were explained and gradually an equitable set of rules was drafted in chaste Bengali. I was also taught how to jot down proceedings of meetings and keep a minute-book. This and other necessary matters, laboriously learnt from my husband, were nonchalantly passed on to the lady who had been persuaded to shoulder the combined duties of Hon. Secretary and Treasurer.

The draft rules were presented, explained and formally passed at a subsequent meeting. With our slender resources paper was provided and as the Samiti had been established 'to work for the welfare of the women of Tamluk', the local press generously printed the little *Book of Rules* free of cost. By this time the members had begun to feel important and realized it was incumbent on them to widen their sphere of activity—but how?

Not far from our bungalow was the small local hospital. The out-door dispensary was always crowded but the two little rooms attached to it were rarely occupied for the people felt admittance to a hospital meant certain death. The last patient was a young English engineer. He had been struck down by cholera while visiting some remote village and brought here the next morning in a palanquin. He never recovered. He had come to Tamluk on tour with his newly wedded wife whom he left with the ladies at the Mission House. The shock and grief of his sudden and unexpected death almost drove her mad. The tragic tale haunted me and I always averted my eyes when I passed the hospital. When my husband suggested we take an interest in it I shuddered but was nevertheless persuaded to pay a visit.

The room meant for men patients boasted of an iron cot with a hard coil mattress under a black striped cover, but the adjoining one had neither of these luxuries. It was quite bare with only a frayed mat rolled upright in a corner. This was spread on the rare occasions when a woman patient was admitted. This I reported to the members of our Samiti and with much righteous indignation it was resolved to rectify the matter. But we were short of funds so it was necessary to raise some money for a bed.

Although I had appeared in public to give prizes, attend a wedding, and visit a hospital, I was still more or less in *purdah* and would only venture forth to nearby homes after sundown. I was accompanied by the secretary and our *chaprasi* [office peon] followed with a hurricane lantern to light the dark and narrow streets.

While distributing my booklets and pleading my cause I had some interesting experiences. Many of the houses had either thatched or corrugated iron roofs with walls and floors of beaten earth. Each home had a veranda where guests were entertained during the hot weather. When visitors arrived in the evening, a reed mat would be spread and a palm leaf fan offered to keep oneself cool while the joys and sorrows of life were discussed. One evening my hostess unrolled the mat and welcomed me warmly. I sat down, drew up my feet and edged towards the wall that I intended to lean against. She sharply told me to move away from the place. Seeing my surprise she pointed to two holes on the earthen wall where I was about to lean and explained that it was at this time 'they' came home. She used the term of respect and I wondered whom she meant. 'Who—?' I stammered. It took me some time to realize who 'they' were and although I had been assured 'they never harm anybody, they have lived here for years' the mere thought of being in such close proximity with two respectable snakes who were considered members of the family, made me lose interest in my mission and I left early.

Then there was that dear old lady who gave me a new angle of vision regarding the Samiti. I had explained to her its aims and objectives and she had given me a patient hearing as she chewed chipped betel nuts. Then she shook her head and mumbled I was far too young for this kind of work and asked how many children I had. Hearing about the one and only six-year old son she made sympathetic noises and wheezed, 'Ah-ha that is why the mind has turned too much to *dharma* and *karma* at this time of your life!' Since 'social work' to her meant, 'the practice of religion through good work', she unhesitatingly made her contribution.

There were many who thought like her and gave their mite in the same generous spirit, but as the majority of them were of the lower income group, we were unable to raise the requisite amount for a new hospital bed. They were far too expensive in those days following the First World War so we had to be content with a second-hand one advertised in the *Statesman.* This was given a coat of paint to make it look more respectable and was duly presented in the name of the Mahila Samiti.

This gave our members a new impetus and there were lively discussions as to how else we might further the interests of the women of Tamluk. Opinions were invited and an old lady asked, 'Can we not have a "lady doctor" for our town?' Then she went on to say how awful one felt to be compelled to call a man doctor to deliver babies during difficult cases and attend to other ailments that a woman's flesh is heir to.' Why,' she quavered, 'he was even called the other day to give a douche—.' Other members now came forward to support her and all unanimously agreed that a medical woman was an essential necessity.

When my husband heard this he felt the local Municipality ought to help and advised us to draw up a memorandum stating our grievances and demanding the services of a suitably qualified midwife. 'Give it to me,' he added, 'I shall see that it is placed before the next District Board meeting.' Before long Tamluk had its first 'lady doctor', a worthy woman whose services were much appreciated by the public and our Samiti began to be looked upon with due respect.

In July 1920 came floods that caused widespread havoc in Tamluk. During the time of the Moghul Emperors, a dyke had been constructed called the Khojar Bund, the dyke of the eunuch. This had been damaged by heavy rains and the swollen river inundated the countryside. Crops went under water, homesteads stood flooded, cattle perished in large numbers. Panic prevailed amongst the people for they feared this would be followed by the terrible tidal wave colloquially called 'Shanra Shanrir Ban'—flood of the male and female oxen.

News poured in daily of death and devastation and I saw little of my husband. For days at a stretch he was out supervising the army of men who were trying their best to repair the breach. The rain was incessant and the work hazardous, but it had to be done, and relief measures had to be taken to alleviate the sufferings of the people. While bicycling over the narrow embankment my husband one evening met with an accident and sprained his ankle. He had to walk a long distance before he reached the traveller's bungalow where his shoe had to be cut away from the swollen foot but in spite of this, his work continued unabated.

On the days he was in town, numerous people would come to see him at our bungalow. These included Calcutta newspaper reporters, prominent members of Congress, veteran relief workers from the Ramakrishna Mission, local officers with the latest information, village headmen from the interior, and many other people whose concern was the flood that was ravaging the country.

The press gave much publicity to the situation and high-ranking Government officers began to make their appearance to make enquiries and inspect my husband's work. Mr. Cook had sent another ICS officer to help. He came from a good old Bengalee family who long ago accepted both the Christian faith and the English mode of life and thought. He was brought up in England in the midst of a very anglicised family. Hearing all this I had recoiled at the idea of his being our house guest but during his stay my husband formed a high opinion of him and the servants were completely won over by his courtesy and consideration. As for me, I never met him. Being in *purdah* could be a blessing, and I was spared the trial of meeting any of these visitors but comfortably viewed them from behind the shutters. My life seemed to be filled with the brewing of countless cups of tea, and enquiring how far the waters were and how long they would take to reach our bungalow. Our little son thought it all great fun and enjoyed bringing in the latest news as passed on to him by his bosom friend, the office peon.

It was at this critical time that I fell ill and made things more difficult. My husband had gone out on tour, leaving me alone. My Samiti friends came to see me and sympathized. Dear Miss Matheson, of whom I had grown quite fond, wore a worried look on her kind face, and assured me I would soon be well. But my temperature rose alarmingly. I shivered under blankets and was incessantly sick. The senior local physician known as Bhutu Doctor, (*bhut* means 'ghost') was called by the Sub-Assistant Surgeon when he found my case beyond him.

Bhutu Doctor had thick spectacles, protruding teeth and was small and smelly. He exuded a strong odour of rank tobacco and when he bent to examine me, breathing heavily on my face, I very nearly became sick all over his stethoscope. His diagnosis was 'bilious fever' and he left a long prescription with the assurance that 'there was nothing to fear'. I took my own temperature, meekly swallowed his powders and pills but gradually grew worse.

Word was sent to my husband who hastily returned and despatched telegrams to both his people and mine about my condition. This brought my tearful mother-in-law and brother-in-law from Murshidabad to have a last look at me, and Mejda from my parents with orders to take me away for treatment. My recollection of this period is somewhat hazy and disjointed. An evil smelling fluid was poured down my throat (later I learnt it was a strong brew of chicken broth well laced with brandy, prescribed by Father), a heavenly ice bag installed on my splitting head, a nightmare journey by train, swaying in a stretcher borne through a milling crowd at the Howrah station... then the old familiar room in my father's home and the anxious face of Mother.

It seems I was suffering from a bad attack of malaria which left only after heavy doses of quinine. Until then I had been rather careless about the anti-malarial measures prescribed for those who resided in the interior districts of Bengal but after that I never failed to take the precautionary dose of quinine each week, kept strict surveillance over the drinking water which was boiled and filtered, and slept, even on the sultriest night, under the stifling mosquito net. We religiously followed these cardinal rules and perhaps it was due to this that we escaped any further attacks of the pernicious malaria that is the bane of Bengal.

My convalescence was long and tiresome. Drained of all energy, I was still in Calcutta in September when everyone was talking about the special sessions of the Congress to be held there. It was to be presided over by Lala Lajpat Rai. I became infected and felt I must witness at least the opening function. My knowledge of politics was nil but I avidly read the newspapers and had heard endless discussions of political matters for this was the one subject that neither men nor boys wearied of. When Annie Besant was interned by the British Government for stirring up the Indian people by her matchless oratory, and then on release had presided over the 1917 session of the Indian National Congress, I had trembled with excitement. Her words, 'to see India free, to see her hold up her head among the nations, to see her sons and daughters respected everywhere, to see her worthy of her mighty past engaged in building a yet mightier future. Is not this worth working for, worth living for and worth dying for?' thrilled me. Perhaps she and Sarojini Naidu, whose melodious words never failed to move me, would be at this Congress session. I was seized with a great longing to behold these leading public figures in the flesh and became very vocal about it.

'You can't,' said Mejda who never was interested in anything serious. 'But why?' I demanded. 'Since your husband happens to be a government officer you are not allowed to dabble in politics;' he replied with a smug smile. 'So what?' I nsapped, 'I owe no allegiance to the British Government!' My illness had left me with rather a frayed temper, but when I remembered that all might be lost if Mejda was not placated, I reasoned that since I was not taking part in any proceedings there could be no harm in just seeing things. But Mejda gloomily shook his head and said the Government was very knowledgeable in these matters and had their special informers. He warned that if I did not curb my unholy desires my husband might lose his job.

With a heavy heart and my enthusiasm considerably dampened, I sought out Dada and confided in him. 'Aren't you going?' I whispered, 'Then you must take me with you, if of course you are quite sure that nothing will happen to him.' 'Him' was my husband. Dada chuckled and said there was no reason why I should not satisfy my legitimate curiosity, that he did not think it would harm my husband and promised to take me with him.

The new daughter-in-law of the family, Abola, clung to me and said I surely would not go without her! Mother was aghast at our doings. Whatever was the world coming to? Here was the *nutan bou* [new bride] with her husband away in England, wanting to attend a Congress meeting! She was much against all these new-fangled ideas and held me to blame for them but since Dada, noted for his sobriety and orthodox views, had sponsored our cause she eventually gave her reluctant permission.

On the day of the opening session we set out very early with Dada. As I clutched my ticket in one hand and held firmly on to Abola with the other, I remembered Mother's warning that the responsibility was mine and that I would have to account for any mishap that might occur to the *nutan bou.* Somehow, I managed to find two good seats in the small enclosed area reserved for ladies. Once seated I looked around for known faces but alas could not find any and voiced my disappointment. 'The Congress leaders have not come as yet,' said the friendly girl by my side. I gazed at the vast sea of faces before me in wonder. 'There they come!' she whispered excitedly. 'Who—?' I asked humbly. 'Why the Ali brothers of course!' and seeing their tall stalwart figures I felt ashamed not to have recognized them before.

One by one they came, the fighters for India's freedom, and I was shocked to the core when a man in front of me stood up and hissed 'Spy!' when Annie Besant entered. 'What does he say?' I whispered in great distress for I could not understand how anyone could use that word to Mrs. Besant. 'Oh, he is quite mad,' was the calm reply. 'Just you watch and wait, you'll find a few more like him.' Then I heard the wonderful address of the President, Lala Lajpat Rai. In forceful language and impeccable English he dwelt on the wrongs done in the Punjab and charged Sir Michael O'Dywer with all the barbarous atrocities that had been inflicted on the poor people of that state.

Sir A. Choudhury gave a spirited speech in faultless English and a rather plump upcountry lady, whose name I learnt was Mongola Devi, spoke in Hindustani and I thought it would have been better if she had not gesticulated so much. After her came a veiled lady who sang a Hindi song which condemned the Hunter Committee, Rowlatt Act and Sir Michael O'Dywer. She lifted up her hands and circled round within the rostrum like a dancer and I closed my eyes and clenched my hands and wondered how she could make that exhibition of herself. Later, when I asked Dada the meaning of this little act, he laughed and said it was to satisfy the masses. I had indignantly replied that if they wanted entertainment of that sort they ought to have gone to a theatre and not come to a Congress Session. We accompanied Dada to the Congress another day and I was relieved to see that the seat next to mine was occupied by the same knowledgeable young woman.

I attempted to take an intelligent interest in the proceedings but my eyes wandered and I found myself absorbed more in my surroundings and the people assembled than in what was said by the speakers. But I well remember the main resolution. Because the ladies' enclosure was on the left side of the rostrum and some distance away, I had only a partial glimpse of the insufficiently clad figure who came to move it.

He spoke clearly and seemed to be very sincere. After mentioning the wrongs done by the British Government in the Punjab, he said there was only one way our people could redress their wrongs, prevent a repetition of the same and vindicate national honour. That was to establish *Swaraj*. And until the wrongs were righted and *Swaraj* achieved, the only course left open for the people of India was to adopt the policy of progressive non-violent non-co-operation. The people were advised to surrender their titles and honorary offices, resign from nominated seats in local councils, refuse to attend Government levees and *durbars*, withdraw their children from schools and colleges owned, aided or controlled by the Government and boycott British goods and buy *swadeshi* cloth to help the millions of weavers in the country and revive the art of spinning and weaving in every home.

I breathlessly watched people speak for and against the resolution. The Ali Brothers supported it as did an elderly man on whom the years sat lightly. 'Pundit Motilal Nehru,' whispered my companion reverentially and I could hardly tear my eyes away from that proud patrician face when I remembered that wonderful portion of his Presidential address from the previous year: 'What is our ultimate goal? We want freedom of thought, freedom of action, freedom to fashion our own destiny and build up an India suited to the genius of her people.... We must aim at an India where all are free and have the fullest opportunities of development, where women have ceased to be in bondage and the rigours of the caste system have disappeared....'

There was a lengthy debate, and much excitement prevailed when C.R. Das, with other leaders of Bengal and leaders of Maharashtra, strongly opposed it. . . there was a great furore near the rostrum and loud shouts from the assembly. 'What's happened?' I asked. 'Why, the resolution is passed,' my companion said gleefully as she settled her *sari* more decorously on her head prior to departure. 'Who was the man who moved it?' 'Oh, that was Gandhi!'

'There!' I told Mother on my return. 'Now see whether your Nutan Bou is intact or not. What an awful task it was to take you with me,' I said turning to the giggling girl. 'Now you can write and tell Chorda that your "Chordi-mani" [small jewel of an elder sister] has brought you back in one piece so he had better bring a nice present for her.'

For many days the amazing resolution was discussed by everyone. Many said the mover was 'mad' for how could one possibly detach oneself completely from every activity and yet exist? But, my husband, when he came the following month, shook his head and said there was a method in the madness and that the resolution would have far-reaching consequences.

The floods had subsided in Tamluk and Mr. Cook had forced my husband to take three weeks leave after his strenuous duties. As we did not like to stay in hotels we gratefully accepted the kind offer of accommodation in Darjeeling from Nutan Bou's people. Accompanied by our cook, bearer, a pert maid called Shoilo and assorted luggage we went to live in 'Ashuntully', a furnished house perched on the hillside.

We were enchanted with our first glimpse of the Himalayas but found the climate rather inclement and crept to bed fully dressed on the first night. Although we had on our overcoats and covered ourselves with all the quilts and blankets that had been brought, we found we were still cold. The novelty of having a fire in our bedroom had delighted us at first, but we nearly set the house on fire by adding extra logs. We became quite alarmed when the flames lept higher and higher and the legs of the bed became heated. But my husband sprung up and somehow adjusted the fuel so that we managed to snatch a little sleep before the arrival of the milkman.

October was very cold and wet in Darjeeling that year and the snows were seldom seen. When a sudden shaft of sunlight disclosed the gleaming peaks of Kunchanjungha there would be much excitement and everyone would leave whatever they were doing to rush out and gaze at the dazzling splendour revealed like a miracle for a few. Once we were assembled in an admiring group when Gouri, our bearer, a raw recruit from the plains of Orissa, came and stood agape at a respectable distance. His face wore a look of puzzled wonder. 'How did you like the snows?' I asked. He rolled his eyes and raised his hands and expressed his surprise very volubly. He could not understand at all how all that ice could have been transferred to such heights and whoever could have taken that huge amount there?

I returned to Tamluk in November and my Samiti members were delighted to see me looking so well. I was glad to be back and had a lovely dream. I dreamt of corn... ripe sheaves of rich yellow corn piled up high in a field beyond which stood a stately home which I knew to be ours. A flock of snow white swans came flying in a line... they flew down in slow motion to pick up the sheaves and rose again. In a stately procession they carried all the corn in their beaks till they alighted in the open courtyard of our home and lay down the sheaves in one great pile. The sheaves gleamed like gold in the sunlight... and I awoke firmly convinced that this foretold good fortune. If someone asked me then what I expected, I would not have been able to answer properly but would most probably have said, 'Something wonderful!'

During my convalescent period I had unlimited leisure and indulged in my favourite habit of introspection. I became more than ever aware of my deficiencies and the yearning to improve myself increased considerably. The daily routine of scripture study, prayer and meditation had been interrupted and taken up later in a perfunctory manner. Now when I attempted to continue the course in earnest it left me strangely discontented. The prayers became mere repetition, the meditation unsatisfactory and the *Gita* more difficult to grasp. The written word no longer sufficed. I felt I must explore and make my own discoveries. So long I had been reading about things, but now... I felt I must find something that would make all the difference to the belief. It was realization I sought but then I did not know it by that name. My mind set out to search and I became irresistably drawn to some knowledge that I was only dimly aware of. It was as if I heard a distant melody of haunting beauty and had only to take a few more steps to find its source. But the light was faint and I could not see the path clearly and became heart sick with longing.

It was at this time that I happened to come across a small white marble symbol of Shiva that someone had given me, and since the name of the great god meant all that was good, true and beautiful, I commenced a ritual worship of the symbol in addition to my usual devotions in the hope of gaining more light. All this made me rather moody and invariably late for breakfast for I never ate before the morning bath and prayers. One day my husband said with gentle smile: 'It is not time for you yet... you must go more slowly on this path.' The truth of his words dawned on me, and a few days later I gave away my symbol of Shiva, curtailed my devotions, and breakfasted at normal times.

13

The year 1921 was a memorable one in many respects. It had begun with a remarkable dream in which I saw the clouds part to reveal the figures of Ganesh, Shiva and Vishnu. In March I found that righteous indignation could stir one to write satirical verses which others termed doggerel.

While in Calcutta my husband had attended a session of the Legislative Assembly where a veteran leader, one of my heroes, was seen canvassing in person for votes. He had already fallen considerably in my estimation by accepting the high office he now enjoyed and when I heard he wanted to retain his seat, I was pained and shocked. That this fiery patriot could become so enamoured of power that he would openly beg for support to serve the Government he had for long years criticized and condemned, moved me to the core.

'Oh how could he?' I wailed, feeling his lapse to be a personal calamity when my husband related the incident to me. He laughed at my outburst, said I was too emotional and that it was the prerogative of politicians to change their views. He hurried away to the office and I spent the afternoon writing what I thought about the whole affair. He was much amused to see what I had written and immediately posted it to the editor of *The Indian Daily News*.

When it appeared in print he marked the portion in red pencil, scrawled 'Congratulations'! and sent me the newspaper from his office. Clutching it in my trembling hands I flopped down on the bed and nearly fainted from joy and shock. *The Indian Daily News* is no more, but I have the cutting still in my scrap book :

A Ditty

'I love and wish to serve thee, dearest',
Thus the love-lorn veteran sighed.
'My heart and thy lotus feet,' said he
'With love knots fast are tied.'

The maiden smiled a knowing smile
But turned him a gracious mien;
In the course of her amours long
The like of him many she'd seen.

Full many a one had come and gone,
Repeating the old, old tale;
But sad to say at love's crucible
She had known them all to fail.

They came with vows and words high-sounding,
To serve her and their love to prove.
But 'Truth will out,' as runs the adage,
Each had his interest to move.

But this hoary-headed war-scarred veteran
Bending on his knee,
Who had so long resisted her,
She had never thought to see.

Long and loud his voice had risen,
Gainst her wiles and smiles,
And the people had uplifted him
Up to the very skies.

So the conquest of this man at last
Was surely no mean feat;
It pleased her much to see him thus
Kneeling at her feet.

Her hand she placed on his hoary head;
Oh, friends, T'was a wondrous sight!
'I accept your love and homage,' she said,
'And appoint you to be my knight.'

'Five thousand silver coins a month
  I give thee as thy fee,
And gird this golden sword as well,
  Arise, Sir Knight,' said she.

When the people came to know about
  This 'latest' of their hero
No wonder their estimation
  Of him rose to zero !

'Woe to the land if man like our hero,
  Hai! Hai !' they lamented, shaking their noodles
'Accept gaudy baubles and sugared fondants,
  And consent to be metamorphosed into poodles!'

While home went the veteran,
  All arrayed in his glory;
And to follow him there
  Would but lengthen my story.

*La Pasquine**

When there were still a few months left for Romu's seventh birthday, he suffered his first sense of personal loss. Every time he thrust his little tongue into the cavity of the missing tooth he would enquire with a furrowed brow when the new one would be likely to appear. The old one had become shaky, he had pulled it out with closed eyes and advised by his knowledgeable friend, the office peon, had deposited it in a mousehole and asked the invisible mouse to take the old tooth and provide a nice new one. He was greatly troubled over the delay in replacement and we also became anxious for him, but on another account.

As we saw him start to lose his baby teeth we realized it was high time for him to be sent to school. But, the Tamluk High English School was too high for him and there were no facilities for teaching boys of his age group. What was to be done? With some other parents who faced the same problem, we

*I had borrowed the '*non de plume*' from the hero of Marie Corelli's *Temporal Power* as it meant one who jests.

persuaded the Headmaster to form a special class. The subjects would be Bengali, English, reading, writing, grammar and arithmetic; the hours 8-10 a.m. and 2-4 p.m.

Romu, together with some young companions, began his education with great gusto and daily brought home some piece of exciting news for our benefit. 'I hope he won't acquire a Tamluk accent,' I said as Romu set off for his first day of school. His father told me not to worry as the Headmaster was taking a personal interest and surely employed a good teacher for this class. If I was going to be finicky he suggested I look after the English myself.

Sometime later when I was enjoying a second bath on a sultry afternoon I heard Romu burst in like a tornado. He called out to me at the top of his voice, then hammering at the bathroom door and yelled; 'Open! Open quickly.' 'Why, what's the matter?' was my cross reply. 'I've learnt a new English word and I'm sure you don't know what it means!' 'What *is* it?' I cried from within. 'Arr—um-pee—t,' squealed Romu in ecstasy, then as he saw his father raise his eyebrows, hastened to add, 'I'm sure you too don't know the meaning of this word that, Sir (all teachers were 'Sirs' to their pupils in Tamluk) taught us today, and guess it yourself—Arr-m-pee-t,' he sang rolling the r's with rich resonance and with a long drawn out ee. 'Arr—um—pee—t!' he repeated capering about the room in high glee. Then seeing our puzzled looks he decided to take pity on our abysmal ignorance and with great zest began slapping his under arm. His father burst into a fit of laughter but I very nearly collapsed. I could not take the armpit as a joke and awaited my son's return each day wondering what he would regale us with next!

From that time on I sat with him religiously as he studied his English lessons. I had to exert all my tact and forebearance to keep his respect for his Sir unimpaired while substituting the pronunciation I had learnt from the good nuns. It was an extremely difficult feat and I doubted my ability to continue for long. But, fate stepped in and his classes were discontinued when he accompanied me to Calcutta a few months later. He was taken under the wing of my old teacher, Sister Teresita of St. Teresa's Convent, where he became a day scholar for the period I was in Kidderpore waiting the arrival of his brother.

Mother came to Tamluk to fetch me in September and all care was taken by my parents so that I might be spared the ordeal of 1914, but it was not to be. Calcutta in the cold weather of 1921 was an agitated city. The Prince of Wales was on a visit to India and C. R. Das who was to preside over the Congress sessions had been arrested and jailed.

Hakim Ajmal Khan who took his place had said in his Presidential address: 'We are not in a mood to accord the Prince of Wales a cordial welcome as long as the two sores of Khilafat and Punjab are still running and *Swaraj* is still unattained.' And C. R. Das, in his undelivered address, had said 'Measures have been taken in order to coerce the people to receive the Prince of Wales but it is the imprisoned soul of Calcutta that will greet his Royal Highness . . . . Freedom is my birthright and I demand a recognition of that right not by instalment nor in compartments but whole and entire.'

Calcutta was seething with excitement in December 1921 when the Prince was expected to visit the city. Notable citizens were invited to greet the Prince on arrival and Father was to be amongst them that morning as one of the representatives of the Bengal Landholders Association. The Congress had appealed to the people to boycott all proceedings relating to the visit of the Prince and our chauffeur absented himself from duty that day. Greatly annoyed, Father waited in frock coat and top hat for his chauffeur, but the Reception Committee had planned for just such an eventuality.

It was imperative that these prominent citizens be present when the welcome address was to be read by a premier nobleman of Bengal so on receipt of the news a young Englishman arrived. We peeked at him from the windows while Father raised his pince-nez for a better view of his new chauffeur. Father returned in fine fettle from the function and not being interested in politics dismissed the episode in his characteristic manner by commenting that he found the Prince to be but 'a stripling'. We heard no more of the event that had created such a commotion in Calcutta.

It was at this very time that my other son chose to come into the world and to the consternation of all concerned, a doctor had to be called to assist in the delivery. Since this was the first time such a thing had happened in the annals of the family there was much talk over the matter.

The services of Khiro Dai had been dispensed with and a hatchet-faced woman by the name of Sumoti installed. 'She is a real midwife,' said sister-in-law Ava, 'and always in demand by the best families.' Mother did not care for her much, nor did I—She was too full of gossip about the 'best families'.

When my time came and I was plunged into the deep waters of pain, she sat and watched me struggle through the long drawn hours of agony. Day passed into night and the dark night into another bright day which came to an end before she realized all was not as it should be, and then frankly confessed her skill was of no avail in a case like mine. It was decidedly 'difficult' and could only be dealt with by a good doctor.

Poor Mother was at her wits end. Never had she seen medical aid being administered by a man in these circumstances and would it be right and proper to bring in one without the permission of my husband and his people? The subject was discussed all through the night while I lay precariously balanced between life and death and Sumoti dropped dark hints that no one should be allowed to blame her if anything happened for she had given sufficient notice. At daybreak Mejda was allowed to fetch Dr. Biman Das Mukherjee only after Mother had decided that there was no harm in him coming to advise Sumoti.

When Mejda arrived he was told that he would have to wait as the doctor was busy with his morning devotions. When he eventually came and had heard Sumoti's version of her 'case', he was of the opinion that there was no time to be lost. But, so great is the power of past tradition that even then, with her love for me and her anguish at my suffering, Mother hesitated to take the decision. This annoyed Dr. Mukherjee so much that he was on the verge of departing when Father appeared on the scene. Hearing everything he requested the doctor to do what he thought best without further delay. And Dr. Mukherjee just managed to save me.

I was unconscious when he came and in those days perhaps

doctors did not follow up their cases with post-natal care so I never had the opportunity of seeing him. But every time my eyes fell upon my sturdy little son I felt this doctor must have been God Himself. The fame of my saviour spread and no one appeared to think of him as anything else but a doctor whose amazing skill had saved our lives. As for Mother, he had won her over completely by addressing me as his Mother. Our age-old custom of establishing a mother-son relationship with its implication of filial respect immediately places the man in a very definite position of privilege and responsibility and helps to break down all barriers. Mother praised his beautiful manners and gentle speech and said he was a great gentleman.

My close proximity with death stirred me to the depths. True, death is inseparable from life, yet as far I was concerned it had been but a word connected with the far off nebulous future. My lengthy convalescence gave me a legitimate opportunity to muse over my experience and I came to the conclusion I had learnt all there was to know of life. World weary with my knowledge, I attempted an 'Ode to Death' which ran thus:

I fear thee not, I dread not thee,
No terror for me oh Death hast thou,
The pageant of life's galaxy
Has lost its charm and glitter now.

For I have drunk to the very dregs
The brimming cup so fair to see,
That had in hand both life and love
Along with youth did hold to me.

Ah, when my thirsty lips did kiss
The magic cup with the crimson brew,
Methought no drink was half so sweet
Ah me, if only then I knew !

'Ne'er the sweet without the bitter,'
We are taught in nursery days,
From out my mind the line did slip
As fell my feet on worldly ways.

If sweet the drink did seem at first
With a sweetness that seemed unsurpassed,
Its sweetness fled too fast alas,
And drear disillusion came at last.

The cup is drained in it I've had
Alike my share of joy and grief,
Why should I shrink since now I know
Life, Love and Youth all, all are brief.

Being very young when my first-born arrived I hardly knew which end of him to hold. I was old enough now to take a pride and pleasure in mothering my new born son but my joy was muted by the knowledge I had derived of death. 'What is the use, of reaching out for things,' I thought, 'Life is only for a very little while. Nothing is stable, all things are fleeting, one can be certain of nothing but death.' Recoiled within itself, my mind enjoyed a calm freedom. It drew its tentacles from all desires and refused to be entangled in the meshes of any kind of emotion. But with the passage of time, the veil that had been lifted a little was drawn again with the hand of mercy and the memory of that brief encounter with death—the ultimate truth—gradually became Him. Nature once again involved me in the game of Life and swung me high and low in the swing of laughter and tears.

Detained by my son's infantile ailments and my own ill health it was not until May 1922 that I returned to Tamluk. As it was not possible for my husband to get any leave we had to abandon the idea of taking our son to the ancestral home at Murshidabad for his *annaprashan* ceremony. Instead it was very quietly performed at Tamluk in June when he received both his first mouthful of rice and the name he would be known by for the rest of his life. His horoscope said his star was *purva phalguni* and his birth sign was Leo. According to this, his proper name must begin with the letter 'M', but his father had thought 'Suchit' a nice name and I had agreed. The difficulty was solved by the priest who decreed that he might still have a name starting with 'M' to be used only for formal religious rites and gave him the name of 'Mahesh'. And Suchit, with the usual family name 'Chandra' after it, would be the name he was known by.

Suchit means 'good-minded' and in those days he was more or less true to his name and never gave me much trouble. But despite all the thought and care expended at his naming ceremony, as he had a habit of banging his toys on the floor while uttering sounds rather like 'Don, Don, Don,' we ultimately called him Donny.

We were nearing the end of our three years in Tamluk and expected to be transferred at any time. In the meantime the heavy monsoons made another breach in the embankment and there was a minor flood that kept my husband busy. There was considerable excitement in the country about the boycott of foreign goods and particularly foreign clothes. We heard of bonfires made of bales of Manchester cloth at public meetings. Some applauded these acts and others criticized them, saying it was a sinful waste when so many in our poverty-stricken country went unclad. Congress volunteers toured the villages and urged the people to eschew foreign goods and buy only those that were produced in their own country. The demand of *Swaraj* was explained and the people were encouraged to revive the cult of the spinning wheel.

When Gandhiji first launched his *charka* [spinning wheel] campaign, a large section of the people lamented at his attempt to turn back the wheels of progress. But, it became the rage nevertheless, 'Have you a *charka*?' was what everyone asked each other. Nearly all tried their hand at it and the majority grew bored. 'The thread breaks, I cannot manage the thing!' some confessed, 'But my little son can'—'my daughter can'. Most of the elders abandoned it but the younger generation took it up in earnest.

The coarse material woven from the hand-spun yarn was called *khadi*, which became the symbol for the national cause. When Gandhiji first preached the virtues of *khadi*, it became the popular craze. For a dress reform movement it was remarkable. Even effeminate fops flung aside their loose flowered organza shirts and proudly disported their *khadi*. With these clothes also went their fine *dhotis* and pointed *lapaita* [slippers]. For, a rough homespun shirt demands a nether garment of like texture and as exquisite footwear failed to fit in with such an outfit, simple sandals became the fashion.

The importance of the spinning wheel was emphasized in the vernacular papers and I remember seeing a coloured front-piece in a journal which portrayed a prominent lady plying a *charka*. She wore a red and gold Benares *sari*, most of her ornaments, and a vapid smile. There was an old folk song at the bottom, that translated would run something like this:

The Charka is my husband and son,
The Charka is my grandson,
By the bounty of my Charka,
An elephant stands tethered to my doors.

We were still in Tamluk when Chorda went abroad and I was breathless with interest when in his letters, he mentioned places connected with the books we had both enjoyed since our earliest years. I could not help sighing with envy as I read of Baker Street, Kensington Gardens, Picadilly, Mayfair and the thrilling Tower of London. He would ask for news but there was little I could give from the secluded life I led in that little bungalow on the outskirts of the town.

Beyond the garden were the red brick court buildings where my husband was nearly always busy. Close to this ran the narrow cobbled road hidden by trees and from this road I could sometimes hear shouts of 'Bande-Mataram!' Congress had chosen this for their slogan and the volunteers were passing it around everywhere. It means, 'Hail to the Motherland!' and comes from an inspiring poem written by Bankim Chandra Chatterjee.

Hail to the Mother!
Richly watered, rich with fruits,
Cool with southern winds,
Green with crops,
The Mother!
Her nights rejoice in moonlit glory,
Her lands are clothed in beautiful trees in bloom,
Sweet of laughter, sweet of speech,

Giver of boons and giver of bliss,
The Mother!

At about this time, Romu returned from school one afternoon greatly excited. In those times he was always bringing home something new for my benefit. That day he burst in with, 'Ma, what does "Bande Mataram" mean? Everyone seems to be shouting this now. And who is "Gandhi"? And is it true that he is a saint? I was told Government had ordered him to be hanged and the rope had split. The Police tried to pierce him through with a sharp spear, Ma, and it broke! And oh, I am ever so hungry—what is there to eat?'

He had delivered all this in one breath and nearly knocked me over with his usual boisterous embrace. I remember the incident well. The influence of Mahatma Gandhi was filtering into remote villages and wild rumours were current. Many were the tales afloat about the man whose name would later become a household word in India.

I heard of many political meetings and processions and my husband's official work increased considerably. He found it difficult to keep his confidential reports from being circulated around the town by his gossip-loving clerk. A small Corona typewriter was purchased, on the instalment system like my Singer sewing machine, and I taught myself to type with two fingers. Before long I was helping him with his correspondence and came to know much about the nature of his work and the trend of the times.

My days passed placidly enough till the end of the rains brought a slow fever to my small son. It persisted in spite of treatment so we took him to Ranchi hoping he might benefit by the change of climate. After we had made a few preliminary mistakes and learnt some bitter lessons over the ways of landlords and their ladies, we eventually settled down in a bungalow on the outskirts of the town. Here I stayed with the two sons and an old aunt and my husband visited us when he could obtain a few days leave.

The cool dry air had its effect and the patient's temperature soon became normal. But, Romu became ill with typhoid fever of a virulent type. Alone in that distant place for three agonizing months with a seriously ill child, I had to exert all my energies to cope with the situation. It was an experience that helped me to grow mentally and strengthened my spirit. Once a day the doctor came to see the child in a horse-drawn carriage and left his instructions. Complications set in and careful nursing became all important but I had neither training nor experience with seriously ill patients.

Putting my small son in the care of my aunt, I tried my best to nurse Romu according to instructions and prayed with a new intensity. Those were nightmare months when the doctor's fees and medicines drained our finances. I began to hate the sight of the hills that had once seemed so wonderful and longed to leave Ranchi; but Romu could not be moved.

On a bitterly cold night when the jackals wailed louder than usual, Romu's condition worsened. Our old cook and maid servant stood near his bed in silence and by the dim light of the oil lamp I could see how spasmodically he was breathing. In that dark hour I found that my faith in God had remained intact. 'This will pass by His grace,' I whispered to myself over and over again. There was little else that I could do—the doctor was far away and we were off the main road in an area where it was said leopards lurked at night. I held Romu's hot little hand and prayed in silence. . .the crisis did pass.

Six weeks later, we brought Romu to Calcutta and only when I had made him over to Mother was I able to relax and have a proper night's rest. As the days passed, I became aware that I had shed many of my inhibitions, grown more self-reliant and replenished my faith through these trials and tribulations.

14

We were still in Calcutta at the end of February 1923 when it was announced that Rabindranath Tagore would be coming with his students from Santineketan to stage *basantotsab*. The 'Spring Festival,' an enchanting programme of song and dance, would be a benefit performance for the North Bengal Flood Relief Fund.

My sisters-in-law and I were eager to see this, but Mother was shocked at the cost of the seats. We told her it was for charity but she was convinced it was too extravagant. Her main objection, of course, was that there were no *purdah* arrangements at the Madan theatre. We promised to sit in the front row where no one else could see us except those on the stage but even then she did not think it advisable. We were in despair until someone foisted four tickets on Mejda. Since it would be a pity to waste them, Mother gave her consent with the injunction that we must not only cover our heads with our *saris* but pin them securely so that they could not fall off. Time and changing views had uncovered our faces, but it was still compulsory to cover our heads and we promised to conform. 'I really don't know what our people will say if they see you there!' wailed Mother as we were about to set off. We vowed we would do our best to keep out of their way.

We avidly enjoyed the feast of song and dance and thought the decor and dresses absolutely marvellous. I had loved Tagore before, but now I adored him and his melodious tunes haunted me for many nights and days.

We had arrived early and taken our seats in a surreptitious

manner but, when the show ended, the crowd made it impossible for us to exit as quickly as planned. My sisters-in-law and I had to slowly weave our way out of the foyer, apprehensive of being recognized by someone we knew, for we were also averse to advertising the fact that we had been bold and bad enough to break away from *purdah*. 'Did you see anyone?' we asked each other anxiously in the sanctuary of Mejda's Citroen. When heads were shaken in the negative, ostrich-like we felt no one could have possibly seen us, we were safe!

After returning from Ranchi I was detained at Kidderpore for a long time. First, it was Romu who needed expert medical treatment to recover from the after-effects of typhoid; then I was ill for several weeks. During my convalescence I once again dreamt of a flight in space...I looked upon a gloomy sea... there was no light except a luminous glow from the grey waters and the foam-tipped waves that lapped the shore. I gazed in despair at the menacing sea and wondered how I was to fly over it. Should I grow weary and fall, the deep waters would close around me and I would be lost forever. I felt the task was beyond me and yet had to attempt it. With an immense effort I lifted myself over the heaving waters and lo! a Voice was heard: 'Fear not,' it said, 'Call on Hari and He will help you cross over.' Hari is one of the many names by which God is called, and I heard myself calling upon Hari. Surrendering myself to Him I felt all fear fall away from me. My heart rejoiced, my flight was smooth and effortless.

I read a lot at that time and remember finishing *If Winter Comes* at one stretch in the early hours of the morning. When the pale light of another day imperceptibly stole in, I was still musing over Mark Sabre and the tragic events of his life. His sufferings became mine and my heart contracted with pain. It was ever like this, what I read nearly always had a profound effect on me. I entered for the time being into the skin of the people in the book and experienced their anguish and bliss in a most disconcerting manner. Hutchinson had replaced Marie Corelli in my affections!

During my enforced leisure I tried to record my thoughts and began with old age—how it can be terrible and pitiful and also beautiful. This effort made me crave self-expression and I continued to write in secret. I think it was my mother's grandmother who inadvertently provided me with the theme of old age.

She was a lady of over eighty years with a small shrunken figure and twinkling eyes that she kept anointed with *kajal.* We did not see her often but she had come once with my grandmother to visit us. One afternoon when we were on the veranda Father happened to pass by and a smile flickered on his face. He remarked that four generations were seldom seen together and that the group ought to be photographed.

'What did he say?'' asked the old lady. Both she and my grandmother had pulled the portion of their *saris* that covered their heads down several inches to conform to decorum in the presence of a son-in-law. When she heard what he had said she was shocked and hurt beyond measure. 'Ah me,' she sighed, wiping her eyes, 'I am ill-fated that I am still alive.' Both Mother and I hastened to assure her that Father had no such intention in his mind and that among European people, living to a ripe old age was thought wonderful. But she would not take it as a compliment. It was all right for men, she quavered, but certainly not for a woman like her who had seen death collect nearly all her loved ones. 'I am of no earthly use to anyone,' she had said, lamenting death's delay in calling her. She would not be comforted and fearing that Father might take her photograph to perpetuate her shame, she left the next day for her village home.

Romu recovered. Returning to Tamluk in June 1923, I gratefully offered my thanks-giving prayers and alms at the ancient shrine of Bhima Devi by the river. It was a halcyon month. Hoping to remain another year in Tamluk all our savings were invested in a motorcycle to facilitate my husbands's tours. This caused great excitement in the countryside and the younger generation would run after it with shrill cries while their elders would rush out to watch it ploughing through the dusty streets.

But soon after its arrival we were plunged in gloom at the news of my husband's transfer to Chittagong. Not only did this mean moving to a remote town in East Bengal but also the lack of a rent-free bungalow such as we were then enjoying. The Government accepted no responsibility for officers posted to headquarters so we would have to find our own accommodation. It was difficult to find a suitable house within one's purse range and in the meantime the officer had to live in one of the dingy rooms of the dismal Inspection Bungalow.

Faced with this bleak prospect we wondered where we were to store our furniture and other belongings till the house materialized. However, our immediate problems were happily solved by a cousin of mine who happened to be posted in Chittagong. He had a spacious bungalow and a generous heart and invited us to stay with him till we could find a home of our own.

The people of Tamluk tried hard to detain my husband. He had endeared himself to them by his service during the devastating floods. But their efforts were of no avail as his allotted term had already been extended by many months. The members of the Mahila Samiti gave me a tearful farewell and I found it hard to part with these kind friends whose warm affection had enriched my life.

In September we reached our new station after a wearisome journey by train and steamer in most inclement weather. I was entranced by the scenery with its wooden hills and undulating roads. My cousin's beautiful bungalow with its well-kept garden sprawled over a low hill. We lived here for three weeks in comfort and came to know the niceties that had to be observed by him and a few others of our country who belonged to the select group of 'covenanted officers'.

Their movement, speech, habits and mode of living were under surveillance and the slightest deviation from approved standards spelt disaster. From what I gathered the unwritten law was : never to be seen except in European clothes, to speak always in English and to adopt the British mode of living and thinking. This of course meant that wives must never observe *purdah*.

Despite the handsome emoluments I could see my cousin chafe under the conditions of his service and harbour bitter hatred for his superior officers, all recruited from the ruling race. Having lived for long years in their country, he was of the opinion that the Britisher at home was of a different breed altogether. He was a dour person, my cousin, endowed with a scathing tongue and a pungent sense of humour and many were the arguments he had with my husband while I sat astounded to hear his view of things.

He regaled us with brief sketches of officers and their families. 'You will have to be careful, nearly all of them are very enlightened.' I tried to look intelligent. 'Yes', he nodded 'they believe our old customs to be superstitious, attempt to embrace every aspect of western culture, and, I might as well warn you, they never worship God with the help of any image, preferring the abstract *Param Brahman* [the Supreme Being without name or form].'

I was abashed and guiltily thought of my Ganesh from Father's Jaipore marbles. Hearing all this and how these polished ladies were the glass of fashion, I was filled with trepidation. Then, he began to deride them mercilessly and went on to say that most of them were artificial and insincere. 'They are divided into three groups', he continued, exhaling a column of smoke from one of his endless cigarettes. 'The *bagha*, the *chaga*, and the *chuno*.' I gasped. Gravely he explained that he had made a scientific study of the species and the first were the 'tigers.' 'Blessed with the knowledge of all that is British and best, by virtue of their trip to Bilat [England],' they were foremost in bank balance plus brains. The next were the 'goats,' who were not so affluent or influential, but bleating acquiesence, meekly tried to follow their leaders. Lastly came the 'small fry'. Numerically they were stronger, but of humble means and station; they valiantly determined to swim in the wake of their superiors.

'And remember,' he added, 'they all consider those who are not of their community to be steeped in darkest ignorance, especially those who are still within the orthodox fold.' Here he wagged an admonishing finger at me with a twinkle in his eyes. With a sinking feeling I began to wonder whether I could ever be a credit to my husband here. Already I had been warned about *purdah* and the prospects were disconcerting. I did not relish the idea of being plunged into Chittagong 'society' as portrayed by my cousin. The idea of meeting quite unknown men with their womenfolk was most depressing.

My husband too was worried, but on a different account. Every day after office he would set out to search for a suitable house and return late, enveloped in gloom. As time passed, it became evident the kind of accommodation we had in mind might not be available.

One afternoon I was taken to see the only 'To let' house in town and was confronted with an ancient two-storied building in an advanced stage of decay. It faced a narrow street close to the bazar. Two bed-raggled ducks squawked on the pea green waters of a pond beside it and just opposite was a tin shanty inhabited by some queer looking people. The women wore outdated frocks revealing a lot of thin dark leg and the hirsute men were in singlets and shorts. Their voices were raised in a sort of pidgin English and their washing was hung in the front veranda. They were all right, we were told; it was only under the influence of liquor that they became a little noisy and truculent.

I looked at the gaunt dilapidated structure and could not help remarking, with a giggle, that it looked like a haunted house. My husband was not amused. 'We cannot live forever on the bounty of your cousin', he muttered. 'You will have to make up your mind about coming to stay here or returning to Kidderpore'. I shook my head vigorously. 'Go back? Certainly not! Let's see what the rooms are like, they might not be quite so bad,' I said with a brightness that was wholly artificial.

As we climbed the rickety stairs our small son stretched out his hand towards the wall . . . I saw a forked tongue flick out like lightening from between the broken bricks and quickly snatched him up in my arms. The two of us almost toppled down the stairs. 'Whatever made you do that?' growled his father with a frown. I told him what I had seen. 'We will have to be very careful,' he said in a low tone.

We moved in. I remember the September rains were rather heavy that year and diverse items were used to hold the water that came through the roof. On top of our mosquito net we would spread out a reed mat and get up at night to empty it, and all over our bedroom was an assortment of buckets and bowls to catch the rain dripping from the ceiling. Another inconvenience we suffered was the number of lunatics who walked into our ground-floor living room and could only be removed with the help of the police.

But after a few months we were fortunate enough to leave this place for a small hill-top bungalow with a beautiful view of the country-side. The layout had been expensive so the previous occupant wanted a high price for it. Although we could ill afford this luxury we complied with his wishes and were thankful when he agreed to accept the sum in instalments and helped us to get the tenancy from the landlord. The bungalow was in a remote area but I loved the solitude and we lived there for the rest of the three years we were in Chittagong.

Romu was now a day scholar in a proper school. He would set off early in the morning swinging his satchel. The school was about three miles away and he would be accompanied by the office peon who balanced on his head the deed box containing official files. The school was close to the law courts where my husband, then the Sub-Divisional Magistrate, later travelled to on his motorcycle.

I joined the *Mahila Samiti* here. The District Magistrate's wife, a large and friendly Englishwoman, was the President. A baby show had been proposed by her and I was called to interpret this to the members since she did not know any Bengali. The response was not favourable. There was an ominous silence. When pressed to disclose why, the women admitted their fear that babies might sicken and even die if their health was favourably commented upon. 'The "evil eye" don't you know?' whispered one of the members confidentially to me. The President smiled brightly. 'Did you tell them about the prizes?' she asked. I nodded and tried again, but the majority of the members were more or less convinced that the baby show would not benefit them or their children.

Finally it was decided that the uninhibited ones should come forward for the good cause. My small son was then a plump two years old and I was asked to set an example by exhibiting him. Wives of other officials were also requested to help in this manner. Apart from these children the only other exhibit was a six-year old girl whose father was the District Magistrate's office peon. Under these circumstances it was thought judicious to award the prize of Rs. 25/- to her and my son was given the second prize of Rs. 10/-. Retaining only the crimson rosette that was pinned on his chest I made over the money to split up into consolation prizes for the rest of the contestants.

The attendance was poor in the morning, but women and children appeared in large numbers in the evening to see the 'bioscope'. It was hoped they would benefit by visual education, but after having followed the vicissitudes of the hero and heroine and finally, their happy union, the audience could not be persuaded to remain any longer. The President implored me to explain the benefits in health and hygiene to be derived from the next item on the programme. I tried my best but the ladies shook their head and with polite smiles, said their children were falling asleep, and commented on the pointlessness of remaining to look at 'mosquitoes and flies.'

The films produced by the Public Health Department of that period seemed to deal mostly with the cause and cure of malaria and cholera. They were referred to as 'Mosquito and Fly' pictures because the unwholesome activities of these pests were featured with much prominence and were coldly received by the public. So, when this educative film appeared on the screen, the seats were practically empty. The President sadly gave away the few remaining oranges and sweets to the drowsy children.

An old lady looked at her contemplatively. 'How many children has she?' she asked. I duly translated the query. 'Ek chokra, do chokri,' replied the President with a bright smile raising the requisite fingers to clarify her statement. But no answering smile lit up the old lady's face, in fact it registered definite disapproval. The President mutely questioned me. I raised my eyebrows and shook my head. For, I could not possibly tell her how shaken an old lady was at her claim to possess 'one male and two female brats.'

My *purdah* was definitely broken at Chittagong when I

began to attend mixed parties. Although they were mostly for tea—very rarely did we dine out and I don't remember hearing of cocktail parties in those days—these were sufficiently exciting to keep me awake the previous night pondering over what to wear and praying fervently for the gift of requisite social graces.

At first we were the only ones with orthodox traditions but we were later reinforced by a rather refreshing family from Allahabad. He was a high Government officer but she had a rural education and did not know a word of English. Although she too was newly out of *purdah* she was quite unperturbed at parties. Both were charmingly unspoilt and adhered to their own customs. They came from a different province and many of our ideas differed, but as we agreed on a few basic fundamentals, their advent made life more pleasant for us.

With them we climbed the steep hill of Sitakund some miles from the town to visit the shrine of Shiva and we went together in a steamer to the island temple of Adinath. Once my husband had some work in Cox's Bazar by the sea and all of us spent a happy weekend in a small bungalow. I remember waking in the luminous dawn to see the sun rise like a globe of fire and the sky shot with rose and orange to herald the miracle of another day. In the evening I would quiver in ecstasy to behold the glory of the setting sun across the glittering stretch of endless waters. These all too brief interludes from our town life were very precious and I cherished the memory of those happy times.

I never succeeded in being at my ease with the people amongst whom we had to move in Chittagong. One of the things that struck me as queer was the habit of talking always in English. It appeared to be the hallmark of excellence to be able to do so and when Bengali was spoken, it was spoken with a foreign accent! Parents spoke to their little children either in English or Hindi.

'I can understand the reason for English,' I told my cousin who never failed to be amused at my reactions, 'but why Hindi?' He shrugged his shoulders. 'I warned you about their oddities,' was the reply, then as an afterthought he added, 'Perhaps they do it to show that their children are looked after by *ayahs*.' 'But,' I stammered, 'What has that to do with it?' 'Everything. Have you an *ayah*?' he asked abruptly. I recalled our simple Mokkhoda from her little village in the backwaters of Bengal, with her bashful veil lowered before 'menfolk' and shook my head. 'No, we have Mokkhoda and you know full well, we don't call the Bengali maid servant an *ayah* but refer to her as *jhi* [a daughter].'

'There you are!' he cried in triumph. 'The majority of us employ the humble *jhi* in Bengal, but the *ayah* comes mostly from the distant North or South, and they speak nothing but English, for even the street beggars there beg in that language. These imported maid servants are generally superior beings. They never cover their faces, hold different ideas of food and accommodation, and demand such high wages that only the foreigners and the wealthy can afford to employ them. Hindi is the mother tongue of the Northern ones so they use this with the children entrusted to their care. As parents and friends only speak English, naturally the little ones learn nothing else. Besides,' he concluded, 'you ought to know that it's very bad form to be acquainted with Bengali.' Here he ended his homily but I was not convinced.

'I have heard them sing Bengali songs—.' 'That is a different matter altogether, why, that must be to show how accomplished they are—'he said, breaking into a gale of laughter at my bewildered look. I never could be quite certain whether he seriously meant what he said. He held in contempt the Chittagong 'set' and was ruthless in his sarcasm. Although he had abandoned our old ways and was what could be termed quite modern, he still retained a deep regard for the traditional.

But I was to learn later that in Chittagong there were men and women who were thinking on different lines. To liberate the Motherland from foreign rule, drastic measures were being decided upon. Their aim was to further the national cause, not as Congress planned but according to daring plans of their own. Oblivious of self, they had dedicated their lives to this ideal and joined secret societies to plot revolution.

One evening, after I had been teaching our cook a new recipe, we sat down late to the evening meal. The children were fast asleep. The stillness of the night was broken by the clamorous cries of countless cicadas and the wail of a jackal from beyond the hills. The kerosene lamp burnt low. I raised the wick and was proudly serving the dish so painstakingly prepared when heavy footsteps on the veranda made our spaniel, Gypsy, bark in excitement.

The servant came to say a police officer wanted to see my husband. He was often called out at odd hours and fearing he would be late, I implored, 'Oh let him wait, you must finish your dinner—' but he shook his head and left murmuring, 'it might be something very urgent.' When he came back he said he must go out to attend to important work and might be late in returning. The look on his face froze the questions that rose to my lips and he immediately set out on his mission.

The untouched food was put away and the servants left. Alone in the solitary bungalow I counted the slowly passing hours . . . it was long past midnight when he returned. I wanted to warm his dinner but he said he had no inclination for food and hearing the nature of the work he had been summoned for, I did not wonder.

He had gone to record the declaration of a dying police officer. This officer had received a note from a friend who asked to meet him that evening in a secluded part of the Parade Ground. The friend insisted he had something important to communicate. After they had chatted for a few minutes, the friend pulled out a revolver and shot him in the chest because the officer had recently discovered his friend's connection with the revolutionary party of Chittagong. The officer was young and newly married . . . he died that night.

I had been aware of political activities—*swadeshi* disturbances as they were called at that time—of people being arrested and jailed because they had gone against the British government but this was the first time I had been brought close to violence and bloodshed in the cause of our country's freedom. I began to ask questions, and from the replies and books and papers that came my way, I realized the tremendous implications of the times we lived in. Long before I had learned of the death of Khudiram, forces had been at work to awaken India to the fact that she must win her freedom from foreign rule.

Many influences had helped to form public opinion to this end and to mould the minds of our young men and women revolutionaries.

Sarat Chandra Chatterjee, the Bengali novelist, vividly portrayed the privations, great sufferings, determination and self sacrifice of these bold revolutionaries in his novel, *Pather Dabi* [The Path's Demand]. Regardless of the price, these young people could justify any means where the liberation of the Motherland was concerned. It was a most human document, written with great courage and understanding which gained instant popularity and was promptly banned.

Whatever is forbidden has a flavour of its own; I longed to get hold of a copy. It was a criminal offence to possess one but somehow it was passed on to me by a young man with a seraphic face when I was once at Kidderpore. I remember the thrill of secretly poring over it in the still nights, locking it up in my drawer and surreptitiously returning it to its owner. The owner, a kinsman of an in-law, was a frequent visitor to our house and always wore exquisite clothing. In fact he greatly amused us by his mincing speech and affected manners and no one would ever associate him with anything serious. But in those days one never knew who was who really, or where one's interests actually lay.

While in Chittagong we heard of Surya Sen, the bold 'terrorist' leader. During the non-co-operation movement he resigned from the school he was teaching in, joined Congress, but eventually left it because it seemed ineffectual. He gathered a group of fiery youths who would further the national cause according to his own ideas. The members of his 'Revolutionary Youth Society' would assemble in the remote hill tracts of Chittagong where he trained them for the work he had in mind. Cool-headed and well-educated, endowed with a razor keen intellect, amazing courage and powers of organization, he carefully chose his 'Revolutionary Army'. He taught them how to handle firearms which had been stolen for this purpose, and how to maintain their physical fitness by strenuous exercises.

Their spirits he strengthened by instilling the essence of selected portions of the *Bhagavad Gita*. It was stressed that it was no sin to slay one's adversary in a righteous battle. His magnetic personality inspired those teenagers with indomitable courage and they were prepared to carry out any command. He had planned to capture Chittagong by first capturing the British residents and paralyzing its administration. Since money would be needed for the purchase of adequate arms and ammunition, a series of daring robberies were carried out. It was mostly the rich and miserly who were relieved of their excess wealth by these '*swadeshi dacoits*'.

In the cold weather of 1923, only a few months before we came to Chittagong, there occurred what was called the 'Pahartali Raid.' Far away from the town lay the Tiger Pass between two hills. At ten o'clock in the morning the pay clerk of the Assam Bengal Railway, accompanied by armed guards, rode in a horse-drawn carriage to the railway office with Rs. 17,000 in cash. Hardly was the party half-way through the pass when a group of youths silently appeared. A pistol was pointed at the coachman and he was ordered to halt. In the twinkling of an eye the others surrounded the vehicle, overpowered the guards, grabbed the clerk, relieved him of the money bag, and were seen no more. We were told this story and warned of the perils of the Tiger Pass and such like solitary places, but except for the murder of the police officer no other incident of this kind occurred during our stay in Chittagong.

When the case came up, every effort was made by the defence to prove that the dying declaration was a concocted document. When my husband was called to give evidence he maintained that he had recorded exactly what the dying man had said. The counsel for the defence was a brilliant barrister who could terrify occupants of the witness box by lashing out with unexpected questions, twisting and turning the answers until he confused them and they blurted out things afterwards to be regretted. This barrister was J.M. Sen Gupta, the nationalist leader of Chittagong, who was later called *desha-priya* [dear to the country].

It was at this time that a postcard arrived with the warning, 'Mazumdar, be careful, don't overdo things,' scrawled in Bengali. Immediately two plainclothes policemen were posted at our bungalow, but somehow I did not feel we were in any danger. From what was known of these terrorists, barring the British victims, they attacked only under grave provocation. My husband had only carried out the routine work of the administration without fear or favour and was well known for his integrity. I knew their bullets were reserved for other types of men and he would remain unharmed.

The rest of our Chittagong days passed smoothly enough. My leisure was enlivened by writing a short story and when it appeared in print, I ambitiously began a novel. I had tried to be clever in this story, sketching the follies of a corpulent superintendent of police who had risen from the ranks. Possessing goodwill but no knowledge of Bengali or of the Indian Penal Code, this middle-aged Englishman floundered in situations that were thought to be amusing. I had called it, 'An Eed Incident', and was thrilled when it appeared in the June 1926 issue of *Illustrated Sisir* along with Chapter XI of Mahatma Gandhi's *Experiments with Truth*!

15

In the autumn of 1926 we moved to Manikgunge, in the district of Dacca. My husband's feeble objection to another East Bengal posting had been overruled by the young Under-secretary who had just arrived from England. 'Why,' he had said with an amiable smile, 'Manikgunge is not far from Calcutta. Let me see (consulting a map), it is only . . . miles as the crow flies . . .' He quoted a reasonable number of miles and was convinced that he was quite fair in posting my husband there after distant Chittagong.

The mileage quoted might have been correct 'as the crow flies'—but by train, steamer, country boat and palanquin, it took us a night and two days to arrive at our destination. This being an outlying sub-division, the officer in charge had a bungalow to live in, and, unfurnished though it was, we were thankful for this amenity provided by the Government.

Manikgunge means 'The Jewel Mart', but how this isolated little town derived such a glamorous name was never known. All that we found in the local market was a plentiful supply of fish and milk and seasonable vegetables. The prolonged and heavy rains caused ponds and ditches to overflow into the lanes and narrow roads, converting the countryside into one sheet of brown water. When this happened pedestrians were seldom seen; nearly everyone plied his own craft. Children went about in rafts which they would punt with a bamboo twice their size and a few daring ones could be seen in enormous black earthen bowls, meant for cow's fodder, coolly steering their way with a couple of sticks. The thin steam that flowed beside our bungalow rose to the level of the red gravel immersing the roots of the tall rain trees that grew by its side. Ferry boats carried on a brisk trade and coconuts and other commodities were brought to our doors in precarious boats from distant villages. My husband toured in country boats and I would occasionally accompany him, spending a leisurely day with some needlework or a book, while our small sons tried to fish from the windows and expressed constant hunger.

I found the local ladies here most friendly and receptive to the idea of establishing a *mahila samiti.* We met periodically and exchanged cooking recipes and designs for needlework, held musical evenings, and subscribed to a monthly journal for circulation amongst members. This women's association became so popular that the leading lady of another village became interested and invited us to hold a meeting at her home. Since this was during the rainy reason, the function had to be after dusk, to allow *purdah* women to travel without being seen. My husband was also wanted there for some work so we would go together. I looked forward to this new experience of visiting a remote village during the rainy season and was thankful for the clear skies that afternoon.

Our host had sent his personal boat, a huge ungainly vessel, with a multi-coloured patchwork sail that made it look quite gay and inviting. The setting sun tinged the waters with a vivid orange and rose as we glided past the Law Court buildings, the Boys' School and the 'mart'. Nosing its way through masses of mauve water-hyacinths the boat gained in speed as the boatmen silently plied their oars. Slowly the skies darkened and night fell and it was pitch dark except for the flickering flame in our hurricane lantern. The stillness of the night was broken only by the lapping of the waters as the boat cleaved its way through shallow water and plants, and I wondered how the boatmen could make out where to go.

Losing count of time, we sailed in silence till at last lights could be discerned in the far distance. Shadowy figures moved forward and by blazing gas lights our boat was tethered. It was a pleasant surprise to step out before a brick building with massive pillars and lime washed walls, as the homes I had visited before had mud walls, with roofs of corrugated iron. The periodical tornadoes that devasted this part of East

Bengal made it convenient to live in these hutments that had a chance of escaping the velocity of the gale and even if swept away, were less expensive to reconstruct than brick and mortar buildings. These were thrifty and conservative people and neither University degrees nor prosperity seemed to change their taste in housing.

We were warmly welcomed on landing. My husband remained with the men while I followed some small girls up a narrow flight of stairs to a large hall lighted for the occasion with rented gas lights. There was a large gathering of women and children of all ages sitting on the gaily woven cotton carpet and I was made to sit on a high back chair draped with gold-embroidered crimson velvet and garlanded with fragrant flowers. A welcome song was sung by a group of pretty young girls and then the widowed mother of our host stood up to read her address. It was remarkably well written and delivered with dignity and ease. Speaking on behalf of those assembled, the speaker emphasized the importance of women's education in this part of the world. They had learnt with pride and joy of the attainments of their foreign and Indian sisters and regretted their own educational inadequacies. They wanted education to make themselves real helpmates of their husbands, to help them rear strong and healthy children, and to give widows and other poor women a way of earning their own livelihood. She concluded with the off-quoted lines, 'Until the women of Bharata [India] awaken, Bharata will never awake!'

Then a very old lady rose, adjusted her *sari*, peered through her steel framed spectacles, and in a quavering voice welcomed me to their village. This once prosperous town was now sadly stricken by poverty and disease. Notable men had been born here, she said, naming a few well-know public figures, but alas, they had forgotten their humble birthplace. If these men would take a little interest in their village, it would flourish. 'Our needs are many,' she continued. 'But the first thing we want is education. We must have knowledge for only this can give us the power to break our fetters of ignorance and superstition and then the women of India will be able to regain the honoured position that was theirs in the golden days of the Vedic age.'

The next speaker was a bright teenage daughter of the house. Eager to learn all that the modern world offered, she was convinced the deterioration of Bengal was closely related to the backwardness of her daughters. Education to equip them for service in the home and perhaps later in spheres beyond the home was badly needed. With ease and conviction she deplored the meagre facilities offered in the village and implored me to exert my influence to improve the Girls' School which she had left long before.

I was moved and impressed. Here were minds different from the fiercely conservative ones I had met in West Bengal. Yet all these women were from orthodox homes. I don't remember what I said in reply, but they had enjoyed voicing their thoughts to sympathetic ears. After the farewell song we moved to the narrow veranda.

Here we had a good view of the magic lantern show held below in the courtyard. Requested by our *Mahila Samiti*, the Publicity Department at Calcutta had sent an officer to give a talk on health and hygiene and exhibit suitable slides. It dwelt on the heart-rending toll of infant mortality with hints on mothercraft and how to avoid malaria and cholera. A large crowd had gathered to witness all this and I was thankful that our luck held and no rain spoiled the show.

It was late. I remembered with alarm my sons, alone in the bungalow, and I shivered as I recalled the snake Romu had so recently found in our bathroom. Anxious to leave I approached my hostess, but she smiled and led me to a sumptuous meal. On the speckless floor a gay carpet had been spread and before it on a gleaming bell-metal plate was piled fragrant spiced rice. Twinkling bowls of curried fish, meat and egg were placed in a semi-circle around this and there was a separate plate of sweetmeats. I was requested to eat well.

I made an honest attempt to please, but failed, and it was felt that I was being bashful. Farewells being finally made, I was about to leave when one of the widowed ladies, a very young one with a wistful face approached me shyly and said in a low voice, 'Sister, I would like to re-touch your vermilion.

Will you allow me? There is nothing more beautiful, it is a woman's glory.' A world of sentiment enfolds the word vermilion as vermilion on the brow indicates a woman is a 'wife'. This is the happiest phase of a woman's life, when she is adored by her husband, proud mother of his children, and honoured mistress of his home.

She brought forth an ancient Benares box from a niche, dipped her forefinger in it and touched the centre parting of my hair. Once, twice, thrice she did this, then, slowly dipping it once more with great care, made a dot in the centre of my brow and repeated the ritual. This rite is a part of one's daily toilette and with the passing of time, becomes automatic, but she performed it with such solemn grace and sincerity that I could feel her good wishes with every touch of her finger. 'Now you are beautiful. Truly beautiful. May you wear your vermilion forever,' she whispered with a smile that brought a lump to my throat.

Joining my palms, I bowed low in salutation. Bereft of all that made life worthwhile, she had ardently wished for a stranger the happiness she had been denied. The dignity and grace of that youthful figure, clad in white, loyal to the memory of her lost beloved, dedicated in loving service to his family, and lovingly wishing me well still lingers in my memory.

In 1927 my mother-in-law assigned a task that flattered my ego but also caused many difficulties. My young brother-in-law, with whom I had flown kites and played marbles, had now taken his M.A. degree from Calcutta University and joined the Bengal Civil Service. My mother-in-law, anxious to see him married, wrote me pressing letters about finding a suitable bride for him and I finally agreed.

This experience, being my first in match-making, had seemed very piquant at first but gradually the responsibility of the thing dawned on me. Parents of our Kayastha caste and Bangaj sect who possessed girls of marriageable age deluged me with proposals, and I had the responsibility of choosing the girl best qualified to make the boy happy. Many youths were then choosing their own brides, at least having a look at the girl before the final word was given, but this brother-in-law of mine had pinned his faith on my choice.

It was a difficult task that he and his mother imposed on me. There had to be brains and beauty plus pedigree, and the horoscopes had to tally. It is possible to omit any of the first three qualities, but nearly all Hindus in Bengal are adamant where the last is concerned; many an otherwise suitable match is broken off where the horoscopes fail to correspond.

I was unfortunately down with an attack of influenza when the first proposal arrived. My husband had suddenly arrived on a couple of days' leave with the news of an exceedingly beautiful girl somewhere in the city of Burdwan. Her people had wired, 'Taking girl to the pagoda at Eden Gardens; please meet us there at four.' Burdwan is a longish distance from Calcutta—three hours run by train—and, if they came to the gardens there, it would not do to disappoint them. Besides, the party was eligible, and 'exceedingly beautiful' girls are not to be met with everyday.

I staggered out of bed, gathered my mother and two sisters-in-law and we packed ourselves into a taxi. Arriving at the gardens just at four p.m., we hastened to the pagoda, but found the place deserted. We loitered aimlessly for awhile. 'The train must be late,' we told each other. Just then a taxi overflowing with women and children stopped at the gate, and, noticing a girl clad in crimson silk among them, we judged it was the Burdwan family at last.

My husband separated himself from us and the gentleman with them lingered behind, while they gradually drifted in our direction. A bend of the bridge hid them. I craned my neck in excitement to catch a glimpse of the girl. When I saw her, disappointment surged through me. So this was the 'exceedingly beautiful' one.

Hurriedly I turned to my sisters-in-law, giddy girls both, none too soon, since already they were smiling. 'Mind you behave yourselves,' I hissed.

'Are you all coming from Kidderpore?' courteously inquired a wearyfaced little woman with a baby in her arms. 'Yes,' assented Mother. 'And you from Burdwan?' The little woman inclined her head. 'Please come this way; it is much too warm here,' I said, leading them to a stone bench under the shade of a tree by the lake. 'This is the girl,' explained the lady with a nervous smile. 'Salute them,' she whispered, and her daughter, bending down, took the dust off our feet.

Arranging her glasses on her nose, Mother peered at the little maiden. She was about fourteen, with a round, pimply face, small, deep-set eyes, a snub nose, thin lips and uneven teeth. Her hair had been hurriedly arranged in a high chignon, and the costly crimson-and-gold Benares *sari* was carelessly wound round her. Glancing at the tired-eyed lady with the four younger children clustering about her, I understood the reason. Mother, engaging her in tactful conversation, discovered a relative or two of theirs whom she happened to know, and in the meantime I tried to think of something to say to the girl.

For courtesy's sake I had to show an interest in her so I asked a few formal questions even though I had mentally ticked her off as impossible. She had a queer hoarse voice and an abrupt way of speaking; and so unlovely was she that I marvelled that anyone had labelled her 'beautiful'. An aunt of theirs had accompanied them, a garrulous body with a spoiled child—a regular *enfant terrible* who mercifully helped to alleviate the awkward pauses.

Later, I learned that nearly every unmarried girl is described as 'beautiful' by the matchmakers. The majority of matchmakers are a class of men who gain a livelihood by informing parents with children of marriageable age of the whereabouts of eligible brides and bridegrooms. Sometimes their task ends here, and they are suitably rewarded after the wedding. But again, at times, if requested, they arrange important matters such as dowry, the date of the marriage, and so forth, in consultation with both parties. Matchmakers of this class are popular, because they demand remuneration only if the ceremony does take place and also because they approach the parents of their own accord.

After several minutes of desultory talk we parted company with the Burdwan girl and her family, and there the proposal dropped. Possibly they had read disapproval in our faces for they never inquired about our opinion. This was as it should have been seeing that they were gentlefolk.

Some months later, my husband, hearing from a friend

about three eligible girls, managed to secure leave again. The first of the three girls was asked to meet us at the Victoria Memorial on the afternoon of the very day we reached Calcutta. There we found one of my brothers enthusiastic over the beauty and speed of his newly acquired six-cylinder motor car, and he persuaded us to go for a spin in it to Barrackpore. We told him of our mission, and he promised to deposit us at the Memorial punctually at four. The drive was pleasant in spite of the dust, and the picnic equally so, but the return was disillusioning. The dusty Barrackpore trunk road caused engine troubles that made us half an hour late for our appointment.

The setting sun shone dazzlingly on the white marble splendour of the Victoria Memorial. Shading our eyes, we tried to pick from among the heterogeneous crowd the people we were to meet. This time, fortunately, my husband had been acquainted with the girl's brother, so recognition was not difficult. Ascending the steps of the Memorial, we found a slim youth in European costume and a short, thick-set, bearded person resembling Tolstoy, in *dhoti* and shawl. Although we had made our way into their presence, it was not thought quite correct to be on speaking terms. Courteously stepping aside, the young man indicated where the ladies were, and our men joined him and his companion while we turned to where he had pointed.

'I say, there's the girl!' whispered one of my sisters-in-law with an excited nudge. Yes, it was easy to distinguish her, with her silver-bordered rose silk *sari* and pearl and diamond necklace and ear-rings. She was about eighteen and tall and slim, with a decided stoop. I observed with disappointment that her complexion was fairly dark. Her features were regular, but her whole face was lacking in any sweetness or charm, possibly because of her receding chin. Stifling my instinctive dislike, I advanced and apologized for the delay to the two ladies who were with her. The elder one possessed a pleasing face, and it was her grandchild, and the other lady, rotund of body with a vacant face, was the mother.

After the usual preliminary palaver was over, I became aware that the grandmother was monopolizing the interview.

In fact, she insisted on answering all the queries we put to the girl; so, leaving my sisters-in-law to entertain her and her daughter as best they could, I strolled away with the girl on the pretext of admiring the marble statues within. My motive was of course, to draw her out, to give her a chance of unfolding her individuality a little. But, alas, she proved uninteresting. Yes, she liked flowers; there was a good garden at the convent where she had gone to school in Rangoon. Yes, she was fond of school. Yes, she liked Rangoon, but Calcutta was better. Yes, she went to the cinema and her particular favourite was Jackie Coogan. Yes, she loved singing, especially songs from Rabindranath Tagore's *Gitanjali.* Many of her likes and dislikes I discovered within that quarter of an hour, but her languishing air and mincing speech failed to impress me favourably; besides, the absence of a good chin lent a somewhat vapid look to her face in spite of the chiselled nose and large eyes. Mentally assessing her, I found her far short of my ideal. No, she would not do. I retraced my steps and returned her to her relatives.

After some polite platitudes, the grandmother cornered me as we were leaving and inquired: 'How do you like our girl? Do you approve of her?' Embarrassed, I was silent for a second. It is not exactly in good taste to ask so delicate a question personally. I mumbled something about her grandchild being very nice. Mercifully, the menfolk approached at that moment and we drifted apart. Later we wrote and said that we preferred a younger girl. It is safe to disapprove of age, but one must be discreet regarding looks. Any remarks on appearance are not considered fair for of course they are spread abroad and injure matrimonial chances elsewhere. The second of the three girls we interviewed was connected with the people of one of my sisters-in-law so the appointment was made in their flat in Calcutta. It would be convenient for them, they had pleaded, and I had to acquiesce.

We went there next morning at nine. They had charming manners and were exceedingly eager to have me approve of their candidate, but my heart sank as I beheld the gorgeously apparelled maiden seated on the carpet with downcast eyes.

She was of lighter complexion than the last one but, alas, distinctly Mongolian in features and copiously freckled. When she rose to salute us, she stood a couple of inches above me—a disqualification for a younger sister.

As I feared they would do, the good people had made lavish provision of food. Refusal was of no avail, and we had to sample the sweets and pastry set before us. 'Sweetening the mouth' of guests is a tradition with us, and in consequence this sort of appointment is generally made for public places. Partaking of people's hospitality and then rejecting the girl they wish to see married is not very pleasant, and I felt hot and uncomfortable as the sad-eyed widowed aunt entreated me to inform them soon of my decision. Assuring her that I would, I managed somehow to wriggle out of the awkward situation. In the car we discussed the girl and, as I had expected would be the case, were unanimous in our disapproval.

As we sped through the crowded areas of Bhawanipore, I quailed over the prospect of interviewing the third girl we had planned to see during my husband's leave. This time some remote relationship had made an aunt of mine arrange the meeting at her flat. 'Why will people insist on having these affairs at home?' I wailed. 'I wonder what this one will be like,' I added as we were about to enter the apartment. 'Not bad,' murmured one of my sisters-in-law under her breath, and sure enough I lost my heart then and there.

She was about sixteen, with clear, candid eyes set wide apart in a perfect oval face, a delicately chiselled nose, dimpled chin and just the right sort of mouth. Her complexion was fairly light, and excitement had lent colour to her cheeks. The pale saffron silk *sari* was wound about her slim form in the correct way, and the simple, short-sleeved blouse was well cut. In contrast to both the other girls, she was unadorned but for a pair of gold bangles. She had a sweet voice and sang well, and was most unassuming. I was amused at her obvious anxiety to leave before twelve o'clock so she could attend her class. While we, the elders, were conversing, her eyes were wandering to the clock very often, and once I caught a quick, suppressed sigh. I smiled as I recalled my own school days.

Yes, she was the right sort, and I made up my mind to have her. In fact, I was so pleased with her that I did not hide my feeling from her relatives. As far as I was concerned, the choice was made, and I told them so as we left. 'That was very unwise of you,' Mother said to me later. 'You should not have given your word to them before consulting your mother-in-law. The girl is all right, of course—but then she is not well-born.' 'But,' I protested, 'my mother-in-law has left everything to my discretion. This girl is charming, and I'm sick of the pedigreed kind. Just think of the specimens we've inspected before'! 'All the same,' Mother argued, 'you have to inform your mother-in-law about the girl's family, and I doubt whether she will consent.' Mother was right; it all happened just as she had foretold.

At first my mother-in-law was in favour of the match, ignoring the fact that the family was not of noble birth, and I sent long and rapturous accounts of the girl to my brother-in-law. But just before the engagement, I received a disastrous note from Mother. It seems she had her suspicions about the family from the first and on inquiries had learned some grisly secrets. Of course we were perfectly aware of the status of the family when we went to see the girl. But how were we to know its previous history? I was loath to give up the girl, enlarging on her qualities to my mother-in-law, but the old lady was adamant. 'Blood will tell,' she wrote; besides, she considered that an alliance like this would be a blot on the escutcheon. My brother-in-law was evasive. 'Do what you think best,' he wrote, 'I leave all to you.' It was a compromising situation. However, I managed to bring my mother-in-law around somewhat. I told her of the dearth of suitable girls and warned her that her next daughter-in-law might be blessed with lineage but would most possibly be sadly lacking in looks.

As she was hesitating about whether to break off the match, my mother, a vigorous upholder of birth and tradition, hurled a thunderbolt. 'I shall have nothing to do with you or yours if you stoop to so lowly an alliance,' she said. 'The honour of the family is at stake; so weigh and consider all this before you finally settle things.' That ended the matter. The match was broken off. My disappointment was acute; for I could not forget the candid-eyed girl and doubted if I should be able to find her equal.

Months passed and I had grown wiser. No longer did I run to see alleged beauties, but requested the candidates to be kind enough to send photographs first. Many arrived, with lengthy descriptions of the girls' attainments, but had to be rejected since the likenesses were such that the most myopic would have labelled them unprepossessing.

When things were going on like this, I one day noticed an advertisement in the paper: 'Daughter of high government official of good family, handsome and accomplished.' The sect, too, was the same as ours, and a good deal of difficulty is experienced in following the social rule of marriage with one's sect. With glee I hurried to my husband and implored him to inquire into particulars. But he was gloomy. 'Advertisements of this sort are fishy affairs,' he said; 'the "high government official" may lick stamps in the Secretariat for all I know.' 'He may, and he may not,' I returned, 'and there's certainly no harm in a mere inquiry.' So the letter was written and posted, and the reply dispelled all doubts. The father was really a somebody in the secretariat and came from a well known stock we knew. The family resided in Calcutta, and he desired us to see the girl there, regretting that he had no recent photograph of her.

At the same time we heard of another good-looking girl, daughter of a police officer in Calcutta. Somehow, I was pessimistic about this girl. Although the family was genteel, the father had risen from the ranks. Now a hopeless stigma is attached to the position of sub-inspector of police here in Bengal and, this man had been one before he rose to be a superintendent of police. 'A *darogha's* daughter'! I murmured in contempt. 'Bah! you are too fastidious,' rebuked my husband. 'You're taking the girl, not the father, and, if the girl is really as beautiful as reputed it's silly to make a fuss over what the father once was. Whatever he may have been, he occupies a respectable post at present and the family connections are irreproachable. What more do you want?' So I had to consent to seeing the girl, though I still held my own views in the matter.

The horoscope of the daughter of the high government officer arrived and both of them tallied with my brother-in-law's. Both girls were desirable and it only rested with me to choose one of them. 'Make haste,' my mother-in-law wrote, 'the coming month is an auspicious one, and I desire to have the wedding then.' So, as soon as my own young son's summer vacation commenced, I packed and prepared to leave for Calcutta. I was getting tired; the novelty had worn off, and I made up my mind to select one of the girls and finish the whole business before returning home. My husband wrote and made an appointment with the police officer, this time at the Calcutta Zoological Gardens.

The monsoons had begun, and we had an unpleasant journey to the steamer station, which was sixteen miles off. When we had gone barely half-way, terrific winds and pouring rain compelled us to stop the motor bus and take shelter in a wayside tin shanty. The storm lasted more than an hour; afterward we started, but found the roads appalling. The wheels sank into the mud, impeding progress, and the driver was in despair. The steamer was due within an hour, and we were still miles off. He said it was a case of either the luggage or us since the old bus was incapable of carrying both. Just then a ramshackle office buggy reeled into view. Hailing this, we deserted the bus and stuffed ourselves in somehow. It was rather a tight fit for us all, but we thought it a god-send.

Our next experience was one to be remembered. The horse did all he possibly could, and, when the wheels stuck absolutely, we left the rickety vehicle and struggled through ankle-deep slush, any moment expecting to sprawl in it. 'Coming events cast their shadows before,' I murmured. 'I'm beginning to wonder what these girls will be like.' 'You are superstitious!' snapped my husband. We managed to catch the steamer, however, and reached Calcutta none the worse for our muddy adventures.

The weather seemed to be dogging us. It drizzled the whole of the next day, and a little before four o'clock, the time of our tryst, it poured. Nevertheless we started. How were we to find the police officer's family in the driving rain, and where should we meet them? It was a problem. At last it was decided to enter Peliti's Pavilion and order some tea. We were a big party; my mother and both my sisters-in-law, my brother and husband and two little ones who had insisted on coming, hearing our destination was the zoo!

In the meanwhile we heard that the girl was in the 'Monkey House'. I could not help laughing. 'Monkey House!' I exclaimed. 'How awfully unlucky!' 'They are not so full of superstition as you are!' retorted my husband. 'Surely the poor people can't be drenched in the rain simply because the animals are considered to be inauspicious!'

The rain had increased; we could hardly hear one another's voices, so deafening was the din. Mercifully we had Peliti's Pavilion to ourselves. Our car was sent to the 'Monkey House', and the police officer's party arrived. It consisted of two elderly ladies and two young girls flashily dressed in champagne-cloured Benares *saris* and a multitude of ornaments. It was surprising; we were there to see only one girl, and here were two obviously brought for our inspection. Our menfolk took chairs at a discreet distance. The mother and thc aunt conversed with Mother while we tackled the girls.

One was about seventeen and the other fifteen. The elder was the one with whom negotiations were broached; the other was a younger sister. The features of both were good, but the elder girl was the darker of the two and a trifle hirsute. Her short-sleeved blouse revealed downy arms, her manners were mincing and her figure was short and stumpy; she did not impress me favourably at all. The younger one was slim and tall and girlish; though her features were finely chiselled, extremely thin lips lent a somewhat hard air to her young face, and her brown eyes accentuated it. Her manners were more pleasing than her sister's since she managed to be natural, but they were both in the same class. The relatives seemed well-bred, but the girls were not quite up to the mark.

After they had departed and I had voiced my feelings, my husband said in despair: 'Why, the elder girl was quite good. You are fearfully fastidious, and you will never come upon your ideal; so we had better give up the idea of the marriage altogether.' The truth was, he was sick of the affair and wanted it finished. But how could I let down those who had trusted me? Besides, since he had not been able to observe the girl closely, his judgement was faulty. Needless to say, all the others were of my opinion. So nothing was definite until we had a look at the advertised girl. It was still raining in torrents when we went to the Eden Gardens, where she was expected. On our arrival we found that her family had been scared away by the weather, and so, disappointed, we returned home.

After endless discussion it was settled at night that if this other girl proved unattractive, then the younger of the two sisters we had just seen would be chosen, provided the horoscopes agreed. If my mother-in-law was really insistent about celebrating the wedding next month, I could do nothing but consent. As for taking the elder girl, I flatly refused to have anything to do with her, though it was she who had impressed my husband more favourably.

The following day was fair, and we went to the zoo again to see the advertised maiden. She proved a dear little soul with a wistful, appealing face and no wonder, since she was motherless. She had beautiful manners and, being the winner of many medals, was very clever. She had clear-cut features and a good figure, but alas she was dark!

Returning home, I sent a detailed account of all three girls to my brother-in-law, begging him to come and choose for himself. I was decidedly in favour of the motherless maiden; for in spite of her complexion she had a sweet face, and she obviously possessed breeding and would make a better wife than either of the others. Receiving no reply, I wired. In answer I got a short note to the effect that my brother-in-law would be satisfied with whomever I chose. I felt fairly mad! A nice dilemma I was in. Personally I still preferred the third girl, but on reflection I came to the conclusion that the boy would naturally prefer a fairer bride and that I ought not to foist a dark one on him simply because she had appealed to me.

Since my mother-in-law was eager for an immediate wedding, I had no alternative but to agree to have the younger daughter of the police officer. But fate willed otherwise. That worthy resented our rejecting his elder girl and wrote some rude letters to my husband, who was so disgusted at this unmannerly behaviour that he said he would have nothing to do with such ill-bred folk. Then the gentleman calmed down and begged us to have the one of our choice if we would but wait for him to find a suitable bridegroom for the elder girl, since it was impossible to give the younger one in marriage before her. Finding my husband adamant, he resolved upon the tactics of winning me over by sending some ladies of his house to influence me. Now, this sort of thing is simply not done. What they were became still clearer when they circulated the rumour that we had given and then withdrawn our word of marriage. We shook them off somehow, but it was a very awkward situation all the same.

My position was embarrassing. I had positively resolved to marry the boy off during the next month, and now all my plans were falling through. Then I had another experience.

One day I saw a photograph of a very pretty girl and on enquiring learned that she came from a good family. Her people lived in an up-country town and wanted us to go and see her there. I was not feeling very well; so my husband went alone. She was really good-looking, he declared, and having his word on this point, I took a desperate step.

I told him to consult the pandits, fix the earliest auspicious date for the wedding and definitely settle the whole business. There was no necessity of my seeing the girl herself since I was quite satisfied with the photograph. Besides, the horoscope was very favourable—curiously, she and I were born under the same star. But fate was against me again. It transpired that the father, a wealthy landowner, was a despicable rake and was intimately connected with many criminal cases as well. Besides, it leaked out that the girl, being an only daughter, was hopelessly spoiled. I waved this fact aside but could not get over the reports regarding the father's character. Lurid tales we were told of that gentleman's activities, and at last we thought it best to withdraw the proposal, because it would have been a degrading alliance in spite of the family lineage. So after all I returned home, leaving my brother-in-law unmarried.

For three months, from the middle of August to the middle

of November, I remained quiescent; they are the inauspicious months for all Bengali Hindus. Then one day I was approached to see a girl at a town nearby. I had grown wary. Before acceding to the request, I learned all the particulars about the family. After being absolutely certain of its status, pedigree and antecedents, I had the horoscope examined and, learning it was favourable, asked for a photograph. Finding it passable, I agreed to compromise myself once more.

The heat was terrible; at a temperature of 117 degrees we arrived at the town after a nerve-racking journey. There were no convenient public places here as in Calcutta; so the local temple was the place selected for the meeting. The place was deserted at eleven in the morning, and there I saw the girl, of about seventeen, who later became the bride. She was accompanied by her sister, and both were obviously well-bred and of modest demeanor. Her complexion was fair, and her features were regular. Although not so accomplished as the girls I had previously come across, she possessed a passable provincial education. Well-born, with irreproachable relatives, she was the best available candidate. Since my mothar-in-law was pressing, I clinched the matter and made the final arrangements for the wedding, which was performed in December 1927.

16

As I had not been well for some time I returned to Kidderpore in August 1928 and soon after underwent a major operation at the Cavel Nursing Home. I remained with my parents to recuperate while Romu, who had to continue his studies in Manikgunge returned with his father. His small brother, fighting to keep back his tears, wailed. 'To whom will I now tell things?' His elder brother was a merciless tease, but life lost its flavour when 'Dada' was not available. He fretted, and so did I. My convalescence was long and as the tedious days dragged I began to write to pass the time. My efforts, entitled "Choosing a Bride in Bengal" and written from my own experience was later published in *Asia*, a New York magazine.

December found me still in Calcutta. I went to a *Purdah* Party given by the National Indian Association for lady Irwin, the Viceroy's wife, and here I met an Englishwoman with whom an enduring friendship developed. During the same month I also attended a function whose purpose was directly opposite to this one. Seeing my interest in the political life of our country, Dada had allowed me to accompany him to one of the Congress Sessions for in that year the All-India Congress Committee was meeting in Calcutta. At the entrance, Bengali youths on horseback kept the crowd in order. They were in smart uniforms and some had gold braid on their shoulders. 'Subhas Bose's volunteers' Dada said with an approving smile. Inside the tent, I noticed a slim restless young man with serious eyes and asked who he was. 'Motilal Nehru's son Jawaharlal Nehru,' Dada replied.

People talked so much about the important event of the

year: the Bardoli rent affair. As the crops had been unsatisfactory, the impoverished peasants were not in a position to pay the enhanced revenue. They had pleaded with the Government to appoint an impartial committee to investigate their condition. When these efforts had been exhausted they accepted Gandhiji's advice and began a non-violent 'No Tax' campaign, to obtain redress. Government's attempts to crush the movement failed and eventually the peasants won their point. It was decided that there should be practically no enhancement of land revenue and the confiscated lands were restored to the people.

In January 1929 I retured to Manikgunge and found everyone much excited about the Annual Exhibition. At the end of October the little town, that had been under water since July, awakened to life with the advent of cooler weather. It was at this time that an exhibition was held. It was planned with care by a special committee headed by my husband, and our *Mahila Samiti* was requested to organize a baby show for the health section. The District Magistrate from Dacca opened the exhibition, officers connected with different Government departments paid flying visits, and village leaders assembled from distant places with their followers. Since people in large numbers flocked from the interior to participate in the proceedings, all manner of programmes were devised for their education and entertainment. The Industrial and Agricultural Exhibition became the main topic of conversation. Sir P.C. Roy, the noted scientist, had been invited to inaugurate a function, and our *mahila samiti* had requested him to give away the prizes to the babies.

Acharya Profulla Chandra Roy was a saintly person very human, vastly learned and full of enterprise. He had kept away from politics and devoted himself to science; he founded the Bengal Chemical and Pharmaceutical Works—the first Indian-owned and Indian-managed concern of its kind. He had never married, spent most of his earnings helping his pupils, and was in turn adored by them. We had heard he was a little unusual and lived very simply, but were quite startled to learn what he wanted during his visit.

He would not like to be the guest of any home having

unmarried daughters and would in fact prefer, if possible, to be accommodated in the Inspection Bungalow. As for meals, no more than 2½ annas were to be spent daily, and, the meals were to be riceless and spiceless, just vegetables boiled with no embellishments. The local people who had earlier rejoiced to learn their town was to be honoured by the visit of this celebrity, were now in despair. 'Even if he stays at the Inspection Bungalow, we must provide his food—.' 'But, boiled vegetables only'! wailed a member of our Samiti. 'However can we place this before a guest?' I was also dismayed and failed to visualize this insipid food on our bell metal plates unaccompanied by rice or *chapatis*. Suddenly, I saw how it might be served on china plates and grew quite excited. I tried to tell our members how his meals could be prepared, but with minds wrapped up in curries, they remained unconvinced and continued to deplore the situation. So, I said I would give him what he wanted and they were not to worry.

The great man arrived. Our modest home had been 'swept and polished and garnished and decked with blossoms sweet'! Consulting Mrs. Beeton's book, but disregarding the injunction on economy, I cooked a western meal. It consisted of soup, chicken stew (and a separate one with only vegetables in case he was vegetarian), a cucumber salad, and boiled custard pudding. I laid our table in Western style and hoped for the best. I warned our woolly headed boy to be on his best behaviour. Enlarging on the merits of our guest, it was only when I added that P.C. Roy had been many times to England that the boy's interest was aroused. Rolling his eyes, he drew in his breath with an awestruck 'Ooh!' and promised to be careful.

I waited for our guest to arrive and wondered what he would be like. A slight figure in a short *khadi dhoti* and a nondescript upper garment, with a small grizzled beard and alert eyes that twinkled humorously through framed spectacles, entered and greeted me. With folded hands I bowed low. 'Ah,' he said smiling as the chicken stew was set before him, 'this meal is certainly worth more than 2½ annas. But, tell me how many daughters. . . .' I hastened to assure him I had only two sons. 'Excellent!' he laughed, 'now I can eat with an easy mind.' He ate heartily.

Then he went on to explain, in a humorous vein, that during his frequent tours he found he was often placed in homes having several children and it troubled him to think that the prospect of providing dowries for the unmarried daughters must be causing his host many sleepless nights. It troubled him still more when, though he had pleaded for simple meals, rich dishes of various kinds were placed before him. This was a waste of good money, not to speak of the labour expended by his hostess and all to no avail. It was only a feast for his eyes, for having a weak stomach he never dared to partake of the food. 'But, believe me,' he added with a broad smile, 'my lot has not been lightened very much since I started to lay down my terms. This is the first time my boiled food has been served in this delicious manner. More often than not, I have been faced with soggy vegetables with only a pinch of salt to season it. Not very appetizing it is true, but it is safer to partake of this than the highly spiced curries swimming in oil and *ghee* that our ladies are so fond of preparing. But without any spices, you have cooked a most tasty meal—.'He paid me many compliments and told my husband it was a stroke of luck to have a wife who was a good cook.

I was beginning to feel smug and conceited when his roving eyes fastened on a framed photograph and turned enquiringly on me. I told him it was my father. 'Ah ha!' he said sucking his after-dinner clove with relish. 'I know him—an absentee *zamindar*.' He was severe with landlords who did not live on their estates. 'So, you are a *zamindar's* daughter! They become hopelessly spoilt,' he told my husband, adding, 'Does she trouble you overmuch?' Then, with twinkling eyes, he turned to me and asked, 'Do you constantly demand to be indulged with fine clothes and jewels?' I burned with rage. What did he take me for? Trying to keep a level voice, I retorted I did nothing of the sort and that he must have met odd specimens of *zamindar's* daughters before. He chuckled.

He would linger long after the evening meal conversing on many subjects. I remember his anguish over the mounting number of educated unemployed, and burning faith that industrial enterprise would be the main remedy. He was ruthless in his criticism of the average Bengali who hankered after clerical jobs. He also talked of his great admiration for many notable people of the West and discussed with zest the life of Andrew Carnegie that he was then reading. I had disliked him at first but afterwards found him most lovable and kind.

Our baby show was a success. It was held in the community hall, a building attached to the temple. It had wooden planks laid across for theatrical performances, religious discourses and such like functions. From far and near, women and children gathered here that day and we never heard of the 'evil eye' that had bothered the Chittagong mothers. The numbers of competitors were more than we could comfortably cope with. In fact, the crowd was so great that the wooden balcony running along three sides of the hall, creaked, cracked and gave way in one place, just at the moment Sir P.C. Roy arrived to distribute the prizes.

The two silver souvenirs that had been presented to him at public functions were made over to me before he left. 'Now, don't you go and keep these for yourself,' he had warned, chuckling at his own joke. 'People give me things but what am I to do with them? There is already a cupboard full in Calcutta. No useful purpose will be served by storing these. Utilize them for some good cause.' He presented me with a small box of toilet articles produced by his Bengal Chemical Works, and evinced a child's delight over the cake I baked for him to eat on the way.

My husband detested the clay water goblet that is usually carried on long journeys and said I was not to encumber him with one as plenty of good aerated water would be available at stations. 'What,' interrupted the great man with a frown, 'and spend three annas for a bottle? You appear to hold most extravagant ideas!' Handing me a stone bottle that had once contained Stephen's Ink, he said I was to fill this with drinking water and that would do for him.

His silver articles weighed heavily on me. Eventually, one was given as a trophy at a local Boy Scout's rally and as for the other, I had most unwisely announced that it would be given to the school girl who wrote the best essay on 'What is meant by a good housewife'. For this rash act I had to undergo the agony of reading through numerous artlessly written entries. At last, one bright girl came up to requirements and the silver vase, suitably inscribed, was thankfully made over to her and I could at last inform the donor that his wishes had been carried out.

We had been in Manikgunge for nearly three years and my husband had had a comparatively easy time as far as the political situation was concerned. There appeared to be a pause after the exciting years that followed the Non-Cooperation Movement of 1920. My only recollection is of an incident connected with Congress volunteers and riding boots. Young boys were given these boots to try on prior to a training scheme planned by Subhas Chandra Bose. Amidst much laughter and badinage they hobbled unsteadily in their unaccustomed footwear and fell flat on the road just across the narrow stretch of water by our bungalow. The sizes were much too large and not all the pairs tallied; this dampened local enthusiasm and I heard no more about the venture.

In this isolated place where very little of consequence occurred except day and night, I was given ample leisure for reading and reflection. What was happening in the brave new world since the thrilling campaign of Non-Cooperation launched by Gandhiji, interested me enormously. Since I was present when the fateful resolution was passed, the fortunes of those who participated in the fight seemed to become a personal concern. What Gandhiji said and did was endlessly discussed. Some said he was a saint, and others shook their head solemnly and thought him to be insane.

When our allotted term at Manikgunge had ended, but before settling down in our new station, we applied for leave and hopefully planned a trip to North India. 'I'll show you the Red Fort at Delhi and the Taj at Agra, they are wonderful,' said my husband. 'But, I wish to see Mathura and Brindaban. . . .' I answered, with visions of ancient temples and the playground of Sri Krishna with whom I had grown intimate through my daily study of his *Gita*. 'The distance is not long from Delhi, but those places are dusty, very dusty—'.'Never mind,' I protested. 'All right,' he laughed, 'We'll see them all.' But, it was decreed I was not to set my eyes on any of these places very soon, and it would be Romu, not his father, who would be instrumental in fulfilling my wishes.

As the day for leaving Manikgunge drew near we realized how fond we had grown of the people and the place. Since gentlewomen did not appear here in public, my husband attended his farewell parties alone and a special one was given for me by the members of the *mahila samiti.* Surrounded by a sea of friendly faces I felt a gentle hand on my shoulder and turned round to find a sweet old lady of whom I was very fond. 'Ah,' I said, 'I feel so sad to leave you all—.' 'Do you know,' she murmured with a diffident smile, 'I had a dream about you.' 'Oh, what was the dream?' I asked with polite interest, but at this moment other members came forward, we drifted apart and I lost sight of her.

We started very early next morning, first using a country boat so that we could catch the steamer across the mighty Padma river and we would then catch the train for Calcutta. On our way the boat got bogged down in mud, for this was October and the waters were receding. We got out and walked slowly through knee-deep slush, using long staffs to prod each place before we took the next step. The hardy boatmen managed somehow to get our luggage across and when we finally put our feet on firm ground, it was only to be told we must run for the steamer station. Panting, we reached the steamer just as she started. But alas, for some reason or other she failed to keep to schedule and we found the Calcutta train had left without us.

With the monument of luggage that always manages to accumulate during transfers and the uncertainty of obtaining accommodation in the next train, tempers were frayed. When the next train had arrived and we were about to enter a compartment at the extreme end of the ill-lighted platform, a blind beggar appeared calling for alms. My husband harshly told him to move aside and pushed in the last piece of luggage as we scrambled into the moving train. My mind, already depressed, became more so as I watched the sightless man left standing on the platform with outstretched palm.

I shall always remember that ghastly journey. The next morning our younger son, then eight years old, had his eyeball gashed open in the running train. It was drizzling and the window by which he was sitting to watch the fleeting landscape had its glass pane partially lowered. Thoughtlessly our young servant had flung a broken china plate through this and it was thus that the grievous injury was inflicted.

No medical aid could be given. The train rushed along, we were still a long way from Calcutta. Unashamedly I wept and prayed aloud as I sat with his head on my lap. 'Never mind Ma,' he consoled me. 'Lord Nelson had only one eye.' Then added slowly after a while, 'Do you know why this happened Ma? I think it's because we never gave the blind beggar any alms.' When we at last reached the noisy, grimy Sealdah station there was no one to meet us; the car and clerk from Kidderpore had left when we had not arrived on the previous train.

We took Donny to Dr. S.K. Mukherjee in Kydd Street, the only optician I knew, and we never regretted it. For long weeks before the bandage was removed, it was uncertain whether the wound had responded to treatment. When at last it was found that sight had been restored I tried to stammer my thanks. But the doctor said, 'Your gratitude should go to God, it is He who has cured your son. I was not very hopeful when he came first to me. But, he must be always very careful. Out of two horses, one is lame and must be considered accordingly.'

Pandit Nehru, presiding over the 44th session of the Congress, declared in an address that the time had come for India to march forward to win Independence. Those who would come forward to free the country from foreign rule would be recompensed with suffering, imprisonment and death he warned. Following this the decision was taken that 26th January would be observed as Independence Day. On this day the Congress flag would be flown each year and the pledge of independence taken.

I do not recollect any great enthusiasm about this amongst the people I happened to meet. Those with vested interests flouted the idea and said the Congress was crazy. Grey heads were shaken in disapproval, it was felt to be a fantastic idea. Only the youthful hearts danced at this daring aim and those who lacked the courage to openly espouse the cause did so in secret.

I was in Kidderpore in January of that year of 1930. We were gathered round the tea table that morning when loud voices in the street drew us to the veranda. It overlooked the large expanse of the 'lotus pond' where at one time, so the legend runs, the flowers really blossomed. A long pole had been planted beside its placid waters and many people were assembled to witness the raising of the flag at the appointed hour.

A young man in white homespun seemed to be incharge of the function. Two motor lorries containing red turbaned constables appeared on the scene. We could not hear what the European sergeant said, but the young man was seen to shake his head firmly in the negative. The police force waited, so did the silent crowd. The clock struck eight. The *khadi*-clad youth moved to hoist the Congress flag, the sergeant quietly intervened. Conforming to non-violence, the youth did not resist, we saw him calmly follow the sergeant to the lorry.

'Bande Mataram!' cried the crowd in one voice and this was repeated again and again till he was out of sight. Another sergeant came to the pole, pulled it up, flung it into the 'lotus pond' and carried away the flag. The people watched in silence. We were about to leave when a sudden ripple of amusement made us turn to see a tiny paper flag fluttering gayly in the morning breeze. The sergeant walked back in silence, plucked the flag and thrust it into his pocket. The crowd tittered and began to disperse; a little urchin came capering along the road and shrieked to another who had just arrived: 'Hah! You didn't see the fun, they took away Gandhi!'

Anyone who came in conflict with the police over the Congress ideals was labelled 'Gandhi' by the common people; in fact the Civil Disobedience movement itself was given this name. For, sometime later at Basirhat, hearing distant cries of 'Bande Mataram!' defiant yells and voices raised in anger, I asked our little sweeper girl what was happening down the road. All she said was, 'Only Gandhi,' as she calmly continued to eat her guava with relish.

When the Viceroy made it clear that Independence for India was out of the question, the Congress Working Committee authorized Mahatma Gandhi to start Civil Disobedience. But, before this was done, a moving letter was sent to Lord Irwin in which Gandhi explained how he desired to convert the British people by non-violence. 'It is my purpose to set in motion the force of non-violence against the organized force of British Rule. This will be expressed through Civil Disobedience. . . .' The Viceroy's answer was unsatisfactory and Gandhiji wrote, 'On bended knees I asked for bread and received a stone instead. The English nation responds only to force and I am not surprised by the Viceregal reply. India is a vast prison house and I regard it as my sacred duty to break the monotony of peace that is choking the heart of the nation for want of free vent. . . .'

Amongst the points that had been presented to the Viceroy were total prohibition, protective tariff on foreign cloth and the abolition of the salt tax. It was felt that salt, like air and water, was the property of the people. On the 12th of March, accompanied by his seventy-nine followers—and my heart pounded to find Sarojini Naidu was in this movement—Gandhiji began his historic march to take possession of the salt depot at Darsana. He reached his destination on the 5th of April.

People poured over the daily papers and discussed the outcome of all this with mounting excitement; it was now realized that non-violence was not a form of negation but a definite scheme of resistance. Civil disobedience came to be termed *satyagraha* [truth crusade]: to be prepared to endure imprisonment, sufferings and penalties for the cause, to never ask for any monetary help, and to implicitly obey the leaders of the campaign. A large number of people became aware of the spirit of his teachings, were stirred to the depths, cast aside worldly considerations and joined his crusade with faith and fervour.

'He has been arrested and taken to Yervada Jail,' Chorda announced mournfully one morning. Then we came to know of the message he had left—that neither the people nor his colleagues should be daunted. He was not the conductor of the fight, that was God who dwelt in the hearts of all. Only faith was necessary, then God would lead them. Entire villages were to pick or manufacture salt; women to picket liquor, opium and foreign cloth shops and, young and old of every home to daily ply the spinning wheel, twirl the *takli* [spindle] to produce plenty of yarn, create bonfires made of foreign cloth.

17

We were at Basirhat when the country was passing through this important phase. An annonymous petition had been made to the District Magistrate asking him to cancel this posting. It expressed doubts about my husband's ability to remain impartial in cases connected with Father's estates since the Sunderbans lie within the jurisdiction of Basirhat. The seasoned District Magistrate scented party factionalism and retained his faith in my husband's ability to steer clear of local politics. I heaved a silent sigh of relief, for Basirhat was not only a pleasant place to be transferred to after the water-logged stations of East Bengal, but from here Calcutta was accessible and I would be able to take Donny for his periodical examinations by Dr. Mukherjee.

The broad river Asrumati flowed in front of our bungalow and beyond the garden at the back was a spacious pool enclosed by high banks. Beyond this was the High School where Donny became a day scholar. He would walk over for lunch and was on the whole fairly happy here. Both he and I learnt to swim in the pool, at first supporting ourselves on huge banana trunks used as floats. We hugged them and kicked our feet immoderately while Romu instructed us. He had learnt to swim at Manikgunge but it was his father, an expert swimmer, who watched us on Sunday mornings to see how far we were progressing.

He had warned us about places that were deep, in that tank two people had lost their lives, and instructed us never to enter the waters alone. I broke my promise once and was very nearly drowned. The waters were high due to untimely rains, and I missed my footing on the slimy steps. I was being carried away when the man who was weeding the garden happened to look up, saw my plight, plunged in and rescued me. Gratefully giving him some remuneration I swore him to secrecy, he was not to tell the Master. But, eventually it was I who confessed and was soundly berated for my rash act.

I remember that for some days after I had a curious sense of detachment from my body. It was a singular feeling. As I applied the usual powder that evening, I seemed to see someone else in the mirror. I looked critically at the reflection and recollect saying aloud: 'What are you trying to beautify. This face that would have been sodden in the waters of the pool and brought forth swollen and ugly,—this husk that your loved ones would have turned away from in horror and made haste to dispose of in the funeral pyre before the dawn of another day? Body and spirit were separate you had heard, but now you know it. Confined in this cage of flesh that decompose, you are but here to play the game of life for a little while till the call comes to leave it. Do not forget this glimpse of the ultimate truth.'

I exalted in this knowledge and grew a little light-headed over the insight gained of my real self. But the glory faded as time passed and the mists enveloped my mind. Once more I fondly fancied the fleeting things of life and the folds of *Maya* [illusion] were firmly retied over my eyes. But the memory of that brief encounter with truth lingered and I yearned to re-experience it.

In the silent afternoons the villagers would pass our house on some errand to town and often their voices would be raised in song. They were songs with a plaintive tune, melodious and haunting, sung in rustic but subtle and sweet words and my mind would turn them over trying to understand their inner meaning. Once a saffron-robed mendicant, plucking at his lyre with its single string, the *ektara*, sang a song that expressed thoughts common to our people. The lilt and beauty of the rhyming words with their puns and alliterations cannot be translated, I can but try to give the sense of the song. The devotee complains his beloved Lord is indulging in a game of blindman's buff with him in life and forever eluding him. And this is what he says in loving reproach:

Oh Lord in this world's play, blindfolded hast Thou placed me
And striking at me sayeth, it's Thy Hand that struck me.
Then I hear Thee say, 'Catch me I am here!'
Lord, it pleases Thee to play, but my heart is struck with fear.
Stretching forth my hands to search, I wander and grow weary,
Thou who art so near and dear, yet remain a stranger.
The day is near its end,
The play when will it end?
Cease Thy game I beg of Thee
I confess I am beaten. I have no strength or skill to catch Thee,
From my eyes untie the folds, let me behold Thee I pray,
And dear Lord in Thy Mercy, take my griefs away.

In April of that year I was in Kidderpore for a few days and one day Mejda returned from his constitutional to announce that something serious was happening. He had just seen lorries full of military men rushing along the road and none could say where they were bound for. It was some weeks later we came to know of the Chittagong affair. While Gandhiji and his followers were engaged in a non-violent struggle to free the country from foreign rule, a group of young people had pledged to use violence to win independence.

In the town of Chittagong a band of young revolutionaries had organized an armed insurrection. Led by Surya Sen, they had sworn death to the enemy or to die in this effort. They planned to seize the armoury, attack the British Auxiliary Force and Police Lines, raid the European club, destroy the telephone and telegram communications, remove railway lines and cut Chittagong off from the outer world altogether. Long preparations had been made for this bold scheme and they did succeed in an amazing manner. But the victory was brief, many were killed, some were captured and the rest went underground.

They had known full well when they undertook this perilous adventure that they might be defeated but it had been hoped that their daring attempt would embolden revolutionaries in other parts of the country. They were but sixty-four who figured in this saga, some of them barely in their teens, and including a dauntless girl who swiftly swallowed poison, preferring death to captivity. Their self-sacrifice, flaming spirit and indomitable courage, left a lasting impression on the people.

Amongst them was a lad who often came to play with Romu at our hill-top bungalow in Chittagong. I remembered Ananda Gupta well. High-spirited and handsome he was very lovable and I nearly wept aloud when I learnt he had been sentenced to 'life inprisonment'—that is, for twenty years. His younger brother was killed in the undertaking.

At that time, the true account of the "Chittagong Raid," as it was called, was not known. News being censored, no one had any idea as to what was happening in that remote town after the revolutionaries had been vanquished. Very little news was allowed to filter out and it was not until a student, returning to his college from his home town, told of the reign of terror and the reprisals dealt by the ruthless military police force. Hearing the grim tale, one of his professors, an Englishman of integrity, was so moved that he wrote an open letter to a leading newspaper. The harrowing details were given but the professor soon lost his job and was shipped back home. It was not known whether he ceased to be a missionary, but he became the idol of the students.

Students in Calcutta during this period gained a lot of experience apart from their curriculum. Guardians and parents were always on tenter-hooks during those troublous times fearing their boys might become entangled in political matters, be harassed by the police, or detained without trial as a state prisoner. News of many students being arrested would reach us and we would warn Romu to be careful. He would only smile and say life at his college was quiet on that score. But years later he related an experience of his undergrad days at Scottish Church College. One night he had been awakened by a gentle tap at the door; opening it, he saw a muffled figure that softly entered and closed the door.

He was asked in a whisper whether he could keep something until it was called for. With a pounding heart he had agreed and a small package changed hands, and his strange visitor departed in silence. Romu recognized him as one of the senior students who hardly ever spoke to him. Soon after there was a hubbub and voices raised crying the Police had come. Shivering, he pulled his sheet over his head and lay still. He heard heavy footsteps on the veranda and the warden explaining outside his doors, that this was not the room, for the boy they sought was on another floor, and the crunching noise of heavy footwear died in the distance.

'What did you do with the package?' I asked. 'At daybreak I took it to the lavatory and placed it well behind the cistern. It was the safest place I could think of and whenever I visited the room, I would stealthily check to see whether it was still there. Sometime later my nocturnal visitor appeared once again in the same manner, I told him where it was and saw him no more.'

Romu had matriculated as a private student at Taki. One of my uncles looked after him very carefully and even took the family priest to bless him in the examination hall, much to Romu's disgust. But I was helpless. My mother's paternal home was at Saidpore and my uncles, *zamindars* there, were delighted at my husband's posting and attempted to help us in every way. This embarrassed my husband and made me apprehensive that all this might cause another petition to be forwarded requesting transfer. But, as the people came to know him, his popularity increased and in fact the next petition was sent three years later requesting that his next transfer be cancelled and he be allowed to remain for a longer period.

In childhood, the happy time spent in Saidpore had been too brief. On my first visit to a village I had been left free to wander at will and my days there were a cherished memory. Mother had told us about the Durga *puja* celebrated at her paternal home with such a wealth of detail that we longed to see it. But during that festive season her duties at Kidderpore never allowed her to leave during my unmarried days, so when my uncles invited us when we were at Basirhat, I rejoiced. My sisters-in-law and their children were with us and we were all invited.

Every god had contributed towards Durga's unsurpassed beauty. It is told how Shiva's energy formed her lovely face, and Vishnu's her eight strong arms. Her beautiful breasts were from the moon, her slender waist from Indra, King of Swarga [Heaven]; her black silken tresses from Yama, the god of death; her shaply ears from Vaiyu, the wind god; and her dazzling eyes from the god of fire. One by one, each part of the body was created to complete the form of a perfect woman. The *devas* [gods] then armed her with celestial weapons, and in the invincible armour given her by Viswa Karma—the Divine Craftsman—she was both beautiful and terrible to behold. The King of all snakes gave her a neck chain of deadly serpents, each with a glittering jewel on its head. The sea clothed her in imperishable robes, crowned her with a dazzling diadem, adorned her with golden bracelets and armlets and a gem-set ring for each finger, and her beautiful feet with ornaments. The sea god's gifts were fragrant lotus, and a garland of flowers that would never fade. And, since the *asuras* [demons] would use ruthless violence to work their will on the world, the fierce lion was given to serve her as her steed. The mighty goddess, resplendent with strength, beauty and power thus arrayed, with flashing eyes laughed aloud as she placed her feet on the lion's back. 'Victory to Simha Bahini!' cried the *devas* joyfully. 'Victory to She who rides the lion.' And, 'Simha Bahini' became one of her names.

It is only in Bengal that with Durga, the symbol of invincible power, is seen lovely Laksmi, the power of wealth, protected by the power of arms in the form of the elegant Kartick, the god of war. On her left stands the shimmering form of Saraswati, the power of culture, guided by Ganesha, the spirit of wisdom, and Demos, the lord of the common people. At the feet of this scintillating group full of beauty and grace, lies brute force, ugly and evil, vanquished by the glorious goddess and thousands stood before her with folded hands to cry 'Bande Mataram,' 'I bow to Thee, Mother!'

She was the patriot's vision of India victorious and free with her wealth and culture restored; the pride of her people, released from bondage at last. To others, she symbolized the yearnings of the spirit towards values that crowned life with fulfilment and bliss—the ultimate aim of human existence.

Durga *puja* in Bengal is celebrated with elaborate ceremony when the heavy rains and gusty winds have subsided and autumn has come. The days of mud and slush are gone, the earth is clothed in tender and bright flowers, the wild tawny rivers are tamed and flow calmly in their course now reflecting the azure heavens. The sun shines from cloudless skies when the monsoons have passed; the days are golden, the bright moon and starlit nights stir the spirit and people are heard to say with a reminiscent smile, "Why, already there is a scent of *puja* in the air!"

The wealthy, the needy, the worldly, the spiritually inclined, the happy-hearted and the miserable, all look forward to this national festival. Though moved by different sentiments the same shining thread will be found to enrich the texture of their lives and thoughts. It is a joyous occasion that helps to spread goodwill and maintain social obligations. It is a time of blissful reunions—children who had left home to seek their fortunes in distant places join their families during the *puja* vacation. It is a season for exchange of gifts, and the weavers who had stored their best *dhotis* and *saris* raise their prices to make a little extra profit, since the traditional presents are clothing. The poor hope to obtain a new garment and perhaps a proper meal, for alms-givings is a special feature of the festival and the rich are reminded of their obligations. The elders make gifts of garments as a token of their blessing and attired in these, the younger generations make their obeisance before the Mother and pray for her benediction. It is only here in Bengal that the spirit of the primordial energy is invoked in sculptured clay. Special craftsmen mold, tint and adorn the image, accurately following the word picture given by the *rishis* [sages] in our scriptures.

The Durga *puja* would be at its best in the village where the festival is celebrated with pomp and circumstance by the local *zamindar*. His tenants, both Hindu and Moslem, received new clothes when they came to their landlord's mansion to join the many activities connected with the ritual worship of the Mother. They feasted here for the four festive days and special attention was given to the poor, for it is said that Daridra Narayana, the Lord Himself in the form of the poor, has come to partake of gifts and hospitality from the home that is blessed with the Mother's presence.

As we reached Saidpore, the tinkle of bells and sound of conch shells proclaimed that the ritual worship of Mother Durga had already commenced. The old house wore a festive look, the courtyard was teeming with people and noisy children were romping about. A group had gathered round the drummers demanding that drums should be beaten right now rather than later at *arati*, when the drum and gong usually go together.

There seemed to be a current of joy in the air when my uncles and aunts and cousins came forward to greet us. We went together to the temple for it was nearly time for the *pushpa-anjali*, the flower-offering ceremony, in which everyone participated.

We stood silently with hands folded before the great sculptured group including Mother Durga and her divine children. The snarling lion at her feet had his teeth on the bleeding monster, Mahisasur, on whose neck was coiled a serpent with outspread hood. This was of particular interest to the younger people, but we only had eyes for the serene face of the Mother. A mysterious smile played on her lips and her eyes were tender. Lights and incense and rich offerings of many kinds, including masses of flowers, were placed before her. There were bunches of bananas, large and luscious fruits, and rough clay plates piled high with sugar cakes and other sweets from village folk who had placed their humble gifts before the Mother in thanksgiving.

Soon, the *puja* was over . . . . "Anjali! Anjali!" the word went round and family members, guests and visitors assembled before the Mother. The priest began distributing flowers to those who had not brought any and hearing a titter I turned. A very young girl stood diffidently at a distance and some girls were looking at her in amusement. She wore a red-bordered *sari*, a broad streak of vermilion between the parting of her hair and a large crimson dot on her brow. Her face was sad and forlorn. With folded hands she was raptly gazing at the Mother. She did not come forward to join us in the floral rite nor was she called for the function which is a common courtesy extended to all devotees at a time like this.

The priest called out from the age-old book of Chandi, the immortal hymn beginning with "Om Sharva Mangala Mangle, Shivey Sharvartha Shadhike . . . . " And I could not help noticing that his pronunciation was faulty, having heard this from Father, whose Sanskrit was faultless. I must confess during community worship my mind wanders a little. When I am in the midst of too many relations in a place like this, it tends to become more or less a social function to be observed with nothing very spiritual in it.

Chiding myself for my unseemly thoughts I turned to find the girl had gone. Beside me was a cousin, a law student with liberal ideas and leanings towards social service. I asked him if he knew the girl. He nodded, we went out and he told me about her. I remembered now that sometime ago when we had met, he had said there was a great commotion at Saidpore because of a neighbour who had been bold enough to contemplate giving in marriage his widowed daughter of fourteen years. The parents were heart-broken when her husband died, a few months after the marriage, and brought the dazed child to live with them. They were disconsolate at the prospect of the bleak life confronting her and bravely sent an advertisement, asking if any young man would be interested in marrying the child widow, to be placed in the matrimonial column of a popular daily paper.

This evoked an answer from a young college student in Calcutta and it was then my cousin was taken into confidence to make enquiries about the lad and find out if the offer were genuine. It was. He was a nice boy with altruistic ideas but had no income and was dependent upon his father who, when he came to know of his son's intention, threatened to disinherit him. But this did not deter the boy and he said he would keep his word. Saidpore people were scandalized, such a thing had never happened in the village. My uncle said he would have nothing to do with the family, but his son, my cousin, helped the parents to solemnise the marriage. I remembered now that he had told me all this and I had given him moral support plus a *sari* and vermilion box as a wedding gift for the girl. It all came back to me. He said at present they were in a sad plight as the boy now homeless, was living with his father-in-law, a needy school master with other children to support.

To make matters worse, the family had been cut off from the group amongst whom they lived and moved at Saidpore. My cousin had pleaded with his father to send the usual *puja* invitation to the girl's parents but his father refused. But every year the child stole away from home for a glimpse of Mother Durga. Later, I went with my cousin to the girl's home and met her parents and husband. They were pleased to have visitors after such a long period of isolation. The father appeared to be optimistic and hoped that his son-in-law, since he had graduated with honours in English, would surely not sit idle for long, and some day be able to provide for his daughter. In the meanwhile he was very welcome. They were content to see their dear one dressing once more in the gay colours of a wife, instead of the austere white of a widow. It had been specially hard on the mother to serve her young daughter with austere food and see her always in mourning clothes with nothing to look forward to in life.

In spite of the Widow Remarriage Act and the fact that many reputable men sponsored the cause, the remarriage of widows was not looked upon with favour. My uncles were kind-hearted but conservative. My aunts were sympathetic but unable to go against the wishes of their husbands, as for the young girls of the neighbourhood, they were thoughtless and jested cruelly about the girl.

Her head was bent. I took her hand, 'Would you like to come for *arati*, evening prayers?' She looked uncertainly at her mother. I hastened to add that I would be there with her. My cousin nodded approval. Together we watched the evening ritual being performed by the priest. The incense was fragrant, the flowers were colourful, the atmosphere was soothing and the Mother of the Universe smiled with benign grace. The girl beside me had her hand in mine, her lips were moving in prayer and the tears flowed . . . . Looking on her, I remembered those beautiful lines of Tagore:

> Mother I shall weave a chain of pearls for thy neck with
> my tears of sorrow.
> The stars have wrought their anklets of light to deck
> thy feet, but mine will hang upon thy breast.
> Wealth and Fame come from thee and it is for thee to
> give or withhold them.
> But this my sorrow is absolutely mine own, and when I
> bring it to thee as my offering, thou rewardest me
> with thy grace.

Glossary

Artha	wealth, prosperity, one of the four ends of life
Bhagavat Gita	song of the Lord, the sixth book of the *Mahabharata* which contains the divine words of Krishna to his disciple and friend Arjuna. It emphasizes the doctrine of Nishkama Karma (work done without seeking any reward) and Bhakti (loving faith in a god of grace)
Bou	bride, daughter-in-law, wife
Boudi	elder brother's wife
Brahma	creator god of the Hindu sacred triad
Brahmin	originally a member of the priestly caste; the highest caste recognized by Hindus
Chorda	youngest of the elder brothers
Dada	eldest brother
Darshan	philosophy, to view with reverence
Dharma	religion, duty, code of right conduct, duty selflessly done
Dhoti	a length of cloth which is draped to cover a man from waist to ankle
Didi	elder sister
Durga	the Mother Goddess, divine energy, Shiva's consort. Durga *puja* is the most important Hindu celebration of the year in Bengal.
Guru	a personal religious teacher and spiritual guide
Kama	desire, physical love; one of the four ends of life

Kayastha	a member of a high Hindu caste, especially numerous in Bengal and Uttar Pradesh. Caste occupations include clerks, writers and accountants
Krishna	the eighth *avatar* of Vishnu who is often the object of devotional worship
Kshatriya	a high-caste Hindu, traditional occupations were military or governing
Mahabharata	one of the two great Sanskrit epics. It is attributed to the sage Vyasa and tells the story of the contest between the Kurus and the Pandavas
Mahila Samiti	women's society or association
Mejda	second eldest brother
Moghuls	Muslim rulers of India from 16th—18th Century
Moksha	liberation from all desire and from the cycle of rebirth, merging of the soul with Brahman
Nawab	a provincial governor of the Moghul Empire, a man of great wealth or prominence
Pandit	a learned man or teacher
Pishi	aunt, father's sister
Pronam	an act of salutation
Puja	an act of worship or propitiation
Purdah	seclusion of women from public; a Muslim custom followed by a number of Hindus
Ramayana	the great Sanskrit epic, attributed to Valmiki. The epic tells of Rama who voluntarily abdicated his right to succeed his father and became an ascetic, taking his wife, Sita, and brother, Laksmana, with him to dwell in the forest. He was in exile for fourteen years and his adventures during this time show his divine greatness
Sari	a garment of Hindu women that consists of yards of cloth draped so that one end forms a skirt and the other a covering for the top of the body
Shakti	dynamic energy personified as a goddess

Shiva	the god who destroys so that progress may ensue, the symbol of divine energy in the evolution of the universe
Swadeshi	items made in one's own country
Swaraj	self-rule
Vishnu	the second god of the supreme triad, the preserver, often worshipped in the form of one of his ten *avatars*, such as Rama or Krishna

Index